Juvenile Justice and
Public Policy

Juvenile Justice and Public Policy

Toward a National Agenda

Edited by
Ira M. Schwartz

Lexington Books
An Imprint of Macmillan, Inc.
New York

Maxwell Macmillan Canada
Toronto

Maxwell Macmillan International
New York   Oxford   Singapore   Sydney

Library of Congress Cataloging-in-Publication Data

Juvenile justice and public policy : toward a national agenda / edited by Ira M. Schwartz.
    p.   cm.
  ISBN 0-669-26902-6
  1. Juvenile justice, Administration of—United States.
I. Schwartz, Ira M.
HV9104.J866 1992
364.3′6′0973—dc20   92-14562
                                                    CIP

Lexington Books
An Imprint of Macmillan, Inc.
866 Third Avenue, New York, N.Y. 10022

Maxwell Macmillan Canada, Inc.
1200 Eglinton Avenue East
Suite 200
Don Mills, Ontario M3C 3N1

Macmillan, Inc. is part of the Maxwell Communication
Group of Companies

Printed in the United States of America

printing number
1 2 3 4 5 6 7 8 9 10

Contents

List of Tables and Figures

Tables

Figures

Preface

Juvenile crime continues to be one of the most significant domestic policy issues of our time. Billions in federal, state, and local dollars are spent on this problem every year. Indications are that juvenile-crime-control activities will consume an increasingly larger share of scarce public resources in the future.

Despite the understandable and pressing interest in this issue, little progress is being made to reduce serious juvenile crime rates. Public policy decisions aimed at preventing and controlling juvenile crime are usually made within an atmosphere characterized by rhetoric and a remarkable absence of facts. In too many instances, policies are developed in response to one or two particularly heinous acts by young people, acts that are the exception rather than the rule. For example, in Massachusetts, the governor recently proposed enacting a law that would automatically result in the prosecution of juveniles in adult courts for crimes ranging from armed robbery to murder. This proposal resulted from an incident involving a sixteen-year-old boy who "sprayed Highland Avenue in Roxbury with gunfire. . . . killing Charles Copney, eleven, and Korey Grant, fifteen" (*Boston Globe,* 17 October, 1991).

This volume examines some of the most critical and troubling issues in juvenile justice. The chapters are written by some of America's most respected juvenile justice scholars and professionals. It is hoped that the contents of this volume will serve as a catalyst and resource for developing sound juvenile justice public policy decisions. This volume also addresses some important areas for further research.

In Chapter 1, Barry Krisberg, president of the National Council on Crime and Delinquency, examines the strengths and weaknesses of various national data bases on juvenile justice and discusses what they tell us about the juvenile crime problem. Krisberg also shares his thinking on an important but severely neglected topic, the need to focus attention and research on juvenile delinquency prevention.

In Chapter 2, C. Ronald Huff, director of the Criminal Justice Research Center and a professor in the school of Public Policy and Management at Ohio State University, shares his views on one of the most controversial and volatile subjects in juvenile justice today, youth gangs. Huff discusses how and why gangs form, the changes that have taken place in gang composition over the years, and target strategies to address this alarming phenomenon.

Although juvenile crime is a serious problem, it is generally acknowledged that far too many cases are referred to juvenile courts. Many experts recognize there are many cases that do not need formal juvenile court intervention and can be resolved outside of the court setting. In Chapter 3, Mark Ezell, associate professor of social work at the University of Washington in Seattle, discusses issues associated with the diversion of young people from the juvenile justice system. Diversion is not a new concept. It is an idea that was tried during the 1970s and early 1980s without much success. Ezell reviews this history and discusses his own research on the topic. He offers some valuable insights on how we can benefit from past mistakes.

Chapters 4 and 5 address one of the most provocative subjects in juvenile justice, the future of the juvenile court. In Chapter 4, Barry C. Feld, professor of law at the University of Minnesota, and one of the leading scholars on the juvenile court, reviews the history, theoretical underpinnings, and results of attempts to reform the juvenile court. Feld concludes his chapter with an important question for policymakers and juvenile justice professionals: "Is there any reason to believe that the contemporary juvenile court can be rehabilitated?"

Judge Frank A. Orlando (Ret.) and Judge Gary L. Crippen are well-respected jurists with considerable expertise in juvenile and family issues. In Chapter 5, they too document the juvenile court's shortcomings in procedural matters and in providing quality treatment. However, unlike Feld, they suggest that the juvenile court might still be redeemed. They conclude chapter 5 with an ambitious list of recommendations for change.

Chapter 6 discusses new and emerging roles for prosecutors in juvenile justice. The chapter was written by James Shine, director of the American Prosecutors Research Institute and Dwight Price, senior attorney, National District Attorneys Association, two highly respected professionals with expertise in the area of juvenile prosecution. Shine and Price discuss the newly developed juvenile prosecutorial standards and their implications for the field. They point out that prosecutors are playing an increasingly larger role in juvenile justice and that this trend is likely to continue in the future.

Chapter 7 addresses the growing interest in interconnections between juvenile justice, child welfare, and children's mental health services. Although these systems serve many of the same children, there is a significant lack of coordination and cooperation between them. Mark I. Soler, one of the nation's most prominent children's public interest lawyers and a student of children's service organizations, explores issues pertaining to coordination of services and highlights some promising national developments.

Ira M. Schwartz, professor and director of the Center for the Study of Youth Policy at the University of Michigan's School of Social Work, and Russell K. Van Vleet, senior associate at the center and former director of the Utah Division of Youth Corrections, are the coauthors of Chapter 8. They examine the costs and benefits of various state and local youth detention and incarceration policies and explore their implications for public policy. They point out that some jurisdictions are utilizing youth detention and correctional system funds far more efficiently than other jurisdictions.

Chapter 9 discusses race, gender, and ethnicity issues in juvenile justice. The chapter includes data documenting recent trends regarding out-of-home placement of females and minorities, discusses the impact of the mandates of the federal Juvenile Justice and Delinquency Prevention Act on females and minorities, and identifies some policy and program-matic questions that must be addressed in the future. The coauthors of this chapter are Katherine Hunt Federle, associate professor of clinical law at Tulane University, and Meda Chesney-Lind, associate professor of sociology and director of women's studies at the University of Hawaii.

The private sector has always played a significant role in juvenile justice, but very little has been written about that role. In Chapter 10, Yitzhak Bakal, director of Northeastern Family Institute, Inc. and Harvey Lowell, director of Special Projects, Northeastern Family Institute, Inc. draw upon their experience and expertise in delivering services and influencing youth corrections policy to discuss the role of the private sector.

Policymakers and juvenile justice professionals often claim they are advocating for policies that reflect public demands. In Chapter 11, Ira M. Schwartz presents and discusses the findings from a 1991 public opinion survey on public attitudes toward juvenile crime. It is the first comprehensive public opinion survey on this topic. Among other things, findings suggest the public is not quite as supportive of "get tough" policies as they have been made out to be by some elected public officials and juvenile justice professionals.

Juvenile Justice and Public Policy

1

Youth Crime and Its Prevention: A Research Agenda

Barry Krisberg

Despite the consistently high level of public concern over youthful criminals, reliable national data on juvenile delinquency are extremely limited. The large gaps in existing statistical data do not help policymakers to effectively respond to public fears and prejudices about youthful offenders. The scarcity of valid information forces program and policy development to be largely dependent on anecdotal information rather than solid empirical data. This problem has become more serious over the past ten years because of minimal federal investment in basic research on the distribution and correlates of delinquent behavior.

In this chapter I will review current data sources on delinquency trends. I will also examine data on the major correlates of delinquency. After describing the shortcomings of our existing knowledge base, I will offer a remedial research agenda.

How Much Youth Crime Is There?

Public opinion surveys consistently show that respondents believe that youth crime is rising out of control (Schwartz & Abbey, 1990; Steinhart, 1988). The general public view is consistently reinforced by politicians who pander to these fears and by a media that is fascinated with heinous offenses committed by young people. Further, there is a seemingly inevitable human tendency for each aging generation to view its young successors as especially threatening to public order (Sanders, 1970).

But what are the facts? Has juvenile crime escalated dramatically in the last ten years? Are young criminals today more vicious and more prone to senseless violence than their predecessors? Are young people commencing their criminal activities at any earlier an age than in previous eras? Unfortunately, the answers to these seemingly straightforward questions are not easy to obtain.

1

As I will discuss later, serious technical problems plague current efforts to describe more accurately the contours of juvenile delinquency. To partially remedy these deficiencies, a genuine financial commitment to sponsor new data-collection efforts and to improve existing data collection will be required. At present there is little evidence that either the federal government or state governments are willing to make this sort of commitment of new research funds. But without new research investments, the knowledge base supporting delinquency prevention-and-control efforts will remain woefully inadequate.

National Data Sources on Youth Crime

All current measures of the nature and extent of delinquency are indirect, at best.[1] The main statistical data sources are essentially indicators of the activities of police agencies, juvenile courts, and juvenile corrections agencies. Put simply, the amount of crime committed by juveniles is unknown and perhaps unknowable. What is known, albeit imperfectly, is the number of juveniles who are taken into custody and processed by the juvenile justice system. The dimensions of youth crime are very poorly captured by juvenile justice agency data.

Data on Juvenile Arrests. The principal national data on youth crime are derived from the Federal Bureau of Investigation's Uniform Crime Reports (UCR) (Sessions, 1990). The UCR present the annual number of persons under age eighteen who were taken into custody, a figure only distantly related to the number of juveniles who actually commit criminal offenses each year. The tenuous link between these two statistics can be easily illustrated by examining the attrition of cases as they pass through the criminal justice system. Each year the Bureau of Justice Statistics conducts a large household survey of the extent of victimization in the United States. These surveys typically reveal that citizens report to the police roughly 30 percent of the crimes that actually occur (Bureau of Justice Statistics, 1988). Law enforcement agencies make an arrest in 20–25 percent of the cases in which they are notified. Thus the pool of persons arrested may represent as little as 6–8 percent of those actually committing criminal offenses. This proportion may be somewhat higher if one assumes that persons who are arrested commit a significant proportion of the offenses that are never brought to the attention of police agencies (Greenwood & Abrahamse, 1980).

To discover how many juveniles actually committed crimes one must examine data gathered at the point of an arrest.[2] But data on trends in youth crime and, more generally, offender characteristics, are highly dependent on law enforcement practices. For instance, the current national "War against Drugs" led to a sudden increase in the number of juveniles and adults arrested for possessing and selling drugs. Indeed, juvenile arrests for drug offenses climbed by 36 percent between 1984 and 1989. But this sudden increase in drug arrests did not mean that illegal drug use among adolescents was rising. Quite the contrary: the annual household survey conducted by the National Institute of Drug Abuse (1988) actually showed a decline in the proportion of American youngsters using illicit substances.

Moreover, arrest statistics are a flawed indicator of youth crime because the FBI counts the number of juveniles arrested. This system skews the data because juveniles, more than adults, tend to commit crimes in groups. This is especially true for offenses such as robbery and aggravated assault. Thus, the group nature of juvenile crime may well inflate the FBI counts.

It is important to note that the FBI provides very sparse information about offender attributes. One can learn about the race, gender, and age of the juvenile. But data on prior criminal histories are not collected and information about the circumstances of the criminal event, including the harm done to the victim, is very limited.[3]

Reviewing FBI data, one would conclude that juvenile crime is on the upswing. Between 1984 and 1989 the juvenile arrest rate for crimes such as homicide, rape, robbery, aggravated assault, auto theft, burglary, theft, and arson rose by 18 percent; the arrest rate for violent crimes increased by 39 percent. But during the period 1979–1984 juvenile arrests were declining, so that total arrest figures in 1989 were still below those of ten years earlier (see Table 1-1). It is worth noting that public opinion polls conducted during periods of both rising and falling juvenile arrest rates found that the citizenry felt that juvenile crime was growing at an alarming rate (Haugen, Costello, Schwartz, Krisberg & Litsky, 1982; Steinhart, 1988).

While much speculation is possible about the reasons for these changes in juvenile arrest rates, few well-tested theories and little empirical research accounts for juvenile crime trends. This lack of theory, combined with the well-documented limitations of UCR data, constrains public policy leaders who wish to comprehend, much less alter, juvenile crime rates.

Juvenile Court Statistics. Another measure of youth crime is provided by the National Juvenile Court Data Archives (NJCDA). Since 1975 the NJCDA has provided information on the number and characteristics of youths flowing through the nation's juvenile courts. The data are collected

Table 1-1
United States Part 1 Arrests by Sex—Juveniles (Under 18 Years of Age) 1979, 1984, 1989

	1979			1984			1989		
	Total Arrests	Rate* per 100,000	Percent** Change 79–84	Total Arrests	Rate per 100,000	Percent Change 84–89	Total Arrests	Rate per 100,000	Percent Change 79–89
Part 1 Arrests									
Male	664,456	2,310.9	−31.6	423,749	1,580.7	18.7	479,812	1,876.3	−18.8
Female	146,896	510.9	−24.3	103,717	386.9	15.8	114,579	448.1	−12.3
Violent Arrests									
Male	75,044	261.0	−24.6	52,758	196.8	38.9	69,894	273.3	4.7
Female	8,566	29.8	−17.5	6,594	24.6	44.0	9,060	35.4	18.8
Property Arrests									
Male	589,412	2,050.0	−32.5	370,991	1,383.9	15.8	409,918	1,603.0	−21.8
Female	138,330	481.1	−24.7	97,123	362.3	13.8	105,519	412.6	−14.2
Drug Arrests									
Male	92,383	321.3	−40.0	51,805	193.3	48.5	73,379	287.0	−10.7
Female	18,155	63.1	−45.0	9,356	35.0	7.0	9,565	37.4	−40.7
Eligible Youth Pop.	28,752,979			26,807,000			25,572,000		

Source: Federal Bureau of Investigations, Uniform Crime Reports, analyzed by the National Council on Crime and Delinquency.

* Rate is calculated on youth age 10 to upper age of juvenile court jurisdiction in each state

** Percent Change denotes change in juvenile arrest rates per 100,000 by sex

from a nonrandom group of approximately half of the nation's juvenile courts. These courts serve jurisdictions in which nearly two-thirds of America's youth reside. However, the nonprobability nature of the sample hinders our ability to generate national estimates from the statistics derived from the NJCDA collection efforts.

Trend data from juvenile courts suggest little change in recent years in the rate of case referrals. For instance, from 1977 to 1987 the rate of delinquency cases referred to court decreased by 4 percent. Despite the overall stability of court referral rates, a greater proportion of these cases were for crimes against persons. Thus, viewed from the vantage point of juvenile court statistics, delinquency rates were stable, even though young people appeared to be committing more serious offenses. As noted below, there are several reasons suggesting great caution in using court data to make inferences about juvenile crime trends.

The NJCDA follows *cases rather than individuals* through the court process. Because one individual may have several charges lodged against him (or her—though much less frequently) and some youth go to court many times in a given year, the resulting data on crime trends and offender attributes are biased to an unknown extent. Moreover, the NJCDA focuses only on cases that are formally referred to the court. Because many cases are diverted so that large numbers of juvenile offenders are handled informally by police, prosecutors, and court intake officers, the cohort of youths referred for official court handling is very different from the cohort of those who were arrested. Here again, the attrition of cases as they pass through the juvenile justice process creates major biases in statistical conclusions drawn from analysis of NJCDA data.

Children in Custody. A final source of data on youth crime and youthful offenders is the semiannual survey of juvenile correctional facilities, known popularly as Children in Custody (CIC). The survey permits limited analyses of trends in admissions and one-day counts for both public and private juvenile correctional facilities. Whereas the coverage on public facilities is comprehensive, there are serious questions about how well CIC maps the universe of privately operated juvenile facilities.[4]

CIC data show a steady growth over the last decade in juvenile incarceration in public facilities (see Figure 1–1). Between 1979 and 1989, juvenile confinement rates rose by 45 percent. These data also show that the proportion of confined youths who are nonwhites rose from 47 percent to 60 percent between 1985 and 1989. However, during that same period the distribution of offenses of incarcerated youths remained virtually unchanged.

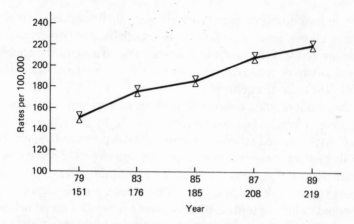

Figure 1-1. U.S. Public Juvenile Facilities One-Day Rates

Source: National Council on Crime and Deliquency Juveniles Taken into Custody Research Program.

The CIC contains some data on youth attributes based on the one-day counts, including commitment offense, gender, race, and age. However, the CIC information is based on aggregate counts, not individual cases. This prevents most multivariate analyses of the available data. Further, the use of the one-day counts creates a statistical bias in favor of those youths charged with more serious offenses who typically have longer institutional stays. For example, in 1989 the CIC reported over 800,000 admissions to juvenile correctional facilities, but the one-day counts only covered approximately 93,000 youngsters. The CIC offers little help in describing the much larger universe of young people who experience short periods of detention.

In sum, current national data are woefully inadequate for answering even the most basic questions about youth crime trends or about the characteristics of juvenile offenders. At best, these data provide an imprecise snapshot of how the juvenile justice system handles the young people who come to the attention of the police and the courts. Depending upon the source of the data they utilized, policymakers would reach very different conclusions about youth crime trends.

Increasing Information on Youth Crime Trends

Other potential sources of data on juvenile delinquency trends are two national probability samples of adolescents: the University of Colorado's National Youth Survey (NYS) (Elliott, Huizinga & Ageton, 1985) and the University of Michigan's Monitoring the Future Project (MFP) (Bachman,

O'Malley & Johnston, 1978). The NYS is a longitudinal survey based on a national probability sample of American youths that was begun in 1976. Data are derived from the self-reports of these young people. The MFP also relies on self-report data, but its annual sample is drawn from the universe of high school seniors. The NYS is particularly valuable for theory testing and research on delinquent careers. But the NYS was not designed to generate regular national estimates of delinquency rates. The MFP misses those youth who have dropped out of school—a very significant omission for delinquency research. On the other hand, the MFP is better designed to yield annual trend data for those adolescents covered in its sample.

The results of the NYS and MFP provide an important supplement to the picture of juvenile crime that emerges from the FBI data. NYS data from 1976 shows that 29 percent of males and 11 percent of females aged eleven to seventeen years committed a Part 1 offense. These percentages are considerably higher than those figures computed from studies based on official data (Elliott, Huizinga & Morse, 1987). The NYS data indicate that birth cohorts born after 1960 have lower delinquency prevalence rates, but those youths who report committing serious offenses also report higher incidence rates (more crimes per offender). The NYS thus suggests that a smaller fraction of the adolescent population is getting involved in serious delinquency, but that this subgroup is committing more crimes. At an aggregate level, these two findings provide a much richer picture of delinquency trends than the UCR figures cited above. Interestingly, the MFP reports very similar findings in terms of declining general prevalence rates and increasing incidence rates for chronic offenders.[5]

The augmentation of the NYS to cover an annual, nationally representative sample of adolescents could greatly enrich our comprehension of juvenile crime trends, especially for particular demographic subgroups. This change would require a regular commitment of federal funding (probably by the U.S. Bureau of Justice Statistics) to sustain the NYS on a consistent basis. While these self-report data would not supplant the need for continued data collection on juvenile arrests, a new NYS would substantially add to our knowledge. Most important, the utilization of self-report data would move us closer toward estimates of the actual extent of juvenile law violations, so that we would not have to rely on the surrogate measurements that are presently collected.

The experience of the National Institute of Drug Abuse (NIDA) household survey on drug abuse could provide genuine guidance for designing annual self-report data collection on youth crime. The NIDA survey has been criticized on two grounds: first, for its exclusion of the incarcerated population, and second, for alleged underreporting of problem behavior by minorities. Each of these measurement and design issues would require careful assessment and might call for refinements in the current methods of the NYS. Further, since the NYS is now designed to produce national estimates, the sample size would have to be significantly increased to provide regional statistics and to adequately cover smaller population subgroups.

Current Issues in Delinquency-Prevention Research

Enhancing Sources of Data

Besides the paucity of reliable data on delinquency trends, the limitations of official crime data inhibit our ability to generate new knowledge in the delinquency-prevention area. The problem of information attrition as one goes from "offenses committed" to "persons arrested" is significant. Further, as researchers' information requests become more complex, the typical data source consists of youngsters in long-term facilities (Beck, Kline & Greenfield, 1988). For instance, virtually all of the studies concerned with the psychological and medical needs of delinquents rely on samples of institutionalized youths (Murphy, 1986). These data are not reflective of the much larger numbers of youngsters handled by the juvenile justice system in community-based programs or those who have never been apprehended. Presumably, studies based on institutionalized youths offer a very distorted portrayal of the "typical" youthful offender.

The use of self-report data also can contribute to a better understanding of the correlates of delinquency. Elliott and colleagues (1987) cite a number of studies that show general agreement on the demographic characteristics of serious juvenile offenders based on either self-report data or official records. Juvenile offenders are disproportionately lower-class, African-American males who reside in urban areas. However, the extent of the overrepresentation of this group varies substantially based on the measure of delinquency that is employed.

Whereas the NYS reports a male/female ratio for serious offenses of 3:1, several studies using arrest data find the ratio is 5:1 (Blumstein, Cohen, Roth & Visher, 1986; Hamparian, Schuster, Dinitz & Conrad, 1978). Similarly, race differences in arrest data are much larger than those found in self-report studies (Huizinga & Elliott, 1987). These findings illustrate the need to supplement delinquency research based on arrest data with comparable studies employing self-report measures. Besides using self-report data, researchers need to employ a wider repertoire of research techniques, especially qualitative studies, to enhance the knowledge base necessary for delinquency prevention. For example, criminology once had a very strong tradition of developing "the delinquent's own story." Clifford Shaw's *The Jackroller* (1966) and his earlier *Brothers in Crime* (1938) and Sutherland's *The Professional Thief* (1937) are classics in this tradition. Sociological biographies of this type can offer important insights that are missed by the more structured questionnaires and official records studies.

A return to "street-corner research" involving intensive ethnographic studies of lower-class youths would be a crucial augmentation of current research. The ethnographic research tradition of Howard Becker (1963), Elliot Liebow (1967), and Harold Finestone (1969) needs to be recaptured. More recently, the studies of juvenile drug trafficking and juvenile gangs by Moore (1978) and Hagedorn (1988) have yielded valuable information to guide theory development as well as new prevention programs.

The Need for Theory-Based Delinquency-Prevention Research

Theoretical work on the etiology of delinquency was once a vital part of criminology. However, the "golden age" of delinquency theory ended abruptly in the mid-1970s. Few substantial and original contributions to delinquency theory have appeared since the work of Hirschi (1969) and Polk and Kobrin (1972).[6] In part, the slowing of delinquency theorizing occurred because federal funding sources during the Nixon, Ford, and Reagan administrations were less interested in theoretical developments, especially those theories that emphasized sociological variables. Conservatives disillusioned with the "War on Poverty" blamed social scientists for the some of the presumed mistakes made in national domestic policy.

Whereas delinquency theory was an integral part of major prevention programs such as the Chicago Area Projects, the Mobilization for Youth, and Haryou-Act, the linkage between theory and practice has been weakened over the last two decades. For example, the Youth Development Strategy promoted by the U.S. Health, Education, and Welfare Department in the early 1970s drew heavily upon the ideas of Polk and Kobrin (1972). But the first major delinquency-prevention initiatives of the Office of Juvenile Justice and Delinquency Prevention (OJJDP) were essentially devoid of either organized theory or systematic research (Krisberg, Austin, Fong & Lawrence, 1981). A subsequent OJJDP prevention program conducted by the University of Washington (Hawkins & Weis, 1985) attempted to more fully integrate theory testing, but this ambitious effort failed to receive sustained funding during the Reagan years.

Delinquency research in the 1970s and 1980s was heavily influenced by the same focus on repetitive criminals that dominated research on adult offenders. Most of the studies conducted during this period relied exclusively on police data, and consequently yielded very limited individual or sociological data for analyses. For example, researchers concentrated on the number, frequency, and temporal ordering of offense "careers." The conclusions of these studies are highly questionable due to serious problems with data reliability and the exclusive focus on youths who were *apprehended* for delinquent offenses.

The theoretically barren delinquency research of recent years offers few clues to prevention strategies. The inventors of these mythical "juvenile career criminals" have either avoided the policy implications of their work or focused on selective incapacitation and intensive surveillance strategies.

Some researchers have attempted to keep alive the rich tradition of theory-based research. In particular, a series of OJJDP-funded studies in Denver, Rochester, and Pittsburgh hold out great promise for generating new insights into delinquency prevention. These studies are all guided by well-developed theoretical frameworks and involve longitudinal data collection. These research efforts are targeted at communities with high rates of serious delinquency and have careful sampling plans designed to tap a large number of high-risk youths (Office of Juvenile Justice and Delinquency Prevention, 1989).

The Rochester Youth Development Study sampled over 1,000 seventh and eighth graders and is testing an interactional theory of delinquency through very sophisticated multivariate data analysis techniques (Thornberry, Farnsworth, Lizotle & Stern, 1987). The Denver Youth Study represents a further refinement of the integrated theory of delinquency developed by Elliott and associates (1985). The Pittsburgh Youth Study examines a range of biological and psychological variables. These studies all attempt to operationalize a developmental perspective on the emergence and continuance of delinquent behavior in adolescence. Results from these studies could offer important new directions for future prevention efforts.

Better Evaluations of Innovative Delinquency-Prevention Programs

The legacy of evaluation research in the prevention field is not a happy one (Krisberg, 1987; Krisberg et al., 1981). Most of the major delinquency-prevention programs were not rigorously evaluated. Other more rigorous evaluations such as the long-term follow-up of the Cambridge-Somerville Project actually showed that at-risk youths receiving intensive counseling became more delinquent than the control group (McCord, 1978).

Research supporting the delinquency-reduction effects of early intervention programs such as Head Start are based on very small samples and these studies have never been replicated (Berrueta-Clement, Schweinhart, Barnett, Epstein & Weikert, 1984).

The current evidence on our ability to prevent troublesome adolescent behavior is not encouraging. For example, major public and private programs to prevent teenage pregnancy have met with little or no success. Efforts to reduce child abuse and school drop-out rates or to increase youth employment have not generated measurable, positive results.

One explanation of these disappointing results may be that existing prevention resources are uncoordinated and, possibly, insufficient to remedy the social problems to which they are targeted. It also must be kept in mind that federal funding for many social problems for the poor were severely cut back in the 1980s (Currie, 1988). Concurrently, changes in the economy and in federal tax policies widened the gap between the rich and the poor (Phillips, 1990). These economic facts combined with powerful social forces that have impacted on the poor, such as growing family instability and the ready availability of cheap, and increasingly lethal, drugs and weapons. Given this environment, the amount of prevention resources that were invested in high-risk families and children was meager.

We do not know the precise mix of prevention services that are required, nor is there hard data on the level of expenditures required to produce noticeable results. For instance, a prestigious Ford Foundation panel estimated that, at a minimum, America needs to spend an additional $30 billion annually to rebuild the welfare system (Ford Foundation Project on Social Welfare and the American Future, 1990).

Research on innovative prevention programs should be given a high priority. Of special importance should be rigorous evaluations of interventions that attempt to test empirically grounded delinquency theories. We need more experimental designs and more longitudinal analyses tracing the long-term consequences of early interventions. Since there may be continuing problems in generating sufficiently large samples in these prevention experiments, emphasis should be placed on multiple replications.

Evaluation research should include both impact and process studies. Assuming that we can learn *what works,* we also need to understand *why programs work.* Research should tell us the necessary and sufficient conditions for prevention efforts to achieve positive results in a broad range of sociocultural settings. Too often prevention practitioners have assumed that programs that work in urban areas can be immediately applied to the rural poor. Similarly, successful programs in some ethnic communities may be totally ineffective in others.

As noted above, there is an urgent need to begin to estimate the community and societal levels of prevention resources that will be required. Suppose a carefully designed study shows that parental training and supportive counseling can reduce delinquency rates. How would such a finding be institutionalized in a neighborhood or on a citywide basis? What level of financial investment over how long a time period could lead to measurable reductions in youthful crime rates? These are difficult questions to answer at present. However, to achieve political relevance, the prevention field must be able to show the "cost-benefit" analyses supporting various prevention strategies. Currently, the alleged costs and benefits of most prevention programs are largely unsubstantiated claims.

New Etiological Factors and New Prevention Strategies

Overlooked Correlates of Delinquency

Traditionally, delinquency research and prevention practice have concentrated on a narrow set of factors. For the first half-century after the juvenile court system was created, the prevention and treatment of youth crime was dominated by psychological theories. Researchers such as Healy and Sheldon and Glueck pointed to inadequate childrearing practices as the source for mental conflicts, poor self-images, and insufficient impulse controls. Although the university-based researchers began to pay more attention to sociological factors such as culture conflict, social disorganization, and social learning, the practitioners held fast to psychological and psychoanalytic theories.

In the 1960s the sociologists emerged to espouse new theories of delinquency and to design new social interventions (Cloward & Ohlin, 1960). Even into the 1970s, sociological perspectives, particularly "labeling theory," exerted tremendous national influence in launching federal programs supporting diversion programs and deinstitutionalization.

The prestige and political clout of sociological theories sharply diminished in the 1980s. But no new theoretical paradigm emerged to replace the sociological theories of the 1960s. Instead, delinquency-control policies were dominated by primitive conceptions about general and specific deterrence (Wilson, 1973) and by moralistic notions advocated by activist conservative religious groups.

The narrow set of theories and popular notions that have dominated the delinquency field have overlooked some of the most powerful correlates of youth crime. For example, the most important variable related to delinquency is gender. Male delinquency rates are three to five times higher than female rates. Yet there are few well-developed theories accounting for gender differences in youthful criminality. Prevention programs have rarely, if ever, addressed gender differences in their choice of intervention strategies. Moreover, Chesney-Lind (1989) argues that the etiology of female criminality appears to be very different than that for males. However, even the best prevention programs rest on theoretical and empirical concepts derived exclusively from research on male delinquents.

Another largely unexplored etiological factor is physical and sexual abuse. Several studies show very high rates of childhood abuse among offender populations (Lewis, Shanok, Pincus, & Glaser, 1979). Few delinquency theories or prevention programs have explicitly recognized the role of child abuse as a cause of future criminal conduct.

A similar observation might be made about mental illness and alcohol and drug abuse. Studies of serious juvenile offenders typically show disproportionate rates of mental health problems, including chemical dependency (Baird, 1987; Elliott, Huizinga & Menard, 1988; Krisberg, Austin, Joe & Steele, 1987). While the national "Drug War" has begun to focus public attention on the nexus between drugs and crime, the needed research and program development in this area is still in its infancy.

We need to launch a concerted research program that examines the complex interrelations between drug and alcohol use, mental illness, and delinquency. Such research must include longitudinal studies and should cover a broad range of ethnic communities in which patterns of chemical abuse and delinquent behavior are very diverse. There also is a crying need for new and much more careful evaluations of prevention efforts in the mental health and drug abuse areas.

Changing the Unit of Analysis

With few exceptions, most delinquency research has focused on the individual offender. The central question of this research was what makes certain individuals engage in repetitive delinquent acts? Other researchers have studied delinquent groups, especially fighting gangs. The major question posed by these researchers was what makes individual youths join gangs? The literature has also addressed how delinquent groups facilitate and propel individuals toward more serious and frequent offending patterns.

The work of Shaw and McKay in the 1940s stands in contrast to traditional delinquency research. Shaw and McKay (1942) were principally concerned with social areas of the city. Their main question was why do certain social areas have higher delinquency rates than others? Shaw and McKay evolved a view of delinquency causation that stressed social disorganization. Their theory was translated into the Chicago Area Project, the nation's first large-scale delinquency prevention effort (Finestone, 1976).

More recently, Linsky and Strauss (1986) have explored regional patterns in crime and illness that are linked to various other social indicators. They show that various measures of societal stress are highly correlated with crime rates. The Linsky and Strauss research suggests that future delinquency research should consider shifting the unit of analysis from the individual to the social area. This "ecological approach" to delinquency is quite promising in terms of conceptualizing community or citywide prevention strategies. It directs our attention to macrolevel variables, including economic factors, health care issues, and housing concerns.

While some recent prevention programs have emphasized organizing neighborhood groups such as "Operation Block Watch," the research results have been modest, at best. Another community-level prevention model, developed by the Eisenhower Foundation, is directed at youth employment and political empowerment strategies. Evaluative studies of the Eisenhower program are still in progress.

In sum, the social area, as a unit of analysis for research as well as a target of prevention intervention, deserves far greater attention from criminologists and program planners.

Concluding Observations

American policies for delinquency prevention and control have not been built on a sound foundation of empirical knowledge. Limitations in existing data on youth crime trends and the virtual absence of rigorous research on prevention programs have handicapped our efforts. Not surprisingly, most programs and policies designed to combat youth crime have failed.

Critics of delinquency prevention have explained these poor results in terms of the general ineptitude of government programs and the alleged intractability of chronic delinquents. These critics have placed their faith in commonsense notions about punishment-oriented or deterrence strategies (Murray & Cox, 1979). The evidence supporting the crime-reduction effect of punishment-oriented policies is lacking or negative (Krisberg, 1987).

As delinquency rates have begun to increase in the last five years, there has been renewed interest in prevention programs. For example, a survey of police chiefs and sheriffs found that 70 percent believed that youth-oriented prevention programs should be the highest priority of their departments. National debate on drug policy has also focused public attention on the value of prevention programs to augment law enforcement efforts.

But to truly advance the "state-of-the-art" in delinquency prevention will require better data and more creative thinking about the causes and correlates of youth crime. In this chapter, I have sketched some parts of the needed research agenda.

Improved information on youth crime will require new data collection, especially the refinement of self-report methods. I also have urged the enhancement of current data through qualitative research strategies such as analytic biographies of youthful offenders ("the delinquent's own story") and ethnographic or "street-corner" research. Research in the future must be more closely tied to theory development and testing.

Prevention programs in the future must be guided by empirically sound research. Funding agencies that support prevention programs should mandate rigorous and thorough evaluations. We also need replications of the studies supporting the value of preventive programs such as Head Start.

Delinquency research and prevention practice should revisit the concept of delinquent areas and examine the contemporary relationships of social disorganization to chronic youth crime. Over fifty years ago, William Healy, one of the early intellectual giants of American criminology, expressed this view:

> If the roots of crime lie far back in the foundations of our social order, it may be that only radical social change can bring any large measure of cure. Less unjust social and economic conditions may be the only way out, and until a better social order exists, crime will continue to flourish and society continue to pay the price.
>
> (quoted in Krisberg & Austin, 1978, p. 30)

More recently, Alden Miller and Lloyd Ohlin reached a complementary conclusion:

> Delinquency is a community problem. In the final analysis the means for its prevention and control must be built into the fabric of community life. This can happen only if the community accept its share of responsibility for having generated and perpetuated paths of

socialization that lead to sporadic criminal episodes for some youths and careers in crime for others.

(Miller & Ohlin, 1985, p. 11)

Commencing the research agenda described in this chapter can only bring us closer to translating these perspectives into social action. Research, of course, provides only the tools. Political courage also is needed to rescue our youths from lives of crime.

Notes

1. The federal Office of Juvenile Justice and Delinquency Prevention has just funded a multiyear project to improve the quality and comprehensiveness of national data on youth crime and the juvenile justice system. It remains to be seen if this ambitious program will receive the necessary funding to achieve its objectives.

2. Some researchers such as Hindelang, Hirschi, and Weis (1981) have asked victims to describe the ages of their offenders. This methodology is only useful in offenses in which there is a face-to-face confrontation. Further, the victim's perception of the offender's age may not be very reliable.

3. The limitations of the UCR are currently being partially remedied through a massive redesign of the system. One component of the redesign will substantially increase the amount of detail collected about the actual criminal event. But implementation of these changes will not occur until well into the future.

4. For a more thorough discussion of these issues, see Krisberg, Thornberry, and Austin, 1989.

5. These findings have also been confirmed by two Philadelphia birth cohort studies conducted by Wolfgang and his associates (Tracy, Wolfgang & Figlio, 1985).

6. The work of Elliott, Huizinga & Ageton, (1985) is a notable exception to the absence of theory-based research in recent years.

References

Bachman, J. G., O'Malley, P., & Johnston, J. (1978). *Youth in transition, Vol. 6.* Ann Arbor, Institute of Social Research, University of Michigan.

Baird, S. C. (1987). *The development of risk prediction scales for the California Youthful Offender Parole Board.* San Francisco. National Council on Crime and Delinquency.

Beck, A., Kline, S., & Greenfeld, L. (1988). *Survey of youth in custody: 1987.* Washington, DC: Bureau of Justice Statistics, U.S. Justice Department.

Becker, H. (1963). *The outsiders,* New York: Free Press.

Berrueta-Clement, J. R., Schweinhart, L. J., Barnett, W. S., Epstein, A. S., & Weikert, D. J. (1984). Preschool's effects on social responsibility. In D. Weikert (Ed.), *Changed lives: The effects of the Perry Preschool Program on youths through age nineteen* (pp. 61–73). Ypsilanti, MI: High/Scope Press.

Blumstein, A., Cohen, J., Roth, J., & Visher, C. (Eds.). (1986). *Criminal careers and "career criminals,"* Washington, DC: National Research Council.

Bureau of Justice Statistics. (1988). *Report to the nation on crime and justice (2nd ed.).* Washington, DC: U.S. Government Printing Office.

Chesney-Lind, M. (1989). Girl's crime and woman's place: Toward a feminist model of female delinquency. *Crime and Delinquency, 35,* 5–30.

Cloward, R., & Ohlin, L. (1960). *Delinquency and opportunity.* New York: Free Press.

Currie, E. (1988). *What kind of future?* San Francisco: National Council on Crime and Delinquency.

Elliott, D., Huizinga, D., & Ageton, S. (1985). *Explaining delinquency and drug use.* Beverly Hills, CA: Sage.

Elliott, D., Huizinga, D., & Menard, S. (1988). *Multiple problem youth: Delinquency, substance use and mental health problems.* New York: Springer-Verlag.

Elliott, D., Huizinga, D., & Morse, B. (1987). A career analysis of serious and violent juvenile offenders. In I. M. Schwartz (Ed.), *Violent juvenile crime: What do we know about it and what can we do about it?* (pp. 23–24). Minneapolis, Hubert H. Humphrey Institute of Public Affairs, University of Minnesota.

Finestone, H. (1969). Cats, kids and color. In D. Cressey & D. Ward (Eds.), *Delinquency, crime and social process* (pp. 788–801). New York: Harper and Row.

Finestone, H. (1976). *Victims of change,* Westport, CT: Greenwood Press.

Ford Foundation Project on Social Welfare and the American Future. (1990). *The common good.* New York: Ford Foundation.

Greenwood, P., & Abrahamse, A. (1980). *Selective incapacitation.* Santa Monica, CA: Rand.

Hagedorn, J. (1988). *People and folks.* Chicago: Lake View Press.

Hamparian, D., Schuster, R., Dinitz, S., & Conrad, J. (1978). *The violent few,* Lexington, MA: Lexington Books.

Haugen, D., Costello, T., Schwartz, I., Krisberg, B., & Litsky, P. (1982). *Public attitudes towards youth crime.* Hubert H. Humphrey Institute of Public Affairs, University of Minnesota.

Hawkins, D., & Weis, J. (1985). The social development model: An integrated approach to delinquency prevention. *Journal of Primary Prevention, 6,* 73–97.

Hindelang, M., Hirschi, T., & Weis, J. (1981). *Measuring delinquency,* Beverly Hills, CA: Sage.

Hirschi, T. (1969). *Causes of delinquency.* Berkeley and Los Angeles: University of California Press.

Huizinga, D., & Elliott, D. (1987). Juvenile offenders: Prevalence, offender incarceration and arrest rates by race. *Crime and Delinquency, 33,* 206–222.

Krisberg, B. (1987). Preventing and controlling violent youth crime. In I. M. Schwartz (Ed.), *Violent juvenile crime: What do we know about it and what can we do about it?* (pp. 35–55). Hubert H. Humphrey Institute of Public Affairs, University of Minnesota.

Krisberg, B., & Austin, J. (1978). *The children of Ishmael.* Palo Alto, CA: Mayfield Press.

Krisberg, B., Austin, J., Fong, M., & Lawrence, W. (1981). *The national evaluation of delinquency prevention.* San Francisco: National Council on Crime and Delinquency.

Krisberg, B., Austin, J., Joe, K., & Steele, P. (1987). *The impact of juvenile court sanctions.* San Francisco: National Council on Crime and Delinquency.

Krisberg, B., Thornberry, T. P., & Austin, J. (1989). *Juveniles taken into custody: Developing national statistics.* San Francisco: National Council on Crime and Delinquency.

Lewis, D. O., Shanok, S. S., Pincus, J. H., & Glaser, G.H., (1979). Violent juvenile delinquents: Psychiatric, neurological, psychological and abuse factors. *Journal of the American Academy of Child Psychiatry, 18,* 307–319.

Liebow, E. (1967). *Tally's corner.* Boston: Little, Brown.

Linsky, A., & Strauss, M. (1986). *Social stress in the United States.* Dover, MA: Auburn House.

McCord, J. (1978). A thirty-year follow-up of treatment effects. *American Psychologist, 33,* 284–289.

Miller, A., & Ohlin, L. (1985). *Delinquency and the community.* Beverly Hills, CA: Sage.

Moore, J. (1978). *Homeboys: Gangs, drugs and prison in the barrios of Los Angeles.* Philadelphia: Temple University Press.

Murphy, D. (1986). The prevalence of handicapping conditions among juvenile delinquents. *Remedial Special Education, 7,* 7–17.

Murray, C., & Cox, L. (1979). *Beyond probation.* Beverly Hills, CA: Sage.

National Institute of Drug Abuse. (1988). *National household survey on drug abuse.* Rockville, MD: Author.

Office of Juvenile Justice and Delinquency Prevention. (1989). *Program of research on the causes and correlates of delinquency.* Washington, DC: Author.

Phillips, K. (1990). *The politics of rich and poor.* New York: Random House.

Polk, K., & Kobrin, S. (1972). *Delinquency prevention through youth development.* Washington, DC: U.S. Department of Health, Education and Welfare.

Sanders, W. B. (1970). *Juvenile offenders for a thousand years.* Chapel Hill: University of North Carolina Press.

Schwartz, I., & Abbey, J. (1990). *1990 Michigan juvenile crime survey.* Ann Arbor: Center for the Study of Youth Policy, University of Michigan.

Sessions, W. (1990). *Crime in the United States.* Washington, DC: Federal Bureau of Investigation.

Shaw, C. (1938). *Brothers in crime.* Chicago: University of Chicago Press.

Shaw, C. (1966). *The jackroller.* Chicago: University of Chicago Press.

Shaw, C., & McKay, H. (1942). *Juvenile delinquency and urban areas.* Chicago: University of Chicago Press.

Steinhart, D. (1988). *Public attitudes on youth crime.* San Francisco: National Council on Crime and Delinquency.

Sutherland, E. (1937). *The professional thief.* Chicago: University of Chicago Press.

Thornberry, T. P., Farnsworth, M., Lizotle, A., & Stern, S. (1987). *A longitudinal examination of the cause and correlates of delinquency.* Albany, NY: Hindelang Criminal Justice Research Center.

Tracy, P., Wolfgang, M., & Figlio, R. (1985). *Delinquency in two birth cohorts: Executive summary.* Washington, DC: National Institute of Juvenile Justice and Delinquency Prevention.

Wilson, J. Q. (1973). *Thinking about crime.* New York: Basic Books.

2

The New Youth Gangs:
Social Policy and Malignant
Neglect

C. Ronald Huff

T
he recent emergence or, in some cases, reemergence of youth
gangs in American cities from the East Coast to Honolulu (with
the "gang capital of the world," Los Angeles, in between) has
received a great deal of attention from the mass media (much of it distorted
and sensationalized) and some attention from scholarly researchers. Gang
research in the United States dates back to Thrasher's (1927) classic work,
and seven decades later the most recent "new wave" of gangs is being
chronicled by such researchers as Campbell (1984, 1990), K. Chin (1986,
1990a, 1990b), Fagan (1989, 1990), Hagedorn (1987, 1988), Huff (1989,
1990), Klein and Maxson (1989), Moore (1978, 1985), Taylor (1990a,
1990b), and Vigil (1988, 1990 [with Yun]).

In this chapter, we will take a closer look at the new youth gangs to see
who they are; who joins them and why; what functions they serve; how
much diffusion has occurred; how gangs have evolved; what linkages exist
between gangs and drugs; and what policies might be considered to
address youth gangs as a social problem. An underlying theme of this
chapter is that youth gangs per se are not *the* problem; rather, they
represent an extreme adolescent subculture, and a symptom of more
fundamental, underlying social and economic problems in our society—
problems that have been largely ignored, or even exacerbated, by our
social policy (or its lack).

Developmental and Definitional Issues

Normal adolescents value their peers far more than they value any other
reference group. Therefore, in analyzing youth gangs, we must begin with
the understanding that it is normal and healthy for adolescents to want to

20

be with their peers. In fact, adolescents who are "loners" are often among the more maladjusted youths. Adolescents go to dances together, party together, shop together (and often shoplift together), so it is not surprising that some of them join together in one type of social group known as a "gang." "Groupness," then, is a familiar phenomenon in the adolescent subculture, and gangs simply represent a more extreme manifestation of that strong preference for "being together" and "belonging to something." In fact, most societies seem to have a term that corresponds, at least loosely, to our own use of the term "gang." Whether it is the *chimpira* of Japan, the *raggare* of Sweden, the Dutch *nozem*, the Italian *vitelloni*, the *stilyagi* of the USSR, the Yugoslavian *tapkaroschi*, or their counterparts in many other nations, there is usually some way of designating youth gangs.

What separates a gang from other adolescent groups is (1) the gang's more routine involvement in illegal activities; (2) a more deliberate quality to these illegal activities; (3) a greater tendency to claim some form of "turf" (though for more recent gangs, this "turf" is not necessarily neighborhood-based); and (4) generally, better-developed leadership. If not for these characteristics, gangs would be largely indistinguishable from other adolescent social groups, such as athletic teams or Boy Scouts and Girl Scouts.

Gang research (Campbell, 1984, 1990) indicates that there are some true female gangs, as well as many female gang "groupies" (females whose gang identity is largely derived from "belonging" to male gang members). However, the vast majority of gang members in the United States are fourteen- to twenty-four-year-old males (though the age range is actually from about ten to over thirty). This may be at least partially attributable to the fact that many gang members come from female-headed households with no adult male present in the home, and often no acceptable adult male role model involved in the youth's life. The proportion of such female-headed households has grown dramatically in recent years. For example, among African-American families, the proportion of female-headed families increased from approximately 18 percent in 1940 to more than 40 percent by the 1980s. Moreover (and with direct implications for youth gang membership), approximately one-half of all African-American families with children under eighteen are now female-headed (Wilson, 1987). The unmet need for "male bonding" on the part of males from such families is all too readily met by nearby male youth gangs. A need that could just as easily be met in a positive, prosocial manner is all too often met through socialization into a gang, with its attendant delinquent/criminal value system.

Though many gang members come from intact nuclear families (Sanchez-Jankowski, 1991), the gang can serve as a surrogate extended family for those adolescents whose own families are perceived as not meeting their needs for belonging, nurturance, and acceptance. Some contemporary youth gangs have even been known to accompany their members to the local cemetery to "grieve" with them on the anniversary of a family member's death, an action that society at large has always viewed as a private family function. Rather than viewing gangs simply as groups of "young criminals," then, we must understand that gangs often do address some important needs of their members, needs such as grieving, male bonding, and protection from rival gangs, though often in a socially and legally unacceptable manner.

In the United States of the 1990s, this scenario is played out daily—not just in the ghettos of Chicago or the barrios of Los Angeles, but in poor neighborhoods in scores of cities from Boston to San Diego and from Seattle to Miami. Many small cities and towns are also experiencing youth gangs, some for the first time. All of these cities have one thing in common: they have never experienced gangs quite like the new gangs.

The New Gangs

Evolution and Diversity

Because Los Angeles, New York, and Chicago are our nation's largest media centers, there has been a tendency to equate gangs with those cities in particular. Whether it was Chicago's Vice Lords and Black Gangster Disciples or the Crips and the Bloods of Los Angeles, each of the past four decades has witnessed some prototype "supergang" (or rival supergangs) that has received national media attention.

Recently, that focus has shifted westward as Los Angeles has supplanted New York City as the nation's media capital and, coincidentally, as its gang capital as well (with a currently estimated 85,000 Crips and Bloods in Los Angeles County alone). Popular culture reflects this shift, with films, novels, and even plays about gangs and gang-related violence shifting from the classic *West Side Story* and *The Warriors*, both of which dealt with New York City gangs, to *Colors, New Jack City,* and *Boyz N the Hood,* all of which concern Los Angeles gangs. The debuts of the latter three movies were all associated with gang-related violence inside and outside movie theaters across the nation, since rival gangs were attracted to these films and found themselves on the same "turf" at the same time.

Gangs have evolved from the classic street-corner, neighborhood-"turf"-oriented gangs such as those chronicled by Whyte (1943) in his classic study of an Italian slum neighborhood in Boston to contemporary gangs that just as often define as "turf" their girlfriends, designated shopping malls, and local skating rinks. Schools, which used to be a sort of "neutral zone" largely immune from gang warfare, are now caught up in gang battles and recruiting wars. Recent research suggests that one of the unintended consequences of court-ordered busing, instituted to address the problems of racial segregation, has been the forced mixing of rival gangs in the same schools (Hagedorn, 1988; Huff, 1989). In the past a neighborhood gang attended a neighborhood school, but now members of gangs from different neighborhoods are bused across the metropolis to schools in which they encounter rival gangs. Schools were never organized with this problem in mind, and many of them are now struggling with new kinds of safety and security issues related to gangs.

Another evolutionary development has been gang migration. In 1986 popular wisdom had it that Los Angeles gangs, especially the Crips, were migrating across America and setting up "franchises" to distribute drugs. Research on Ohio gangs, however, provided reasons for skepticism because during the years 1986–1988 every identified Ohio gang leader who had moved to Ohio from Los Angeles, Chicago, or Detroit was in Ohio because his parent(s) had moved to Ohio. Several of these young males had, indeed, been involved in gangs in Los Angeles, Chicago, or Detroit, and their experience certainly made it relatively easy for them to start new gangs in Ohio and assume leadership roles in their respective new gangs (Huff, 1989), but field research never produced any evidence to support a continuing, direct connection between the new Ohio gangs and the cities of origin of their respective leaders. There were no Ohio "chapters" of L.A. gangs, for example. This finding (Huff, 1989) confirmed studies in other locations that were "noncore" gang cities, such as Evanston, Illinois (Rosenbaum & Grant, 1983) and Milwaukee (Hagedorn, 1988), whose local gangs consisted of local youths, although the gang graffiti and other gang symbols in both those cities were definitely influenced by Chicago gang graffiti and gang symbolism.

In the past several years, however, all of this has changed dramatically. By 1989, members of Los Angeles gangs had been identified by law enforcement agencies in nearly all fifty states, mainly involved in drug trafficking (U.S. Department of Justice, 1989). In Ohio, for example, L.A. gang members have been arrested in cities as small as Hamilton, Lorain, and Canton—and they were not in Canton to visit the Pro Football Hall of Fame! Undeniably, what is termed "gang migration"—actually, gang *member* migration—has increased markedly in the past few years. Why?

Field research on gangs, interviews with other gang researchers, and Los Angeles and local law enforcement officials, and information from the Drug Enforcement Administration, indicates three main reasons:

1. There is less intense competition for "drug turf" in the nation's smaller cities than in Los Angeles, where the competition has sometimes been on a block-by-block basis.
2. There is greater potential profit to be made in the smaller cities. For example, one "rock" of "crack" cocaine sells for about $3–5 in Los Angeles or Detroit, but will bring $15–25 in smaller midwestern cities.
3. Because the crack problem is a more recent one in smaller cities, there has been less intensive law enforcement "heat" on the drug-trafficking networks. This situation is changing rapidly, however, as the smaller cities recognize the extent of their respective drug problems and intensify their law enforcement efforts.

As Carl Taylor has commented with respect to Detroit gangs, "When young Detroiters invade the state of Ohio, they are in pursuit of the American dream. That dream may appear distorted to middle-class or working-class America, yet it is truly business, the spirit of American entrepreneurship" (1990b, p. 115).

How do incoming gang members get a foothold in local communities? Typically, they either have a local contact with whom they live and work as a "base" or they engage in one of three other strategies. The drug entrepreneur can use the "Double Down" or "The Tenth Rock" strategy, wherein the drug distributor either offers a local person twice as much "supply" as he is accustomed to getting for a given dollar investment or gives the person ten rocks of crack cocaine to sell, with the incentive that he need only pay the distributor for nine of them, keeping the profit from the tenth rock for himself. Obviously, an entrepreneurially minded amateur might be enticed with such a "nest egg."

Or he can use the "Welfare Mother Scam." This strategy involves approaching a welfare mother and offering to pay her rent and/or supply her with drugs in exchange for the use of her house. She may not even be informed as to the purpose for which the house is to be used. In many of these cases, there comes a time when the drug distributors stop paying the rent. A not uncommon scenario is for the woman to protest and demand that the agreement be kept, at which point she (or even her children) may be assaulted or even killed. Some women, hooked on drugs, have even agreed to exchange sex for drugs (in L.A. they are cynically referred to as "rock stars" or "hubba whores" by those who use and abuse them).

Or the distributor can use the "Intimidation through Violence" strategy. To discourage competitors for drug turf, the distributor can employ brutal beatings, heinous murders, mutilations, and other incidents of dramatic violence designed to shock competitors and enemies.

It would be misleading to imply that all gangs or all gang members are involved in drug distribution. That is certainly not the case. In one of the best studies of the gangs/drugs connection, researcher Jeffrey Fagan reached the following conclusion:

> Although gangs may be distinct social networks that are involved more extensively than other networks in substance use and crime, there appears to be diversity among gang members and gangs in their participation in these behaviors. Both gang and non-gang youths are involved in serious delinquency and substance use, although perhaps fewer non-gang youths participate in these behaviors and do so less often. (1990, p. 210).

The lucrative drug market, an "equal opportunity employer," has recently attracted gang members who are now showing up in drug distribution networks that may or may not be controlled by the gang, depending on which city is being analyzed (gang *control* of drug markets appears to be extremely rare other than in Los Angeles). The most frequent scenario appears to involve *individual* gang members in drug distribution networks that are not gang-controlled activities.

One of the classic questions posed about gangs is, how does one tell the difference between a group and a gang? Although no single definition of "gang" has ever met with universal approval, historic events have now forced us to move on to a new question, one that is confronting law enforcement agencies and gang researchers every day. That question is, how does one tell the difference between a gang and organized crime? The line dividing gang and organized crime activities has blurred in the past few years as gang behavior has changed and as new criminal organizations have arisen, often composed of either immigrant groups or hard-core, sophisticated, lethal street gangs who are often making enormous profits via drug sales.

Three Nontraditional Criminal Groups

According to the U.S. Senate Governmental Affairs Committee's Permanent Subcommittee on Investigations and the General Accounting Office, five nontraditional criminal groups are now posing significant challenges to law enforcement and drug control efforts. These five are Colombian drug traffickers, Jamaican posses, Chinese gangs, Vietnamese gangs, and Los Angeles street gangs. The absence of a national agenda, outdated investigative techniques, and cultural barriers, along with a lack of cooperation and coordination among agencies, were cited as major impediments to our success in controlling the criminal activities of these groups (U.S. General Accounting Office, 1990). Three of these five nontraditional criminal groups fall within the purview of this chapter, and deserve a closer analysis.

Los Angeles Street Gangs: Crips and Bloods. At present, the two most notorious street gang names in the United States are "Crips" and "Bloods" (aka "Pirus"). They are important not only because of their size, their violent behavior, and their extensive involvement in drug distribution, but also because members of these gangs have been showing up in nearly every part of the nation in the past few years. What began as a "Los Angeles problem" has quickly evolved into a nationwide problem impacting scores of cities from coast to coast.

A profile of the Crips and the Bloods can be drawn based on scholarly research, mass media accounts, law enforcement reports, and personal interviews conducted with law enforcement and investigative personnel over the past five years. Both the Crips and the Bloods began as primarily black and Hispanic local (south L.A.) street gangs circa 1969. The Crips were first; then the Bloods developed to provide protection against the Crips. These "supergangs" do not have centralized leaderships. Instead, they are organized into numerous "sets" (individual gangs), usually based on a particular location. Unlike the image portrayed in the movie *Colors* (reasonably accurate at that time), there is little loyalty now within these gangs. Crips will kill fellow Crips and Bloods will kill other Bloods if such bloodshed will produce greater drug profits. There can be as much variance and conflict between different *sets* of the *same* gang as there is between *rival* gangs.

Members of these gangs generally range in age from the midteens to the midthirties, although there are photographs of as many as three generations of gang members in one family wearing their colors at a family get-together.

Street gangs such as the Crips and the Bloods generally have a membership that is stratified by age, sophistication, and level of commitment. Membership reflects three major groupings: leaders, "hard-cores," and marginals or "wanna'-be's" (they "want-to-be" a hard-core member of the gang). Leaders and hard-core members are fully committed to the gang, including its delinquent and criminal activities. Generally, they have been with the gang for a longer period of time and are somewhat older and more sophisticated. They would *never* associate with other gangs. The marginal associates, or "wanna' be's," on the other hand, are not fully committed to the gang and its agenda and might even hang out with rival gangs. They are "trying it out" to see if they like it. One of the dangers to be avoided by police is *overreacting* by prematurely classifying ("labeling") these marginal "wanna' be's" as gang members and targeting them for arrest. In fact, some gang members got their first real gang identity courtesy of the police, who saw them associating with a gang and therefore assumed they were committed to that gang (see, for example, Hagedorn, 1988). Once the word gets out that a youth is "with" a certain gang, he then may feel *compelled* to join that gang, if only for protection from rival gangs who will now see him as "the enemy."

Age is often reflected in different "sets" of Crips or Bloods. For example, younger Crips may be members of the "Junior Crips" or the "Baby Crips" until they gain experience and/or attract notoriety through their acts. Older members may call themselves "OG's" ("Original Gangsters" or "Old Gangsters") or employ some similar designation to indicate their seniority.

Street gangs such as the Bloods and the Crips also have distinctive symbols and clothing that designate their gang affiliations. Children have been murdered simply because they were wearing the "wrong" color hat, handkerchief, or shoelaces (red for Bloods, blue for Crips) and were mistaken for "the enemy." Increasingly, the clothing of choice includes expensive warm-up/jogging suits (for example, L.A. Dodgers blue or Oakland Raiders black for Crips; Cincinnati Reds red for Bloods). In fact, the symbolic meaning of clothing can be as subtle as wearing British Knights clothing because of the "B.K." logo contained on its merchandise: "B.K." logo is ideal for a Crip who wants to advertise that he is a "Blood Killer," or one who is loyal to the Crips and will kill (or has killed) Bloods.

These gangs also use distinctive graffiti, in terms of both content and form, to mark their "turf," celebrate their perceived dominance of their area, and sometimes "put down" rival gangs (for example, by crossing out the rival gang's name, writing over it, or writing that gang's name upside-down). Such "put-downs" are frequently the immediate precipitant of violent assaults ("paybacks"). Los Angeles, for example, has been averaging nearly five hundred "gang-related" homicides per year; even though the L.A. police department's definition of "gang-related" is much broader than, for example, Chicago's (see Maxson and Klein, 1990), there is unquestionably a great deal of gang-related violence in the L.A. metropolitan area. Moreover, about half of all the victims of gang-related homicides in L.A. are not gang members but innocent citizens, including many, many children.

Chinese Gangs. We are only beginning to acquire systematic knowledge concerning Chinese street gangs and Chinese organized crime. Prior to 1965, crime rates in Chinese communities were, with rare exceptions, quite low (Beach, 1932; MacGill, 1938) and delinquency was unusual (Sung, 1977). One of the main reasons for these low rates of crime and delinquency is the fact that prior to 1965 there were few Chinese adolescents living in the United States, due to the Chinese Exclusion Act of 1882 and the National Origins Act of 1924 (Fessler, 1983; Sung, 1979).

According to Kwong (1987) and Takagi and Platt (1978), the watershed year in Chinese immigration was 1965 due to the passage of the Immigration and Naturalization Act of that year. This act granted China preferred nation status and established priorities for immigration. Chinese immigration to the United States has grown dramatically in the intervening twenty-five years and has impacted significantly upon Chinese subcommunities, whose families, district associations, and social agencies were not prepared to help the large number of immigrants adjust to their new communities (R. Chin, 1977; Hung & Pilisuk, 1977). Crime increased significantly and Chinese gangs developed in San Francisco, Los Angeles, Boston, Toronto, Vancouver, and New York City. Although it has been estimated that there are fewer than 2,000 Chinese gang members in the United States, they have been involved in some very serious gang violence and heroin trafficking (Daly, 1983; U.S. Senate, 1986).

Most of what we have learned about Chinese gangs is based on the work of Miller (1975), Loo (1976), Robinson and Joe (1980), and especially that of Ko-lin Chin (1986, 1990a, 1990b), whose research provides the basis for the following discussion. We know that Chinese gangs are predominantly male (girls hang around with the males and may carry guns for them, but they do not become initiated members). Most gang members are in their late teens or early twenties, with the known age range running from thirteen to thirty-seven. In the 1960s and 1970s most gang members were from Hong Kong, but since the late 1970s members have also come from mainland China and Chinese communities in Southeast Asia, especially Vietnam. Some recently established Chinese gangs have even included Korean youths.

The typical Chinese gang includes about twenty to fifty hard-core members, along with some inactives and marginals. Current estimates indicate that New York City has about nine active Chinese gangs, with a total membership between two and four hundred. Organizationally, most

Chinese gangs have one or two leaders, except for the Ghost Shadows, who have four or five *tai lou* (big brothers) at the top. Next in the hierarchy are the lieutenants or associate leaders who are in charge of the rank-and-file street soldiers (*ma jai*, or "little horses"), who control neighborhood "turf" and commit extortion, robbery, and street violence. The leaders also serve as liaison with the elders of the local tongs and they receive payment from these elders or from the local gambling houses. Leaders rarely participate in street violence, but they do give the orders, provide ammunition, and pay rewards for "contract hits" that are carried out by "shooters" at the street-soldier level.

Initially, most Chinese gang members joined the gangs voluntarily and there was a great deal of camaraderie. In the past fifteen years, however, there has been a large increase in the use of intimidation and coercion, including assault, to recruit new members. Those targeted for recruitment are often lonely and vulnerable youths who are dropouts, speak little English, appear to have a lot of idle time on their hands, and seem to have few if any job prospects. If a youth decides to join a Chinese gang, he will experience an initiation ceremony in which he takes oaths, burns yellow paper, and drinks wine mixed with blood.

Chinese gangs tend to have two or more cliques who dislike and distrust each other. Intragang tension and conflict is common, often erupting when one clique perceives that there has been an inequitable distribution of criminal profits, for example. Leaders constantly plot to have one another killed, and a Chinese gang leader is, in fact, more likely to be killed by his own associates than by a rival gang (K. Chin, 1990b). Tong elders also sometimes provoke conflict, which serves to keep the gangs divided rather than united, thus ensuring that the gangs will not acquire enough power to challenge the tong's status.

K. Chin (1990b) has identified seven unique characteristics that distinguish Chinese gangs from other ethnic gangs:

1. They have close associations with powerful community organizations.
2. They invest in legitimate businesses and spend considerable time doing legitimate business.
3. They are part of national or international networks.
4. They reflect the heavy cultural influence of Chinese secret societies and the Triada.
5. They immediately involve themselves in serious crime.
6. They control large amounts of money, and monetary profit is their main goal.
7. They systematically victimize local businesses.

Vietnamese Gangs. Due to their more recent development in the United States, less is known about Vietnamese gangs than about other kinds of gangs. Based on the research of Vigil and Yun (1990) concerning Vietnamese gangs in southern California (where nearly half of all Vietnamese in America live), we know that the Vietnamese youth gangs, like the Vietnamese communities from which they come, developed as a result of immigration following the end of the Vietnam War. Although the initial wave of Vietnamese refugees were relatively well educated, highly urbanized, young, and of high socioeconomic status, the subsequent migration of the "boat people" brought to the United States a large number of poorer, less educated, less urbanized, less "employable" Vietnamese who were much less prepared to adapt to American society (Bach & Bach, 1980; Grant, 1979; Marsh, 1980; Nguyen & Henkin, 1982; Skinner, 1980).

While the average Asian-American household income in 1980 was approximately $22,000 per year (above the national average), the average annual income for Vietnamese households in Los Angeles County is currently approximately $9,000 (Larson, 1988). Many Vietnamese immigrants, just like their Mexican counterparts, are unfamiliar with their legal rights and work for as little as $1 an hour in illegal sweatshops in the garment industry. Cutbacks in federal assistance and the high cost of living in California have combined to create severe economic constraints for these Vietnamese immigrants, who are frequently attracted to the underground economy as a means of survival.

Certain Vietnamese cultural beliefs and traditions have made the Vietnamese more vulnerable to exploitation by youth gangs. For example, it is common for Vietnamese to shun banks and keep cash and gold bars in their homes (Berkman, 1984). In addition, they are frequently alienated from law enforcement and often refuse either to report crimes or to cooperate in police investigations, in part due to their fear of reprisals and their belief that the police cannot adequately protect them. This, of course, leaves them quite vulnerable to extortion. There is also a significant cultural gap between the Vietnamese and local police, who only recently have begun recruiting officers who can speak Vietnamese (Morganthau, Contreras, Lam & Sandza, 1982).

The Vietnamese gangs themselves appear to include primarily youths in their mid- to late teens and early twenties (they often refer to themselves as "boys," to distinguish themselves from the older Vietnamese involved in organized crime groups such as the Frogmen, the Paratroopers, or the Black Eels). These youths are often several years older than their officially reported ages, because it is common among Vietnamese parents to underreport their children's ages by several years so that they can be enrolled in lower grades in school to compensate for their inadequate English language preparation. This practice, however, has led to great embarrassment for many Vietnamese youths, who have often been taunted and ridiculed at school for being in class with younger children.

Such ridicule at school, along with academic failure, non acceptance in the community, culture conflict, and anti-Asian racism creates a great deal of anger and frustration for these youths, who also find it difficult to acquire the material goods advertised in the mass media. All of these factors appear to contribute to their susceptibility to gang involvement. The gangs can offer a surrogate family, money, recreation, and a sense of autonomy.

The acquisition of money is often accomplished via car theft and robbery and, later on, by extortion. It is reported that by intimidating Vietnamese citizens in their own homes, gang members can usually get about $15–20,000 per residence (Vigil & Yun, 1990). Such residential robberies of fellow Vietnamese may seem paradoxical, given the ethnic pride found among Vietnamese, but the Vietnamese gang members prefer to rob fellow Vietnamese rather than whites or other racial groups who "know a lot of law and don't keep cash [within their homes]" (Vigil & Yun, 1990, p. 158).

The Vietnamese gangs tend to be very pragmatic, not only in their selection of victims, but also in their avoidance of visible gang symbols, violent conflict over neighborhood turf ("that's stupid"), and drug dealing (perceived as unnecessary because of the ease of residential robbery and also because start-up costs are too high). Vigil and Yun (1990) also report that Vietnamese gangs are extremely fluid, claiming no turf, having little or no differentiation of roles within the gang, and allowing members to drift into and out of the gang and even into other gangs. They are also fluid in terms of travel, with informants reporting that they had traveled to many states, committing robberies along the way and sharing one motel room (among fifteen or twenty persons of both sexes), rather than renting multiple rooms and thus inviting suspicion (Vigil & Yun, 1990).

The Social Policy Vacuum: Malignant Neglect

In the United States youth gangs are not a new problem. As indicated earlier, Thrasher's classic study of youth gangs was published in 1927. By the 1950s youth gangs were regarded as a serious problem in the major cities of our country. The problem has only grown worse in the past decade. Walter Miller of Harvard University, who has devoted a substantial part of his distinguished career to the study of youth gangs, recently observed that, "Youth gangs of the 1980s and 1990s are more numerous, more prevalent, and more violent than in the 1950s, probably more so than at any time in the country's history" (1990, p. 263).

Miller went on to assess why the nation has failed to solve its youth gang problem, identifying the following major reasons: (1) failure to develop a comprehensive gang-control strategy; (2) failure to take a national, rather than a local, perspective on the problem; (3) failure to insist on a close linkage between solid theoretical rationales and program design; (4) failure to insist on rigorous program evaluation; (5) failure to provide resources commensurate with the severity of the gang problem; (6) failure to establish a central clearinghouse or organization with primary responsibility for gang prevention and control; and (7) failure to recognize the implications of the social context of gang life (1990).

Analogues for these failures could be cited for other major social problems, ranging from health care to homelessness. These failures reflect a social policy malaise in the government of the United States. Problems such as gangs, crime, inadequate health care, and homelessness require public policies based on long-term planning and effective long-term strategies for prevention and control. But long-term planning is foreign to our impatient society whose values are more closely reflected in the prevalence of fast food, microwave ovens, and fifteen-second "sound bites" of news, and whose political system rewards only short-term "quick fixes" that can be used as ammunition for reelection—the ultimate triumph of form over substance!

Youth gangs are not "the problem." Rather, they are one symptom of more fundamental, underlying socioeconomic problems—problems with both macrolevel components (e.g., structural unemployment and children living in poverty) and microlevel components (e.g., racism and its daily social/psychological effects). The opinion that youth gangs and their members are the problem and that the answer lies in simply arresting gang members, convicting them, and locking them up is a view that is futile and that has now been rejected even by most law enforcement leaders. Los Angeles offers a lesson concerning the futility of that policy, which is one reason why the Los Angeles Police Department created the D.A.R.E. (Drug Abuse Resistance Education) Program and has begun to emphasize *prevention* as the key. Some of the more enlightened law enforcement organizations, such as the Honolulu Police Department, work actively with community agencies to ensure that prevention receives sufficient emphasis in local and state responses to gangs and crime.

The aggressive enforcement and deterrence approach can at best be only one part of the solution. While we need "sticks," we also need "carrots." Most youths will respond to carrots (properly structured incentives and rewards), but not all will. It is perhaps especially unlikely that those who have experienced substantial profits from criminal behavior (e.g., drug sales, auto theft) will respond favorably to anything less than "big money." For some, we will always need sticks (sanctions), including incarceration for those who pose a clear and present danger to public safety.

The fundamental, underlying socioeconomic problems of our society have both macrolevel and microlevel components. But most of the microlevel components, such as the daily effects of racism on the quality of one's life and the "rage" that such racism fuels, are directly related to macrolevel variables such as structural unemployment. One need only look at a wide array of data comparing blacks and whites to see this truth. Everyone knows that life expectancy is lower for African-Americans as a group than for whites as a group. But what happens if we control for socioeconomic *class?* Middle-class African-Americans compare closely to middle-class whites on most important outcome measures, such as life expectancy, precisely because education and income *do make an important difference* in the quality of one's life and in one's ability to avoid criminality, as well as other social and medical pathologies. And it is amazing what a measure of success will do to reduce one's internal rage at the society in which one lives!

We are not plagued by middle-class gangs. This is not to say that middle-class kids don't break the law. They do, and sometimes they even commit violent crimes. Some of the most dysfunctional families in America are middle class or upper class, in which children are given plenty of money and Nintendo games, but little of their parents' time or love. But the *gang* problem of America overwhelmingly involves members of the urban underclass. Gangs in America consist overwhelmingly of poor, inner-city, African-American and Hispanic youths, with some poor whites and some recent Asian immigrants thrown into the mix. These are the dispossessed members of our society. Cloward and Ohlin (1960) would point out that they are, by and large, pursuing "success" via illegal means because they believe that the legal routes to success are not available to them.

And why shouldn't they believe that? Because it's "un-American?" Horatio Alger stories notwithstanding, the realities of contemporary American life suggest that Underclass America does not see steady employment in its future. Instead of being motivated to complete high school and move on to college, as so many middle-class kids are, most poor kids grow up wondering what good it would do to finish high school in the 1990s, since that accomplishment usually doesn't lead to long-term, decent jobs for their brothers and sisters. Even if they were to complete high school and were judged admissible to college, few of them believe they could ever afford a college education.

But they want material success, in the form of conspicuous consumer goods such as flashy cars, $150 sneakers, and the latest designer clothing, those symbols of success in Consumer America that are depicted on national television every single night of their lives. So, if IBM, the NFL, the NBA, MBL (Major League Baseball), or even a respectable career in a lower-paying profession are not in their future, they might still believe they can buy nice "wheels" and nice "threads" if they can make enough money by selling drugs, serving as a lookout for a crack house, pimping, prostituting themselves, stealing cars, or pursuing any one of dozens of other illegal ways of making money. And with children constituting the largest and fastest-growing impoverished group in the United States, the implications for the "pool" of potential gang members are clear.

If we, as a society, do not provide better social support and better access to the legal routes to success, we are ultimately guilty of "blaming the victims" when some of these young people turn to gangs and crime to fulfill their needs. This argument does not *excuse* or *condone* their illegal behavior, but it certainly helps to *explain* it! The question is, what can we do about it?

Remedies for the Gang Problem

Gangs are a symptom of broader socioeconomic problems—a *dependent* variable, not an *independent* variable! Therefore, the strategies that are likely to have a positive impact on gangs are also likely to impact upon crime, mental illness, homelessness, and other forms of "social pathology" in our society. Four such strategies are (1) the development of a full-employment economy; (2) the development of a program of targeted youth service and youth employment; (3) nationwide, mandatory pre-school Head Start; and (4) targeted, community-based public/private nonprofit intervention projects in "high-risk" areas of our cities.

Development of a Full-Employment Economy

One of the findings from recent youth gang studies is that gang members tend to remain in their gangs longer than used to be the case. Instead of "maturing out" of the gangs, it is frequently the case these days that a gang member will begin his gang activity in his early to mid teens, "do time" for delinquent and/or criminal offenses, then return from the correctional system and go right back to the gang (see, for example, Hagedorn, 1988). One of the main reasons for this is the shift in our economy from an industrial to a post industrial, service-oriented economic system.

Gang members often drop out of high school as a reaction to disciplinary measures, academic failure, rebellion, and/or the numbing effects of sometimes unresponsive teachers and a curriculum perceived as irrelevant. Nonetheless, it used to be the case that such a high school dropout could find a decent job if and when he became motivated to do so. Not every good job required a high school diploma. One could work in the steel mills, the auto plants, or other industrial jobs (especially in the northeastern and midwestern industrial states). Many of those jobs are gone. Some have either disappeared entirely; others have been shifted to Sunbelt locations away from major urban areas or out of the United States entirely. Many of the cities that are currently plagued with gangs do not have jobs for which gang members can qualify. An uneducated youth who couldn't find a decent job used to be able to join the military as a final resort. Today, that is not the case, for the shrinking armed forces have raised their minimum standards and now routinely demand a high school diploma.

What does that leave? Increasingly, these youths turn to "street hustling," robbery, auto theft, playing some role in a drug distribution network, stealing from vending machines, and other illegal means to support themselves. Since drug distribution and other illegal enterprises tend to be "equal opportunity employers," the youths find more of a "level playing field" on which to compete than is generally the case in the legal economic markets. They are functioning entirely within what is known as "the hidden economy" of our nation. They do not pay taxes on their earnings. What they earn sometimes carries with it great risk—risk to themselves and to innocent victims. In a recent study following up on the thirty-seven founding members of Milwaukee's African-American gangs, Hagedorn (1991) found that 59 percent were involved in drug trafficking within five years, while only 19 percent had full-time jobs. Similarly, Spergel (1990) found that of 276 gang members on probation in San Diego County, fully 75 percent had been convicted of drug offenses at one time or another.

Unemployment and underemployment in our society impact disproportionately upon minorities, who are also disproportionately represented in the juvenile and criminal justice systems. But, as Moynihan (1973) noted, the United States alone among the industrial nations failed to institute a postwar economic policy that placed continued full employment at the top of the priority list. Unlike some of the European nations, we did not develop systematic apprenticeship programs, job retraining, public job creation, or long-term planning to anticipate and prepare for the shift to a post industrial economic system. Instead, we opted to allow "market forces" to dictate employment prospects, a form of Social Darwinism and malignant neglect from which we have never recovered.

It is imperative that legal economic opportunities for our youth—and their parents or guardians—be able to compete successfully with illegal economic opportunities. Today, in many cities, that is not the case. The de facto reality is that the hidden economy, as an "equal opportunity employer," often offers more opportunity to some of our citizens than do the "official" economic systems. Given this situation, it requires strong internal values and external support for a poor youth to resist illegal activities. The *structural* incentives are in the opposite direction, so it is not very surprising that a lot of kids—and adults—break the law to make money.

The best way to address this problem is to commit ourselves to a full-employment economy so that every American of working age who is able to work and who wants a job has one. This will require significant redistribution of both our priorities and our resources, but it is worth doing. It will also require more cooperation among federal, state, and local governments (including local schools) as well as the private sector. The private sector has a direct interest in such a policy because it would eventually lead to a better educated, better prepared labor pool, without which neither our cities nor our employers have much of a future. The schools will have to reassess their curricula in order to prepare a declining number of youths to be productive workers.

Our economic survival depends on all of this, because our population is aging and the proportion of workers to retirees is declining dramatically. Thus, it is both more feasible and more timely now to propose a full-employment economy. Surely we could accomplish this with a greatly diminished pool of available labor. Just as surely *we must*, if we want to maintain a competitive economic position globally and support our own elderly, retired citizenry?

Targeted Youth Services and Youth Employment

The population most at risk for gang involvement are males aged fourteen to twenty-four, especially those living in poor inner-city neighborhoods, according to most recent gang studies (Huff, 1990). As an adjunct to the goal of developing a full-employment economy for all working age citizens, we should develop a program of targeted youth service and youth employment to address the specific "window of vulnerability" of unemployed, disengaged young people. At a time in their lives when they desire independence most of all, youths are legally, socially, and economically dependent upon adults. Those who drop out of high school (and even many who complete high school) are, as noted above, increasingly unable to support themselves legally because they do not have marketable job skills. In addition to reassessing school curricula to determine how well we are preparing youths (other than the "college prep" kids) for our society, we should also create a targeted national youth service and employment program.

The targets of this proposed program would be youths between the ages of fourteen and twenty-one. These youths, unless (1) enrolled in an accredited school, college, university, or vocational training program; or (2) enlisted in military service; or (3) employed on a full-time basis; or (4) required to be at home for valid reasons; or (5) severely physically or mentally disabled, would be required to complete one year of national service. National service programs could include a national youth conservation corps, job training corps, premilitary "boot camps" (not for a presumed "rehabilitative effect," but to prepare them to enter the military service), or any one of dozens of other imaginative and useful programs that might be developed to provide service to the nation and to prepare youths for productive lives.

Then, following one year of service (subsidized at a basic subsistence level, plus the cost of the training component being delivered), these youths would be assured of one year of subsidized employment. This employment would be provided by either the private sector (with tax incentives provided by the government to encourage them to hire these youths and give them a chance to prove themselves); federal, state, or local governments (using federal funds); or the military (in the case of the "boot camp" graduates). After one year of training and one year of paid work, these young people will have had an opportunity to mature, to develop better work habits and more marketable job skills, and to present to prospective employers a much more impressive resume than would have been the case just two years previously.

This plan would not include every youth between fourteen and twenty-one. As long as these youths are productively engaged in one of the activities listed above (or if they are physically or mentally unable to participate), they would not be included in this targeted program. Although a *universal* program of national service (similar to the Israeli requirement, except broader than military service) has many appealing aspects, the fact is that this is not the time in U.S. history to introduce such a program. With a declining pool of young people moving into productive positions and preparing themselves to replace those who are retiring, we simply cannot afford to interrupt the education and training of the very people we need in place quite soon. Moreover, those youths between fourteen and twenty-one who are productively engaged in jobs, education, training, or military service are dramatically lower risks for criminal involvement. Finally, targeting the program would facilitate its administration, since it would by definition be a smaller program than would a universal one.

A Mandatory National Head Start Program

We know that most delinquents and criminals did not get a "head start" toward success in our society. Quite the opposite: typically, adult criminals started life as infants at risk. To address these problems, which elevate not only a child's risk of becoming involved in crime but also his or her risk for other social problems, we should adopt a national mandatory Head Start program. Ideally, all children should begin the program at age three, so that we can more fully utilize the extremely important early learning opportunities available at that age. Such a program would help prepare kids to succeed in school, would help reduce child abuse at home by providing much-needed assistance to stressed-out parents, would improve the daily nutrition of these children, and would assist them in developing cognitive and social skills, including conflict resolution skills, at a critical age.

And we know that Head Start works! We have longitudinal evidence concerning the 123 African-American youths of low socioeconomic status (at risk of school failure) who participated in the 1962 Perry Preschool Project in Ypsilanti, Michigan. (This project was the forerunner of the national Head Start program.) At ages three and four, these children attended a high-quality preschool program. Researchers tracked them annually from age three to age eleven, then again at ages fourteen, fifteen, and nineteen. Data were also collected for a control group of sixty-five children. After analyzing the involvement of these children with the legal system, the researchers found that 69 percent of the experimental group had no reported offenses (compared with only 49 percent of the controls) and only 16 percent were arrested at all as juveniles, compared with 25 percent of the controls (Berrueta-Clement, Schweinhart, Barnett, Epstein, & Weikert, 1984).

Finally, we know that Head Start and other preschool programs represent real bargains for the American taxpayer. According to the Committee for Economic Development, composed of American corporate executives, "It would be hard to imagine that society could find a higher yield for a dollar of investment than that found in preschool programs for its at-risk children. Every $1.00 spent on early prevention and intervention can save $4.75 in the cost of remedial education, welfare, and crime further down the road" (Eisenhower Foundation, 1990, p. 11).

Targeted Community-Based Programs

We should develop programs designed to impact upon the most at-risk areas of our nation's cities. There are many troubled rural and suburban areas as well, but in terms of density of population and getting more return for our investment, it makes sense to focus on the large populations residing in underclass, socially disorganized urban areas. This proposal would work as follows:

1. The federal government would make available sufficient funds to carry out empirical, descriptive studies in all fifty states. These studies would be designed to determine the costliest areas of our cities in terms of crime, commitments to juvenile and adult correctional institutions, commitments to mental hospitals, proportion of public assistance recipients, percent unemployed, and other empirical indicators of "social pathology." All of these data are routinely collected by agencies and are recorded by zip code, at least. Once the researchers had these zip code data, they could investigate further the exact addresses of the individuals involved and organize them by census tract, by neighborhood, or whatever was the lowest applicable common denominator available. It is highly probable that a relatively small number of zip codes or census tracts account for a relatively large proportion of crime, delinquency, mental illness, homelessness, unemployment, child abuse, and other costly social and economic problems in any given state. Although we may hold different theoretical views as to *why* this may be the case, we may at least be able to agree on the *ecological areas* to be targeted for intervention.

2. The most problematic areas, in terms of costs to the state, would then become the target areas for intervention programs. The states would then issue requests for proposals to public, private, and not-for-profit agencies and organizations, describing the target areas and inviting innovative ideas that would help. Programmatic thrusts could include the rehabilitation of housing, parental effectiveness training, alcohol and drug abuse counseling, improved prenatal and neonatal care, problem pregnancy counseling, job training programs, and a host of other worthwhile ideas.

3. Those intervention proposals that were funded would be required to cooperate in monitoring and in both formative (process) and summative

evaluation efforts designed to learn about the programs as they unfold and to improve program designs around the nation, thus facilitating the transfer of knowledge from one community to others.

Summary

The malignant neglect of urban problems, begun in the 1970s and continuing today, must be reversed. The indiscriminate cuts in federally supported urban programs eviscerated promising initiatives along with those that deserved elimination. The "centerpiece" of our renewed commitment to our cities should be based conceptually on the Eisenhower Foundation's (1990) "community enterprise" development strategy for the inner city. Recognizing that the corporate response to labor-market demographics of the 1990s is likely to be grossly inadequate, the Eisenhower Foundation concluded:

> That "trickle down" approach has been tried; it has had little success, especially compared to our "bubble up" approach of directly empowering nonprofit minority community organizations. . . . The private market has repeatedly pronounced its judgment on the current condition of the inner cities. Without substantial change, these communities will remain too volatile, their work forces too poorly skilled and unstable, to attract private enterprise consistently.
> (Eisenhower Foundation, 1990, p. 75)

The Eisenhower Foundation's strategies include linking public-sector job creation and local community needs via economic development programs led by private, nonprofit-sector entrepreneurs. The foundation, as well as the earlier National Advisory (Kerner) Commission on Civil Disorders (1968) and the National Commission on the Causes and Prevention of Violence (1969), focused on the need to improve the quality of urban life and the chances of success for youth living in our cities. The specific job creation scheme of the Eisenhower Foundation focuses on rebuilding the physical infrastructure of our communities—such as roads and housing—utilizing the labor of youth presently at high risk of joining gangs, abusing/selling drugs, and entering into criminal careers. The foundation's community-enterprise development strategy is conceptually sound and should be carefully considered by policymakers, along with other important components of the foundation's "Youth Investment and Community Reconstruction" strategies (Eisenhower Foundation, 1990).

Why not develop a public policy response that recognizes the long-range importance of local community development and empowerment? One way to pursue that worthy goal is to rebuild our physical infrastructure and our human infrastructure at the same time, by linking the needs of both and creating public-sector jobs, managed by private nonprofits, training and employing at-risk youth. The success of such initiatives could not only remove some of the important incentives to join gangs and commit crime, but could generically address the roots of related social pathologies such as mental illness and drug and alcohol abuse. Equally important, it would give the United States a chance to remain globally competitive when our current children assume their roles in the labor force of our nation.

Is all of this a massive undertaking? Absolutely! We are at a point in our history where we need a sort of domestic Marshall Plan. Is all of this too expensive? Compared to what? For too long, we've short-changed ourselves and our young people, mortgaging the nation's future by putting many of our youth at risk of failure. The new youth gangs and other forms of social and economic pathology bring a new urgency to the need for reform. For too long, we've treated problems much as gangs or crime in isolation from other problems.

We can pay for the initiatives outlined here, primarily through reductions in Defense Department spending that is nonessential, especially in view of recent improvements in surveillance technology that forewarn us of potential military actions and in light of the reduced threat from the Soviet Union. The Eisenhower Foundation (1990) has identified billions of dollars in defense spending that even *conservatives* agree is unnecessary to our national defense.

The fact is that we cannot make headway against these problems until we can begin to address the basic underlying problems of inequality and social injustice. We can retain the incentives that are the best part of capitalism and still broaden the opportunities for our less fortunate citizen. It is not necessary for an affluent nation to retain in its socioeconomic system the vestiges of Social Darwinism to which we cling. In the final analysis, global competition and the aging of our own population put *all of us* in the United States at risk, at least as a world economic power. We will need the productive labor of *all* of our citizens to meet this challenge. Will we adapt in time or will we, as a society, be the victims of our own malignant neglect?

References

Bach, R. L., & Bach, J. B. (1980). Employment patterns of Southeast Asian refugees. *Monthly Labor Review, 103*, 31–38.

Beach, W. G. (1932). *Oriental crime in California.* Stanford, CA: Stanford University Press.

Berkman, L. (1984, Sept. 30). Banks catering to Asians facing a culture gap. *Los Angeles Times*.

Berrueta-Clement, J. R., Schweinhart, L. J., Barnett, W. S., Epstein, A. S., & Weikert, D. J. (1984). Preschool's effects on social responsibility. In D. Weikert (Ed.), *Changed lives: The effects of the Perry Preschool Program on youths through age nineteen* (pp. 61–73) Ypsilanti, MI: High/Scope Press.

Campbell, A. (1984). *The girls in the gang*. New York: Basil Blackwell.

Campbell, A. (1990). Female participation in gangs. In C. R. Huff (Ed.), *Gangs in America* (pp. 163–182). Newbury Park, CA: Sage.

Chin, K. (1986). *Chinese triad societies, tongs, organized crime, and street gangs in Asia and the United States*. Unpublished doctoral dissertation, University of Pennsylvania.

Chin, K. (1990a). *Chinese subculture and criminality: Nontraditional crime groups in America*. Westport, CT: Greenwood Press.

Chin, K. (1990b). Chinese gangs and extortion. In C. R. Huff (Ed.), *Gangs in America* (pp. 129–145). Newbury Park, CA: Sage.

Chin, R. (1977). New York Chinatown today: Community in crisis. *Amerasia Journal, 1*(1), 1–32.

Cloward, R. A., & Ohlin, L. E. (1960). *Delinquency and opportunity: A theory of delinquent gangs*. New York: Free Press.

Daly, M. (1983, February). The war for Chinatown. *New York Magazine*, pp. 31–38.

Eisenhower Foundation. (1990). *Youth investment and community reconstruction: Street lessons on drugs and crime for the nineties*. Washington, DC: Author.

Fagan, J. (1989). The social organization of drug use and drug dealing among urban gangs. *Criminology, 27*, 633–669.

Fagan, J. (1990). Social processes of delinquency and drug use among urban gangs. In C. R. Huff (Ed.), *Gangs in America* (pp. 183–219). Newbury Park, CA: Sage.

Fessler, L. W. (Ed.). (1983). *Chinese in America: Stereotyped past, changing present*. New York: Vantage Books.

Grant, B. (1979). *The boat people*. Sydney, Australia: Penguin.

Hagedorn, J. M. (1987). *Final report: Milwaukee Gang Research Project*. Milwaukee: University of Wisconsin.

Hagedorn, J. M. (1988). *People and folks: Gangs, crime and the underclass in a rustbelt city*. Chicago: Lake View Press.

Hagedorn, J. M. (1991). *Gangs, neighborhoods, and public policy*. Unpublished paper. University of Wisconsin, Milwaukee.

Huff, C. R. (1989). Youth gangs and public policy. *Crime and Delinquency, 35*, 524–537.

Huff, C. R. (Ed.). (1990). *Gangs in America*. Newbury Park, CA: Sage.

Hung, K., & Pilisuk, M. (1977). At the threshold of Golden Gate: Special problems of a neglected minority. *American Journal of Orthopsychiatry,* *47,* 701–713.

Klein, M. W., & Maxson, C. L. (1989). Street gang violence. In N. A. Weiner and M. E. Wolfgang (Eds.), *Violent crime, violent criminals* (pp. 198–234). Newbury Park, CA: Sage.

Kwong, P. (1987). *The new Chinatown.* New York: Hill and Wang.

Larson, D. (1988, October 23). Honor thy parents. *Los Angeles Times.*

Loo, C. K. (1976). *The emergence of San Francisco Chinese juvenile gangs from the 1950s to the present.* Unpublished master's thesis, San Jose State University, CA.

MacGill, H. G. (1938). The Oriental delinquent in the Vancouver juvenile court. *Sociology and Social Research, 12,* 428–438.

Marsh, R. E. (1980). Socioeconomic status of Indochinese refugees in the United States: Progress and problems. *Social Security Bulletin, 43,* 11–12.

Miller, W. B. (1975). *Violence by youth gangs and youth groups as a crime problem in major American cities.* Report to the National Institute for Juvenile Justice and Delinquency Prevention.

Miller, W. B. (1990). Why the United States has failed to solve its youth gang problem. In C. R. Huff (Ed.), *Gangs in America* (pp. 263–287). Newbury Park, CA: Sage.

Moore, J. W. (1978). *Homeboys: Gangs, drugs, and prison in the barrios of Los Angeles.* Philadelphia: Temple University Press.

Moore, J. W. (1985). Isolation and stigmatization in the development of an underclass: The case of Chicano gangs in East Los Angeles. *Social Problems, 33*(1), 1–10.

Morganthau, T., Contreras, J., Lam, H., & Sandza, R. (1982, August 2). Vietnamese gangs in California. *Newsweek.*

Moynihan, D. P. (1973). *The politics of a guaranteed income.* New York: Random House.

National Advisory Commission on Civil Disorders (1968). *Final report.* Washington, DC: U.S. Government Printing Office.

National Advisory Commission on the Causes and Prevention of Violence. (1969). *Final report.* Washington, DC: U.S. Government Printing Office.

Nguyen, L. T., & Henkin, A. B. (1982). Vietnamese refugees in the United States: Adaptation and transitional status. *Journal of Ethnic Studies, 9*(4), 101–116.

Robinson, N., & Joe, D. (1980). Gangs in Chinatown. *McGill Journal of Education, 15,* 149–162.

Rosenbaum, D. P., & Grant, J. A. (1983). *Gang and youth problems in Evanston: Research findings and policy options.* Evanston, IL: Center for Urban Affairs and Policy Research, Northwestern University.

Sanchez-Jankowski, M. (1991). *Islands in the street: Gangs and American urban society.* Berkeley and Los Angeles: University of California Press.

Skinner, K. (1980). Vietnamese in America: Diversity in adaptation. *California Sociologist, 3*(2), 103–124.

Spergel, I. A. (1990). *Youth gangs: Problem and response.* Chicago: University of Chicago Press.

Sung, B. L. (1977). *Gangs in New York's Chinatown* (Monograph No. 6). New York: Department of Asian Studies, City College of New York.

Sung, B. L. (1979). *Transplanted Chinese children.* New York: Department of Asian Studies, City College of New York.

Takagi, P., & Platt, T. (1978). Behind the gilded ghetto. *Crime and Social Justice, 9,* 2–25.

Taylor, C. S. (1990a). *Dangerous society.* East Lansing: Michigan State University Press.

Taylor, C. S. (1990b). Gang imperialism. In C. R. Huff (Ed.), *Gangs in America* (pp. 103–115). Newbury Park, CA: Sage.

Thrasher, F. M. (1927). *The gang: A study of 1,313 gangs in Chicago.* Chicago: University of Chicago Press.

U. S. Department of Justice, Office of Juvenile Justice and Delinquency Prevention. (1989, September). *Community-wide responses crucial for dealing with youth gangs.* Washington, DC: Author.

U. S. Senate (1986). *Emerging criminal groups* (Hearings before the Permanent Subcommittee on Investigations of the Committee on Governmental Affairs). Washington, D.C.: U.S. Government Printing Office.

Vigil, J. D. (1988). *Barrio gangs.* Austin: University of Texas Press.

Vigil, J. D., & Yun, S. C. (1990). Vietnamese youth gangs in southern California. In C. R. Huff (Ed.), *Gangs in America* (pp. 146–162). Newbury Park, CA: Sage.

Whyte, W. F. (1943). *Street corner society: The social structure of an Italian slum.* Chicago: University of Chicago Press.

Wilson, W. J. (1987). *The truly disadvantaged: The inner city, the underclass, and public policy.* Chicago: University of Chicago Press.

3

Juvenile Diversion: The Ongoing Search for Alternatives

Mark Ezell

A central theme in the history of the juvenile court is the endless search for effective alternatives. The juvenile court itself was established as an alternative to handling juvenile cases in adult criminal court; houses of refuge were built to remove young offenders from jails; and probation was introduced as an alternative to reform schools. Diversion is one of the more recent chapters in this search for alternatives in that juvenile diversion programs are intended to operate as alternatives to the traditional processing of youth through the juvenile court. Diversion necessarily involves a decision by a court official to turn the youth away from usual juvenile justice system handling, and usually includes the provision of such services to the youth as individual, group, or family counseling, remedial education, job training and placement, drug and/or alcohol treatment, and recreation. Most diversion programs are funded from public resources, staffed by both professionals and volunteers, and include numerous rules and regulations with which the youth and sometimes the family must comply.

As we move into the 1990s, with a rise in juvenile arrests expected, the need for diversion remains and even increases. We will be faced with large numbers of minors for whom formal court action is ill-advised largely because alternative approaches can be more effective and efficient in reducing delinquent behavior. The purpose of this chapter is to describe and analyze the diversion process and diversion programs. The analysis is organized into the following series of questions: (1) What is diversion and why is it practiced? (2) What is the history of diversion? (3) What are the various types of diversion programs? (4) How well does diversion work? and (5) What are the critical research and practice issues?

What is Diversion and Why is it Practiced?

Although there is little agreement on a specific definition of diversion, the concept generally involves a decision to turn youth away from the official system and handle them via alternative procedures and programs. The expectation is that diverted youth will be more successful (i.e., recidivate less) than similar youth processed in a traditional manner. Alternative definitions of diversion revolve around several questions. First, does diversion necessarily include the referral of the youth to an agency for services or does it simply mean screening the youth from formal processing? Cressey and McDermott (1973) define "true diversion" as the complete separation of the juvenile from the system with no strings attached. However, they found that instances of true diversion are rare. In most cases, the process of diversion is complemented by one or more diversion programs. Rutherford and McDermott (1976) make a useful distinction between diversion as a process and diversion as a program. Diversion as a process refers to the use of discretion by an agent of the juvenile court to remove certain cases from court jurisdiction. A diversion program receives the diverted youth for some type of intervention. The diversion process can operate without a program, but not vice versa.

Another question relates to the auspices of the diversion program. Is diversion really diversion if the agency hosting the diversion program is part of the justice system? One's answer to this question depends on one's position on labeling theory. Labeling theory would predict the following scenario:

> Official reaction to deviance invokes stigma that sets an individual apart from others as a "deviant person." Furthermore, formal dispositions are likely to entail both coercion, by threatening sanctions in response to any lack of cooperation with officials, and social control, through placing the individual under strict rules of behavior. Such coercion and social control reinforce the message that the individual is not a normal person. They also make the individual subject to further official reactions for behavior that is acceptable from others (such as violating rules of probation). These processes can lead the individual to consider him- or herself a delinquent, which will lead to increased delinquency. Official reactions thereby become the cause of further delinquency.
> (Osgood & Weichselbaum, 1984, p. 35)

Generally, proponents of labeling theory insist that the service agency to which the child is diverted be independent of the juvenile justice system so that stigmatization is less likely; Empey (1982) believes that allowing justice agencies to operate diversion programs subverts the goals of diversion. Others, however, are unconcerned about program sponsorship and feel that diversion's real value comes from minimizing a youth's penetration into the system. Research findings by Elliott, Dunford, and

Knowles (1978) make this a meaningless debate. They found that diverted youth perceived high levels of labeling regardless of whether services are delivered through a traditional justice setting or through a separate diversion agency.

More important than the auspices of the diversion agency, however, is the question of whether the court has closed a divertee's case or retained jurisdiction. Does the youth voluntarily receive services from the diversion program? If a youth's case is still considered open by the court, then the agency, notwithstanding its official auspices, can be considered an agent of the court. Agency personnel will be expected to report the youth's attendance and/or performance to the court and the court will take whatever actions it deems necessary in that case. If the youth is cooperative and successfully completes the requirements of the particular diversion program, the case will usually be closed, but if the youth fails to attend, to cooperate, or unsuccessfully terminates with the program, the court has the option to schedule an adjudicatory hearing and prosecute the original charges. In order for this scenario to occur, the youth and his or her parents probably would have agreed to waive their rights to a speedy trial. If diversion is voluntary, as many insist it should be, the youth's decision about whether to cooperate with the diversion program should have no legal ramifications.

Another common definition of diversion is any action, decision, or program that minimizes a youth's penetration into the juvenile justice system. In this view, probation is considered diversion if the youth might otherwise have been committed to a residential program. Similarly, placement in a group home diverts youth from institutions.

This chapter specifically focuses on pretrial diversion, that is, on those practices and programs that divert alleged delinquents from juvenile court prior to an adjudicatory hearing. The concept of diversion used here specifies that a youth not headed toward the court cannot be turned away: "diversion programs must handle only youngsters who otherwise would enter . . . the justice system" (Klein, 1979, p. 153). In practice, many diversion programs operate as alternatives to station adjustments with no referrals as opposed to alternatives to traditional court processing. This practice is discussed more fully in the subsection on net-widening.

What is the History of Diversion?

Since the beginning of the juvenile court, thousands and thousands of juvenile delinquency cases have been handled informally, "adjusted" in some fashion such that the youth's case was either closed or referred to a noncourt agency. These diversions of cases away from the formal juvenile justice system were permissible because of the broad discretionary powers inherent in the jobs of law enforcement officers, court intake workers, prosecutors, and judges. Prior to the 1960s, therefore, diversion was an informal disposition used by juvenile justice officials and specific programs were rarely labeled or funded as diversionary alternatives.

As juvenile crime increased in the 1960s, the juvenile court encountered strong criticism both for its failure to reduce delinquency and for making it worse by negatively labeling youth and by mixing serious juvenile offenders with first-time, minor offenders. Most juvenile justice professionals felt that the court would do a better job by focusing on the smaller number of serious juvenile offenders and by developing alternative approaches for youth charged with less serious offenses. As a result of recommendations made by the President's Commission on Law Enforcement and Administration of Justice (1967), and because of the subsequent availability of federal grant funds, there was a rapid proliferation of diversion programs throughout the country. Sometimes formal diversion programs were implemented in addition to the existing informal diversionary practices in a community, but many times the new programs supplanted the discretionary case adjustments that had effectively functioned for decades. I will return to this issue when I discuss net-widening.

What Are the Various Types of Diversion Programs?

As a result of significant levels of federal funding in the late 1960s and early 1970s, a panoply of diversion programs were created, such as youth service bureaus, job training and placement programs, alternative schools, and family counseling (Roberts, 1989). Youth are either referred directly to these programs by law enforcement officers, court intake workers, prosecutors, or judges, or they are first referred to caseworkers at a youth service bureau who subsequently refer the case to one or more diversion programs.

Gensheimer and associates' (Gensheimer, Mayer, Gottschalk & Davidson, 1986) study of diversion found that all but 11 percent of the diversion interventions took place in nonresidential programs; that the median length of intervention was approximately fifteen weeks; and that the median number of contact hours was fifteen hours of service. They also found that service brokerage was the most common intervention and that group therapy was very frequently utilized.

Since the 1980s, when the juvenile justice paradigm began to shift from rehabilitation to accountability and sanctioning, there has been an increase in the use of restitution and work programs for diverted youth. Diversion program staff locate and supervise community work sites such as public parks, nursing homes, and childcare centers at which diverted youth work for a specific number of hours. Diversion staff also monitor diverted youths' progress toward making restitution to the victim(s) of the crime.

Another increasingly popular diversion program is juvenile arbitration (Ezell, 1989). Mediation and reconciliation programs are somewhat similar depending on how they are implemented. There is great variation in the implementation of arbitration, but generally the youth is referred for an arbitration hearing at which a single arbitrator or a panel decide on the appropriate sanctions. Depending on how a particular community implements this program, the crime victim may be present and participate in the hearing. The resulting arbitration agreement is flexible in that the youth can be required to do one or more of the following: pay restitution, perform community service work, write or make a personal apology, attend a class on the consequences of crime, or participate in a counseling or drug/alcohol treatment program. If the youth complies with the arbitration contract, his or her case is closed; if not, the prosecutor has the option of taking the case to court.

There is nothing unique about a diversion intervention that differentiates it from interventions used for adjudicated delinquents. For example, a "Scared Straight" type of program can be used for either diverted or adjudicated youth or both. The key criterion for identifying a true diversion program is to determine the stage of juvenile court processing reached by the youth who is participating in the program.

How Well Does Diversion Work?

The diversion research literature is quite extensive and has been reviewed numerous times. Comprehensive reviews of the diversion literature have been prepared by Klein (1979), Blomberg (1983), and Polk (1984). In addition, Gensheimer and associates (1986) conducted a metaanalysis of 103 published and unpublished outcome studies between 1967 and 1983. The purpose of this section is to summarize the current state of knowledge, add some of the more recent research findings, and highlight the issues in the recent debate over diversion. In general, "conclusions drawn by reviewers of the literature have generally painted a pessimistic view for the promise of diversionary efforts" (Gensheimer et al., 1986, p. 42).

The impact of diversion (either as a process or as a program) is expected to occur at both the individual and the system level. Theoretically, diverted youth will avoid both the stigmatization of official court handling and the criminogenic effects of associations with other delinquents, and, as a result, will not commit subsequent delinquent acts. These behavioral effects are expected to occur not only because of avoidances but also because the youth may be receiving some ameliorative service from a diversion program. At the system level, pretrial diversion is expected to reduce the number of juvenile arrests and the number of cases that go to court. In other words, if the diversion process operates as intended, the entire flow of cases into and through the juvenile justice system should be altered. When diversion is successful, and all other factors that influence juvenile arrests remain constant, arrests should decrease due to a reduction of secondary deviance as well as a less-burdened, more-efficient, and more-effective juvenile court. Notwithstanding diversion's impact on arrests, the flow of cases to juvenile court should decline.

Numerous studies have been conducted on diversion and its effect on individual youth, their families, and the court. Blomberg (1983) critically assesses both the state of knowledge about diversion and the adequacy of the research techniques employed. He concludes that "the reported findings from various evaluations of diversion programs have been mixed and fragmented" (p. 24). There have been contradictory reports of lowered rearrest rates for diverted youth versus increased misconduct and accelerated penetration into the formal system. Blomberg suggests that knowledge is incomplete regarding which diversion services are most effective for various kinds of youth, and argues that this issue should be at the top of the research agenda.

Binder and Geis (1984) recently took a strident position in defense of diversion. They argued that a cult of sociologists have "substituted rhetoric for logic in their argumentation . . . in opposition to diversion programs" (p. 624). Their prodiversion stance is not, however, bolstered by strong empirical findings. Their arguments rely solely on strong language.

The only real contribution Binder and Geis have made to the state of knowledge about diversion and related issues is the response they provoked from Polk (1984). After a careful review of diversion's record, Polk concludes that "the data on impact do not permit us at this time to reject the hypothesis that the services may be either of no benefit or even harmful to the clients experiencing the diversion program" (p. 658).

The results of the metaanalysis conducted by Gensheimer and associates (1986) are noteworthy. They conclude, "Overall, findings from this analysis do not provide substantial evidence for the efficacy of diversion programs. . . . diversion interventions produce no strong positive or strong negative effects with youth diverted from the juvenile justice system" (p. 52). The authors argue that their findings should not be the basis for the abandonment of diversion. The typical diversion client in their sample of studies was an adjudicated delinquent; they admit that this client population compromised their ability to generalize their findings to traditional diversion clients (i.e., those diverted from court prior to any adjudication).

In addition to their finding that diversion has no effect, either positive or negative, Gensheimer and associates identified two important correlations: first, the younger the diversion client, the more likely that intervention will have a positive effect; and second, "the greater number of contact hours between the youth and the service deliverer, the greater the positive effect on outcome measures" (p. 52).

Empirical studies of many community corrections reforms in general and diversion programs in particular have documented these programs' propensity to widen the net of the justice system, an unintended increase rather than an alteration of the court's reach. Explanations for the sidetracking of diversion differ somewhat, but all are in agreement that most, if not all, diversion programs have "widened the net" of the juvenile justice system. Rather than providing a true alternative to court, diversion programs have merely supplemented the court function and increased both the number of youth brought to the attention of the juvenile justice system and the number under court jurisdiction. A substantial proportion of youth served by diversion programs would not have received services and/or been supervised by the court had these programs not existed.

Saul and Davidson (1983) describe net-widening as the major unintended consequence of juvenile diversion. Instead of reducing the number of youth under court supervision, as intended, diversion has increased it. Blomberg (1983) agrees, pointing out that net-widening extends the reach of the juvenile justice system by increasing the overall proportion of the population subject to court services or control.

Esbensen (1984) indicates that no clear definition of net-widening has been agreed upon, but the following question raised by Polk (1984) accurately articulates the issues: "Is diversion serving as a process for moving young persons who have 'penetrated' the justice network outward and away from that system, or has it become a device for incorporating a whole new class of clients inside an expanding justice system?" (p. 654).

While numerous studies have documented that net-widening is one of the outcomes of diversion programs, few studies have been able to adequately identify and follow those youth who would not have been processed by the court to determine whether participation in the diversion program was harmful or beneficial. The few that have examined this question, or made conjectures about the issue, conclude that the effects of net-widening are detrimental both to individual youth and society at large (Blomberg, 1977; Fishman, 1977; Klein, 1975). Blomberg (1984) believes that net-widening reduces individual freedom, increases the number of rearrests, contributes to behavioral difficulties, and facilitates unnecessary intrusions into families. For example, Blomberg (1977) documents a case in which a youth and his family were required to attend family counseling. As a result of the father's failure to fully cooperate, and presumably other considerations, not only the boy who was originally in trouble but also his two brothers were removed from the home.

Others are equally concerned about the coercive nature of diversion programs and the complete disregard for a youth's democratic rights that diversion programs entail (Nejelski, 1976). According to Austin and Krisberg (1981), "instead of justice, there is diversion" (p. 171). In addition, Scull (1984) comments that the distinction between guilt and innocence is increasingly blurred as a result of the extension of social control.

Others see different consequences and attach different meanings and importance to net-widening. Binder and Geis (1984), for example, question the implicit assumption that no intervention is better than diversion intervention. They argue that because of net-widening, services such as counseling are provided to youth and their families where none was provided before. They add that it is doubtful that youth will outgrow their misbehavior without some societal response. Further, they are unconcerned about potential infringements of individual freedom. Youth have chosen to engage in behavior that merited intervention, and if they wish their lives to remain unconstrained by rules and regulations, they should behave accordingly, or not get caught.

Using multiple research methodologies, including a time-series design with a comparison group, Ezell (1989) documents net-widening and other unintended effects of a diversion program. Based on his research, it appeared that the operation of the diversion program caused prosecutors to reduce the probability of an alleged delinquent being sent to court but did not alter the probability of an arrested youth being placed under court supervision. The operation of the arbitration program succeeded in keeping many youth out of court but not out of the system. In addition, Ezell documented other changes in the processing of youth through juvenile court: the probabilities of youth who went to court being placed on probation or committed to a residential program both increased.

Even though it has enjoyed mixed results, diversion continues to be a popular policy. Blomberg (1983), Klein (1979), Austin and Krisberg

(1981), and Lemert (1981) conclude that the promise of diversion has not been fulfilled. Lemert suggests that diversion programs have been coopted by law enforcement agencies and transformed to be more consistent with their primary goal of social control. Klein reviews a "litany of impediments" to diversion and indicates that poorly developed program rationales, the failure to target appropriate youth, and professional resistance, among other things, are largely to blame for inappropriate implementation. Both Austin and Krisberg and Blomberg argue that diversion's less-than-satisfactory results are a result of a variety of organizational dynamics.

What Are the Critical Practice and Research Issues?

In this section, I will identify and discuss several important issues relating to the development and operation of diversion programs as well as crucial research issues.

Practice Issues

First, better prospective targeting of the youth who should be diverted would prevent (or at least reduce) net-widening. Many juvenile diversion programs focus on youth who would not have gone to court and those who would have received little or no official response. The political and organizational forces that cause diversion programs to accept the "wrong" youth are extremely powerful and are very difficult to alter once a program is operating. Profiles of targeted youth can be developed by examining data on cases handled informally, put on probation, and committed to residential programs. Agreements on targeted youth should be achieved between law enforcement agencies, prosecutors, judges, and program staff before the program opens its doors. Better client targeting can also clarify whether the community diversion program is intended to deal with youth who were definitely headed to court or to serve as a community alternative to doing nothing. While it is true that many youth who commit minor offenses, as well as their families, are in need of social services, juvenile courts and diversion programs are not adequately designed, funded, or administered for the delivery of a wide range of human services. Court officials and diversion program staff should make referrals to appropriate community agencies; if needed services are not currently available, officials and staff should work to secure their funding. In short, diversion programs should avoid trying to be all things to all people and should focus on a limited set of service objectives.

Second, diversion programs and court officials should pay greater attention to the due process rights of juveniles accused of delinquent acts who are being considered for diversion. Currently, little attention is paid to whether the youth actually committed the alleged offense that originally brought him or her to the attention of authorities. In fact, many prosecutors divert youth on whose cases they had inadequate evidence. Therefore, the difference between guilt and innocence is left unaddressed, much less resolved. In some jurisdictions youth must admit guilt before being diverted. In others, they are not asked about their guilt but are asked to "accept responsibility" for the event. If they assert their innocence, they will not be diverted and their case will proceed to court if the prosecutor so chooses.

All too often, the youth and his or her family are asked to make their decisions without the advice of an attorney and/or in what might be considered coercive circumstances. At times, it is questionable whether the parents have the youth's best interests in mind when they agree to diversion or whether they are trying to avoid the social embarrassment of having their son or daughter go to court.

Third, juvenile justice officials should improve their ability to match diverted youth to appropriate diversion interventions and needed services, while, at the same time, communities should develop a broad variety of diversion interventions. Research as well as common sense tells us that no single intervention will work for all youth, but most communities have only one type of juvenile diversion program. This is the strength of the original conceptualization of the youth service bureau as a broker of services for diverted youth. More systematic attention should be given to matching youth to services with successful track records for youth from similar circumstances.

Fourth, in addition to developing a broad array of interventions for diverted youth, much greater care should be taken to operate programs in a way that avoids stigmatizing the participants. If labeling theory is one of the rationales for diversion, then it should be reflected in program operations. This mandate requires creativity on the part of program administrators and court officials, but by recruiting nondelinquent participants and carefully marketing the program to the community as well as other professionals who work with these youth (e.g., teachers, social workers, etc.) the self-fulfilling prophecy predicted by labeling theory can be avoided.

Research Issues

While many researchers' attempts to answer the question Does diversion reduce recidivism? have led to inconclusive answers and great debates, some are realizing that they have been asking the wrong question. A more appropriate question is What alternative works best for which types of youth? (Blomberg, 1983). Research needs to be designed so that we know which types of youth are most positively affected by an intervention. Maybe restitution programs "work best" for males and community service work is better for older youth. This type of research has to be done in order for court officials to match diverted youth to the best program as discussed above.

Researchers also need to improve the descriptions and measurements of the diversion interventions so the programs can be replicated when they are found to be effective with certain youth. Questions such as the following need to be addressed: who works with the diverted youth, what are their credentials (e.g., MSW, Ph.D., etc.) and training; what is the nature, intensity, and duration of the intervention and what theory or rationale guides it; and what are the short- and long-range goals of the intervention?

Finally, researchers should pay greater attention to the agency context of the diversion intervention and the organizational requisites for administering the program. For example, is the agency public, private for-profit, or nonprofit; what are the caseloads of the diversion staff and how are they supervised and supported; is there an automated client information system; is the agency large or small, hierarchical or flat, centralized, formalized or participatory, for example. Characteristics of the agency and its work culture have a major impact on the delivery of services but are rarely described or assessed by researchers. For example, Ezell (1989) suggested that the fact that the arbitration program he studied was organizationally located in the prosecutors office, as opposed to an external nonprofit organization, might have influenced the high level of net-widening that occurred. Not only will this information aid in the replication of successful diversion programs, but it will provide information to diversion program managers so that they can more effectively set priorities, supervise staff, and acquire and allocate resources.

Conclusion

There is a repetitive quality to the history of juvenile justice reform (Rothman, 1984). An examination of this series of reforms, from houses of refuge to reformatories, from probation and the juvenile court to diversion, reveals what may be viewed as well-intentioned changes that produced either dissatisfying or unknown outcomes. It also reveals a pattern of enthusiastic ideological support for innovations combined with an unwillingness or inability to critically scrutinize both the implementation and the performance of the innovation. The history of juvenile justice is an evolution of an ever-enlarging and ever-changing social control apparatus.

At the time when each reform was enacted, it appeared so sound and humane to its supporters that critical scrutiny seemed unnecessary. When viewed over a longer history, however, the policies and innovations of one generation are rejected as mistaken by the following generation, which in turn implemented new reforms that in their turn were eventually rejected, and so on.

In the 1960s, with rapidly increasing juvenile arrests and the growing belief that the juvenile court was failing, diversion became popular. While the community corrections movement created optional placements within the juvenile justice system, diversion was envisioned as an alternative to the system altogether. It was only in the late seventies that diversion began to be empirically scrutinized. Diversion's ability to reduce recidivism has received mixed reviews by researchers. However, it has consistently produced a panoply of unintended consequences, positive and negative, at both the individual and the system levels. Most diversion programs are capable of widening the net of the justice system, extending instead of altering the overall proportion of youth subject to some form of state control or supervision.

In summary, an examination of the history of juvenile justice reform reveals the following pattern. First, program and policy innovations are introduced with great enthusiasm. Accompanying the excitement is an "illusion of knowledge" (Blomberg, 1984), that is, a widely held belief that technological advances will effectively eradicate crime and delinquency. Subsequently, dissatisfaction with the outcomes grow and numerous unintended consequences are recognized. The disparity between rhetoric and reality, between intentions and outcomes, is slowly but surely documented. There is little understanding, however, of why or how this disparity arose, or from where the unanticipated outcomes came. This position is largely a result of narrowly conducted, post implementation research. A new reform is introduced and the cycle repeats itself.

With the growing fiscal crisis in America, the use of community-based alternatives to institutionalization will continue, as will efforts to divert youth from the court. In order for diversion to be effective, however, researchers and diversion staff need to cooperate to a greater extent when programs are planned, implemented, and studied. This partnership is crucial to avoid the frustrating cycle of juvenile justice reform.

References

Austin, J., & Krisberg, B. (1981). Wider, stronger, and different nets: The dialectics of criminal justice reform. *Journal of Research in Crime and Delinquency, 18,* 165–196.

Binder, A., & Geis, G. (1984). *Ad populum* argumentation in criminology: Juvenile diversion as rhetoric. *Crime and Delinquency, 30,* 624–647.

Blomberg, T. G. (1977). Diversion and accelerated social control. *Journal of Criminal Law and Criminology, 68,* 274–282.

Blomberg, T. G. (1983). Diversion's disparate results and unresolved questions: An integrative evaluation perspective. *Journal of Research in Crime and Delinquency, 20,* 24–38.

Blomberg, T. G. (1984, April). *Criminal justice reform and social control: Are we becoming a minimum security society?* Paper presented at the Symposium on the Decentralization of Social Control, Burnaby, British Columbia.

Cressey, D. R., & McDermott, R. A. (1973). *Diversion from the juvenile justice system* (National Assessment of Juvenile Corrections). Ann Arbor: University of Michigan Press.

Elliott, D. S., Dunford, F. W., & Knowles, B. (1978). *Diversion: A study of alternative processing.* Boulder, CO: Behavioral Research Institute.

Empey, L. T. (1982). *American delinquency: Its meaning and construction.* Homewood, IL: Dorsey.

Esbensen, F. (1984). Net widening? Yes and no: Diversion impact assessed through a systems processing rates analysis. In S. H. Decker (Ed.), *Juvenile justice policy analysis trends and outcomes* (pp. 115–128). Beverly Hills, CA: Sage.

Ezell, M. (1989). Juvenile arbitration: Net-widening and other unintended consequences. *Journal of Research in Crime and Delinquency, 26,* 358–377.

Fishman, R. (1977). *Criminal recidivism in New York City: An evaluation of the impact of rehabilitation and diversion services.* New York: Praeger.

Gensheimer, L. K., Mayer, J. P., Gottschalk, R., & Davidson, W. S. (1986). Diverting youth from the juvenile justice system: A meta-analysis of intervention efficacy. In S. J. Apter & A. P. Goldstein (Eds.), *Youth violence: Programs and prospects* (pp. 39–57). New York: Pergamon Press.

Klein, M. W. (1976). Issues and realities in police diversion programs. *Crime and Delinquency, 22,* 421–427.

Klein, M. W. (1979). Deinstitutionalization and diversion of juvenile offenders: A litany of impediments. In N. Morris & M. Toney (Eds.), *Crime and justice: An annual review of research* (pp. 145–201). Chicago: University of Chicago Press.

Lemert, E. M. (1981). Diversion in juvenile justice: What hath been wrought. *Journal of Research in Crime and Delinquency, 18,* 34–46.

Nejelski, P. (1976). Diversion: Unleashing the hound of heaven? In M. K. Rosenheim (Ed.), *Pursuing justice for the child* (pp. 94–118). Chicago: University of Chicago Press.

Osgood, D. W., & Weichselbaum, H. F. (1984). Juvenile diversion: When practice matches theory. *Journal of Research in Crime and Delinquency, 21,* 33–56.

Polk, K. (1984). Juvenile diversion: A look at the record. *Crime and Delinquency, 30,* 648–659.

President's Commission on Law Enforcement and Administration of Justice. (1967). *Task force report: Juvenile delinquency and youth crime.* Washington, DC: U. S. Government Printing Office.

Roberts, A. R. (1989). The emergence and proliferation of juvenile diversion programs. In A. R. Roberts (Ed.), *Juvenile justice policies, programs, and services* (pp. 77–90). Chicago: Dorsey.

Rothman, D. J. (1984). *Conscience and convenience: The asylum and its alternatives in progressive America.* Boston: Little, Brown.

Rutherford, A., & McDermott, R. (1976). *National Evaluation Program Phase 1 Summary Report* (U.S. Department of Justice, Law Enforcement Assistance Administration, National Institute of Law Enforcement and Criminal Justice). Washington, DC: U.S. Government Printing Office.

Saul, J. A., & Davidson, W. S. (1983). Implementation of juvenile diversion programs: Cast your net on the other side of the boat. In J. R. Kluegel (Ed.), *Evaluating juvenile justice* (pp. 31–45). Beverly Hills, CA: Sage.

Scull, A. T. (1984). *Decarceration: Community treatment and the deviant—A radical view* (2nd ed.). New Brunswick, NJ: Rutgers University Press.

4

Criminalizing the Juvenile Court: A Research Agenda for the 1990s

Barry C. Feld

Historical Background

T The United States Supreme Court's decision *In re Gault* (1967) began transforming the juvenile court into a very different institution than the Progressives had contemplated (Rothman, 1980; Ryerson, 1978). Progressive reformers envisioned an informal court whose dispositions would reflect the "best interests" of the offender. The Supreme Court engrafted formal procedures at trial onto the juvenile court's individualized treatment sentencing schema. Although those decisions were not intended to alter the juvenile court's therapeutic mission, in the past two decades legislative, judicial, and administrative responses to *Gault* have modified juvenile courts' jurisdiction, purpose, and processes (Feld, 1984, 1988b). As a result, juvenile courts now converge procedurally and substantively with adult criminal courts (Feld, 1981b, 1984, 1988b).

Three types of reforms—jurisdictional, procedural, and jurisprudential—provide a vehicle for examining the contemporary juvenile court. The Supreme Court's recognition that juvenile courts often failed to realize their benevolent therapeutic promise has led to two jurisdictional changes: removing status offenses from juvenile court jurisdiction or limiting the dispositions courts may impose on noncriminal offenders, criminalizing serious juvenile offenders. These jurisdictional modifications narrow the scope of juvenile courts at the "hard" end through the removal of serious juvenile offenders and at the "soft" end through the removal of noncriminal status offenders. As juvenile court jurisdiction contracts, the sentences that delinquents charged with crimes receive increasingly are based on "just deserts" rather than their "real needs." Proportional and determinate sentences based on the present offense and prior record, rather than on the "best interests" of the child, dictate the length, location, and intensity of intervention (Feld, 1988b). Now that punishment plays an increasing, if not dominant, role in sentencing juveniles, issues of

59

procedural justice, especially the delivery of legal services, have emerged. Although theoretically the formal procedural safeguards of juvenile courts closely resemble those of criminal courts, in reality the quality of justice routinely afforded juveniles is far lower than the minimum insisted upon for adults.

These four procedural and substantive developments—removal of jurisdiction over status offenders, waiver of serious offenders into the adult system, increased punitiveness, and procedural formality—contribute to the criminalizing of the juvenile court. These changes raise the question whether anything unique remains of the Progressives' vision of a therapeutic welfare agency. And yet, even with the juvenile court's transformation from an informal, rehabilitative agency into a scaled-down criminal court, it continues to operate virtually unreformed. As juvenile courts converge with their criminal counterparts, is there any reason to maintain a separate court whose sole distinguishing characteristic is its persisting procedural deficiencies?

The Progressive Juvenile Court: Procedural Informality and Individualized, Offender-Oriented Dispositions

By the end of the nineteenth century, America had changed from a rural, agrarian society to an urban, industrial one (Wiebe, 1967). Modernization, urbanization, and immigration posed new problems of social control, and a reform movement, the Progressive movement, emerged to address them. As economic life shifted from the family to other work environments, family structure and function changed: family life became more private; women's roles became more domestic; and the numbers of children born per family declined (Kett, 1977). By the close of the nineteenth century, more modern concepts of childhood and adolescence had emerged; children were seen increasingly as vulnerable, innocent, passive, and dependent beings who needed extended preparation for life (Hawes & Hiner, 1985). This newer view of children altered traditional child rearing practices. Many Progressive programs shared a unifying child-centered theme (Platt, 1977). Juvenile courts, child labor laws, and compulsory school attendance laws reflected and advanced the changing conception of childhood (Wiebe, 1967).

Progressive criminal justice reforms in the early twentieth century, including the creation of the juvenile court, reflected changes in ideological assumptions about crime and deviance. While classical explanations attributed crime to free-will choices, positive criminology assumed that crime was *determined* rather than *chosen.* By attributing criminal behavior to antecedent forces, criminologists reduced actors' moral responsibility for crime and focused on reforming offenders rather than punishing them for their offenses (Allen, 1964; Matza, 1964; Rothman, 1980). Applying medical analogies to the treatment of offenders, a growing class of social science professionals fostered the rehabilitative ideal (Allen, 1981). Whether viewed as a humanitarian movement to "save" poor and immigrant children (Hagan & Leon, 1977; Sutton, 1988), or as an effort to expand social control over youths (Fox, 1970; Platt, 1977), juvenile courts were envisioned to be benign, non punitive, and therapeutic.

Juvenile courts used informal and flexible procedures to diagnose the causes of and prescribe the cures for delinquency. Progressives invoked the legal doctrine of *parens patriae,* the state as parent, to legitimize intervention and used informal, discretionary procedures to diagnose the causes of and prescribe the cures for delinquency. As a scientific and preventive alternative to punitive criminal law, rehabilitating delinquents precluded uniform treatment or standardized criteria (Platt, 1977; Ryerson, 1978). By separating children from adults and by providing a rehabilitative alternative to punishment, juvenile courts rejected the jurisprudence of criminal law and its procedural safeguards such as juries and lawyers. Because its jurisdiction encompassed youths suffering from abuse, dependency, or neglect, as well as those charged with criminal offenses and non criminal disobedience, proceedings were characterized as civil rather than criminal. Theoretically, a child's "best interests," background, and welfare, rather than the crime committed, guided dispositions. Since a youth's offense was only a symptom of his or her "real" needs, sentences were indeterminate, nonproportional, and potentially continued for the duration of minority.

The Constitutional Domestication of the Juvenile Court

The Supreme Court's *Gault* (1967) decision mandated procedural safeguards in delinquency proceedings and focused judicial attention initially on whether the child had committed an offense as a prerequisite to sentencing (Feld, 1984, 1988b). In shifting the focus of juvenile courts from "real needs" to legal guilt, *Gault* identified two crucial disjunctions between juvenile justice rhetoric and reality: the theory versus practice of rehabilitation, and the gulf between the procedural safeguards afforded adults and those available to juveniles. Several years later, in *In re Winship* (1970), which required proof of delinquency by the criminal standard "beyond a reasonable doubt" rather than by lower civil standards of proof, and in *Breed v. Jones* (1975), which applied the ban on double jeopardy to convictions in juvenile court, the Court posited a functional equivalence between criminal trials and delinquency proceedings.

In *McKeiver v. Pennsylvania* (1971), however, the Court denied juveniles the constitutional right to jury trials and halted the extension of full procedural parity with adult criminal prosecutions. The Court feared that jury trials would adversely affect traditional informality, render juvenile courts procedurally indistinguishable from criminal courts, and call into question the need for a separate juvenile court *(McKeiver v. Pennsylvania*, 1971). The Court in *McKeiver* justified the procedural differences between juvenile and criminal courts on the basis of the former's *treatment* rationale and latter's *punitive* purposes, although it did not analyze the differences between the two that warranted different procedural safeguards (Feld, 1987, 1988b).

Since those decisions, legislative, judicial, and administrative actions have transformed the juvenile court. Four developments—removal of status offenders, waiver of serious offenders to the adult system, increased punitiveness, and procedural formality—provide the impetus for criminalizing the juvenile court. These reforms have not been implemented as intended, nor have they had their expected effects. As a result, the juvenile court has been transformed but remains unreformed.

Juvenile Court Jurisdiction Over Noncriminal Status Offenders

The historical changes in normative assumptions about childhood and the social control of youth resulted in juvenile court jurisdiction over status offenses (Kett, 1977; Sutton, 1988). Progressives regarded youthful autonomy as malign and authorized coercion of unruly children to reinforce parental authority or to allow the state to intervene (Platt, 1977; Sutton, 1988). Status jurisdiction reflected a strategy of predelinquency intervention to prevent youthful misconduct from escalating into full-blown criminality.

While the idea of helping troubled children is inherently attractive, the definition and administration of status jurisdiction has been criticized extensively in the post-*Gault* decades (Allinson, 1983; Teitelbaum & Gough, 1977). These criticisms focused on its adverse impact on children, its disabling effects on families, schools, and other agencies that refer status offenders, and the legal and administrative issues it raises for juvenile courts. Beginning with the President's Crime Commission in 1967, many professional organizations have advocated reform or abolition of status jurisdiction (Rubin, 1985).

Until recent reforms, status offenses were classified as delinquency, and status delinquents were detained and incarcerated in the same institutions as criminal delinquents even though they had not engaged in criminal conduct. Juvenile court intervention at the behest of parents overloaded courts with intractable family disputes, diverted scarce judicial resources from other tasks, and exacerbated rather than ameliorated family conflicts. Social agencies and schools used the court as a "dumping ground" to impose solutions rather than making their own efforts to address the source of conflict. Status jurisdiction raised legal issues of "void for vagueness," equal protection, and procedural justice (Rubin, 1985). Curbing unruliness, incorrigibility, or immorality necessitates a broad grant of standardless discretion whose invocation primarily reflects the values or prejudices of the judges who administer it. The exercise of unstructured discretion fosters racial, class, and sexual discrimination: poor, minority, and female juveniles have been disproportionately over represented among the ranks of status offenders (Chesney-Lind, 1988; Sussman, 1977). Many procedural safeguards that delinquent youths receive are denied to those charged with noncriminal misconduct.

Three recent trends—diversion, deinstitutionalization, and decrimin- alization—reflect judicial and legislative disillusionment with the response to noncriminal youths, concern about the effectiveness of intervention, reservations about stigmatizing transitional deviance, and a desire to reduce juvenile courts' caseloads. The Federal Juvenile Justice and Delinquency Prevention Act (1974) required states to begin a process of removing noncriminal offenders from juvenile detention and correctional facilities (Schwartz, 1989b). Federal and state restrictions on comingling status and delinquent offenders in institutions provided the impetus to divert some status offenders from juvenile courts and decarcerate those remaining in the system.

Diversion

Since *Gault,* virtually every state has amended its juvenile status jurisdic- tion. Many of these amendments focus on providing services on an informal basis, primarily through diversion programs (Klein, 1979). Just as the original juvenile court was intended to divert youths from adult criminal courts, now diversion is supposed to shift away from the juvenile court youths who would otherwise enter that system. It is questionable whether diversion programs have been implemented in a coherent fashion or been effective when attempted (Klein, 1979; Polk, 1984). Theoretically intended to reduce the juvenile court population, diversion has had the opposite effect of "widening the net of social control" (Polk, 1984). Diversion provides a rationale for shifting discretion from the core of the juvenile court where it is subject to a modicum of procedural formality, to its periphery, which operates on an informal, pre-*Gault* basis with no accountability (Sutton, 1988).

Deinstitutionalization

Federal and state bans on secure confinement provided an impetus to deinstitutionalize noncriminal youths. Although the numbers of status offenders in the most secure facilities declined somewhat by the mid-1980s, only a small proportion of status offenders had ever been sent to secure institutions. Historically, most status offenders who were committed to institutions were sent to forestry camps, home schools, and other medium security facilities; despite *Gault,* many status offenders continued to be confined in such places, albeit with different procedural rights than those afforded delinquents given the same dispositions. Moreover, 1980 amendments to the Juvenile Justice Act weakened restrictions on secure confinement; status offenders who run away from nonsecure placements or violate court orders can be charged with contempt of court, a delinquent act, and then incarcerated (Schwartz, 1989b). Many nuisance juveniles today are charged with minor criminal offenses instead of status offenses, for which there are no dispositional limits.

Decriminalization

Historically, status offenses were classified as a form of delinquency. Now, almost every state has reclassified conduct that is illegal for children *only* into nondelinquent categories such as Persons or Children in Need of Supervision (PINS/CHINS) (Allinson, 1983; Rubin, 1985). Such changes simply shift youths from one jurisdictional category to another without significantly limiting courts' authority. Using a label of convenience, status offenders can be relabeled downward as dependent or neglected youths, upward as delinquent offenders, or laterally into the private sector (Klein, 1979).

Many children who formerly would have been labeled status offenders, especially those who are middle class and female, now are shifted into the private mental health or chemical-dependency treatment systems by diversion, court referral, or voluntary parental commitment (Schwartz,

1989a, 1989b; Weithorn, 1988). In *Parham v. J.R.* (1979), the Supreme Court ruled that the only process juveniles are due when parents commit them to secure treatment facilities is a physician's determination that such commitment is medically appropriate. While some children's psychological dysfunctions or substance abuse require medical attention, many child commitments are based on mere social or behavioral conflicts, self-serving parental motives, or the desires of medical entrepreneurs coping with underutilized hospital bed space (Schwartz, Jackson-Beeck & Anderson, 1984; Weithorn, 1988). Although data on voluntary commitments to private psychiatric facilities are scarce, it appears that the numbers of juveniles entering the "hidden system" of mental health or chemical-dependency social control has increased dramatically as a direct consequence of the decline of routine incarceration of status offenders and nuisance juveniles (Schwartz, 1989a, 1989b). Social policies to *de*institutionalize may inadvertently have resulted in *trans*institutionalization, transferring some juveniles from publicly funded facilities to private agencies administered by entrepreneurs and financed by insurance plans (Lerman, 1984). Whether incarceration is characterized as in their "best interests," for "adjustment reactions" symptomatic of adolescence, or for "chemical dependency," these trends revive the imagery of diagnosis and treatment on a discretionary basis without regard to formal due process considerations.

The appropriate response to minor, nuisance, and noncriminal offenders goes to the heart of the juvenile court's mission, the normative concept of childhood upon which it is based, and remains one of the critical, polarizing issues of juvenile justice. The policy debate pits advocates of authority and control against those who see intervention as discriminatory and a denial of rights (Rubin, 1985). Within the past decades, several states have totally divested juvenile courts of status jurisdiction and now allow noncriminal intervention only in cases of dependency or neglect. Juvenile court judges strongly resist such jurisdictional divestiture, since any contraction leads to further convergence with criminal courts (Klein, 1979). The simultaneous emergence of the "hidden system" raises questions about the effectiveness of diversion, deinstitutionalization, and decriminalization reforms. Are former status offenders simply being subjected to other forms of coercive controls with even less formal supervision than available through the juvenile court? And if so, what accounts for the societal propensity to incarcerate young people "for their own good"?

Waiver of Juvenile Offenders to Criminal Court

Historically, juvenile court sentences were discretionary, indeterminate, and nonproportional so as to achieve the offender's "best interests." The post-*Gault* era has witnessed a fundamental change in sentencing policies, for now considerations of the offense, rather than the offender, dominate the decision. A shift from rehabilitation to retribution is evident both in the response to serious juvenile offenders and in the routine sentencing of delinquent offenders (Feld, 1987, 1988b).

Whether persistent or violent young offenders should be sentenced as juveniles or adults poses difficult theoretical and practical problems. The decision implicates both juvenile court sentencing practices and the relationship between juvenile and adult court sentencing practices. Virtually every state has a mechanism for prosecuting some chronological juveniles as adults (Feld, 1978, 1987). While numerically few, some criminal youths challenge juvenile courts' assumptions about rehabilitation and nonpunitive, short-term social control (Feld, 1990).

Two types of statutes—judicial waiver and legislative offense exclusion —highlight the differences between juvenile courts' and criminal courts' sentencing philosophies (Feld, 1978, 1987; Thomas & Bilchik, 1985). Since juvenile courts theoretically emphasize individualized treatment of offenders, with judicial waiver a judge may transfer jurisdiction on a discretionary basis after a hearing to determine whether a youth is amenable to treatment or a threat to public safety. With legislative offense exclusion, by statutory definition, youths charged with certain offenses are simply removed from juvenile court jurisdiction.

Judicial waiver's focus on the offender and legislative exclusion's emphasis on the offense illustrate the contradictions between treatment and punishment. These are mutually exclusive penal goals. Punishment is *retrospective* and imposes unpleasant consequences because of past offenses, while therapy is *prospective* and seeks to improve offenders' future welfare (Feld, 1988b; Gardner, 1982). Sentences based on past conduct are typically determinate and proportional, while sentences based on the offender are typically indeterminate and non proportional (Morris, 1974; Packer, 1968; Von Hirsch, 1976, 1986). When youths are transferred to criminal court, legislative exclusion uses the seriousness of the offense to control decisions about adult status, whereas judicial waiver relies upon clinical assessments of amenability to treatment or dangerousness to decide child versus adult status (Feld, 1990).

Viewed this way, waiver statutes present the same policy issues that indeterminate or determinate sentencing guidelines raise for adult offenders. In the adult context, determinate sentences based on just deserts provide an alternative sentencing rationale to indeterminate sentences (Petersilia & Turner, 1987; Von Hirsch, 1976, 1986). Just deserts sentencing emphasizes equality, defines similar cases as similar based primarily on the offense and prior record, and precludes consideration of individual status or circumstance. By contrast, individualized justice includes all personal characteristics as relevant and relies heavily on professional discretion to weigh every factor (Matza, 1964). Proponents of just deserts sentencing reject individualization because of the demonstrated ineffectiveness of treatment programs (Greenberg, 1977; Lab & Whitehead, 1988; Martinson, 1974; Sechrest, White & Brown, 1979), the vast discretion it vests in presumed experts who cannot justify their differing treatment of similarly situated offenders, and the unequal and unjust results clinical subjectivity often produces (American Friends Service Committee, 1971; Feld, 1988b, 1990; Von Hirsch, 1976, 1986). The just deserts sentencing philosophy has influenced several states' juvenile waiver and sentencing statutes (Feld, 1987, 1988b).

Waiver decisions raise two interrelated sentencing policy issues: the bases of juvenile courts sentencing practices, and the relationship between juvenile and adult criminal court sentencing practices. The first involves individualized sentencing and the tension between discretion and the rule of law. The second focuses on harmonizing social control responses to young offenders across the two systems. Legislatures address both issues by using offense criteria as dispositional guidelines in judicial waiver proceedings to limit sentencing discretion and improve the fit between waiver decisions and criminal court sentencing practices or to automatically exclude certain youths from juvenile court jurisdiction (Feld, 1987).

Judicial Waiver: Individualized Offender-Oriented Dispositions

Judicial waiver embodies the juvenile court's approach to individualized sentencing. Although two Supreme Court decisions formalized the procedures in waiver hearings (*Kent*, 1966; *Breed*, 1975), it is the substantive bases of the waiver decision that pose the principal difficulties. Asking a judge to determine whether a youth is amenable to treatment or poses a threat to public safety implicates fundamental issues of penal policy and juvenile jurisprudence (Feld, 1978, 1987). Although the Progressives assumed that juveniles are especially amenable to treatment, the question of "what works"—whether rehabilitation programs systematically produce lasting change—remains highly controversial. Evaluation research counsels skepticism about the availability of programs that can effectively rehabilitate adult or serious juvenile offenders (Greenberg, 1977; Lab & Whitehead, 1988; Martinson, 1974; Sechrest, White & Brown, 1979). The conclusion that "nothing works" in juvenile or adult corrections has not been persuasively refuted (Melton, 1989). Clearly, some offenders do persist in crime despite treatment, and clinical tools are lacking with which to predict whether a particular individual will be a recidivist. Similarly, waiving jurisdiction because a youth poses a threat to public safety requires judges to predict future dangerousness even though a clinical technical capacity to predict future criminal behavior is lacking (Morris, 1974).

In effect, judicial waiver statutes are broad grants of standardless discretion. Like individualized sentencing statutes, the subjectivity of waiver decisions produces inequities and disparities. Judges cannot administer waiver statutes on an evenhanded basis; within a single jurisdiction, "justice by geography" prevails as courts interpret and apply the same law inconsistently (Feld, 1978, 1987, 1990; Hamparian et al., 1982). Evaluations of judicial waiver nationwide provide compelling evidence that it is arbitrary, capricious, and discriminatory (Hamparian et al., 1982). A youth's race, as well as geographic locale, influences waiver decisions (Fagan & Deschences, 1990; Fagan, Forst & Vinona, 1987). Judicial idiosyncrasies or the location of the hearing are more important to the transfer decision than the nature of the crime.

Ultimately, waiver involves the appropriate dispositions of offenders who chronologically happen to be juveniles. The traditional distinction between treatment as a juvenile and punishment as an adult is based on an arbitrary line that has no criminological significance other than its legal consequences. There is a strong relationship between age and crime: crime rates for many offenses peak in mid- to late adolescence (Farrington, 1986; Greenwood, 1986; Petersilia, 1980). Rational sentencing requires a coordinated response to young offenders on both sides of the juvenile/adult line by using a standardized means to identify and sanction serious young criminals (Greenwood, 1986).

A "punishment gap" occurs when juveniles make the transition to criminal courts. Most juveniles transferred via judicial waiver are charged with property crimes like burglary, not with serious offenses against the person. When they first appear in criminal courts as adult first-offenders, they typically receive community dispositions rather than incarceration (Greenwood, Lipson, Abrahamse, & Zimring, 1984; Greenwood, Petersilia & Zimring, 1980; Hamparian et al., 1982). Because prior records cumulate, however, criminal courts tend to sentence older offenders more severely just when their rate of criminal activity is actually on the decline, while they sentence younger offenders more leniently even though their criminal careers are increasing or at their peak (Boland, 1980; Feld, 1983). Differences between juvenile and adult sentencing practices thus work at cross-purposes when youths make the transition from the one system to the other.

Although juvenile and adult courts' sentencing practices are contradictory when youths make the transition, judicial waiver serves important political and organizational functions for juvenile courts. By relinquishing a small fraction of its clientele and portraying these juveniles as the most intractable and dangerous in the system, juvenile courts create symbolic scapegoats, appear to protect the public, preserve their jurisdiction over the vast bulk of juveniles, and deflect more comprehensive criticisms (Bortner, 1986; Feld, 1978, 1987).

Legislative Exclusion of Offenses

As contrasted with judicial waiver, legislative waiver excludes from juvenile court jurisdiction youths charged with specified offenses (Feld, 1987). Legislatures create juvenile courts and may modify their jurisdiction as they please, although they often fail to make explicit their sentencing goals. Exclusion could be justified, for example, if the minimum period of appropriate confinement is longer than the maximum sanctions available to juvenile court, that is, if a serious offender could not be confined long enough if sentenced as a juvenile (Feld, 1990; Zimring, 1981).

Legislatively defining adulthood entails a value choice about the quantity and quality of crime that will be tolerated before a more punitive response is mandated (Twentieth Century Fund Task Force on Sentencing Policy toward Young Offenders, 1978). Since most youths will not receive better services in the adult correctional system than are available in the juvenile system, the decision to try a youth as an adult must be defensible on grounds of social defense. Offense exclusion enhances community protection, increases deterrence through the certainty and visibility of consequences, and reaffirms fundamental norms *only* if longer adult sentences are imposed. However, adult prosecution is appropriate *only* if the seriousness or persistence of offending warrants confinement for substantially longer than could be imposed on a juvenile.

Using the present offense and prior record to structure waiver decisions rather than amorphous clinical considerations can integrate juvenile and adult sentencing practices and enable criminal courts to sentence violent or chronic juveniles more consistently (Feld, 1978, 1990).

It is incongruous when youths who presumably require longer sentences than the juvenile system can provide are judicially waived and then are not imprisoned when sentenced as adults (Hamparian et al., 1982).

Within the past decade, just deserts rather than individualized clinical assessments has come to dominate this sentencing decision (Feld, 1987, 1990). Legislatures use offense criteria either as dispositional guidelines to limit judicial discretion or to automatically exclude certain youths. More than twenty states have amended their judicial waiver statutes to reduce their inconsistency and inequality and to improve the fit between juvenile and criminal court sentencing policies (Feld, 1987). Some states specify that only serious offenses such as murder, rape, or robbery may be waived (Feld, 1987). Restricting waiver to serious offenses limits judicial discretion and increase the likelihood that significant adult sanctions will be imposed if waiver is ordered.

More importantly, about half of the states have rejected the traditional juvenile court sentencing philosophy, at least in part, emphasized retributive policies, and excluded youths charged with serious offenses from juvenile court jurisdiction (Feld, 1987). Some states only exclude youths charged with murder, capital crimes, or offenses punishable by life imprisonment. Others exclude broader categories of offenses, such as rape or armed robbery, or youths charged with repeat offenses (Feld, 1987). Regardless of the legislative details, these statutes remove judicial sentencing discretion entirely and base the decision to try a youth as an adult exclusively on the offense charged. These exclusion statutes provide one indicator of the shift from an individualized treatment sentencing philosophy to a more retributive one and reflect legislative distrust of juvenile court judges' discretion. Using offenses to structure or eliminate discretion repudiates rehabilitation, narrows juvenile court jurisdiction, reduces its clientele, and denies it the opportunity even to try to treat certain youths.

Using offense criteria to structure or eliminate judicial discretion constitutes a rejection of traditional juvenile court jurisprudence, but to what extent does it accomplish its intended goals of rationalizing and maximizing social control of serious offenders? Do waiver-sentencing guidelines and/or excluded offenses effectively identify serious juvenile offenders, or do they simply provide legislators with an opportunity to posture politically about "getting tough" on crime? Do the juveniles identified under these amended statutes subsequently receive longer sentences than they would have if they had been tried as juveniles, or is the legislation overly inclusive, identifying youths whom adult courts are reluctant to incarcerate? How do these statutory changes affect the racial composition of juveniles waived to criminal courts? Finally, how do the changes in waiver legislation affect the capital punishment of juveniles (*Stanford v. Kentucky*, 1989)?

Punishment in Juvenile Courts: Offense-Based Sentencing Practices

States apply just deserts principles to the routine sentencing of juveniles as well as to waiver (Feld, 1988b). The *McKeiver* Court rejected procedural equality between juveniles and adults because juvenile courts purportedly *treated* rather than *punished* youths. Increasingly, however, juvenile courts pursue the substantive goals of the criminal law (Feld, 1984, 1988b). The shift to punishment has occurred because therapeutic individualization neither reduces recidivism nor provides a principled basis for coercive intervention, produces unequal results among similarly situated offenders, sanctions minor offenders excessively, and serious ones leniently (American Friends Service Committee, 1971; Cohen, 1978; Feld, 1988b; Institute of Judicial Administration-American Bar Association, 1980; Von Hirsch, 1976, 1986). Whether a juvenile court is punishing a youth for a past offense or treating for future welfare is reflected in statutory purpose clauses; juvenile court sentencing statutes and actual sentencing practices; and conditions of institutional confinement (Feld, 1987, 1988b). All of these indicators consistently reveal that treating juveniles closely resembles punishing adult criminals, even though the *McKeiver* Court justified the juvenile court's procedural differences by its therapeutic mission. (The legislation summarized in this chapter is analyzed extensively by Feld [1988b] in an article that contains a statutory table and complete citations.)

The Purpose of the Juvenile Court

Most state juvenile codes contain a "purpose clause" or preamble that provides a statutory rationale to aid courts in interpreting the legislation (Feld, 1988b; Gardner, 1982). Since the creation of the original juvenile court in Cook County, Illinois, in 1899, the historical purpose of juvenile court law has been "to secure for each minor . . . such care and guidance . . . as will serve the moral, emotional, mental, and physical welfare of the minor and the best interests of the community." Many juvenile codes supplement that original purpose with the additional goal of removing "the taint of criminality and the penal consequences of criminal behavior, by substituting therefore an individual program of counselling, supervision, treatment, and rehabilitation" (Feld, 1988b).

But in the past decade about one-quarter of the states have redefined the purposes of their juvenile courts (Feld, 1988b, p. 842, n.84). These amendments deemphasize the role of rehabilitation and the child's "best interest," and elevate the importance of public safety, punishment, and individual and juvenile justice system accountability (Walkover, 1984). These purpose clauses emphasize protecting public safety, enforcing children's legal obligations to society, applying sanctions consistent with the seriousness of the offenses, and rendering appropriate punishment to offenders (Feld, 1988b; Walkover, 1984). Many courts recognize that changes in purpose clauses signal a basic philosophical reorientation, even as they endorse punishment as an acceptable juvenile court disposition (*D. D. H. v. Dostert*, 1980; Feld, 1988b; *In re D. F. B.*, 1988; *In re Seven Minors*, 1983; *Lawley*, 1979; *Schaaf*, 1988).

Just Deserts Dispositions: Legislative and Administrative Changes in Juvenile Courts' Sentencing Framework

Sentencing statutes provide another indicator of whether a juvenile court is punishing or treating delinquents (Feld, 1988b). Originally, juvenile court sentences were indeterminate and nonproportional to achieve the offender's "best interests." Most states' juvenile sentencing provisions continue to mirror their Progressive origins, provide a range of alternatives (dismissal, probation, out-of-home placement, or institutional confinement), and give judges broad discretion to impose any disposition (Feld, 1988b). Within these substantial ranges, the court's authority is formally unrestricted: dispositions may run for the duration of minority or until some other statutory termination. Even states that use indeterminate sentences recognize that offenses may constrain dispositions and instruct judges to consider the seriousness of the offense, the child's culpability, age, and prior record (Feld, 1988b).

Determinate and Mandatory Sentences in Juvenile Court. Despite the court's history of indeterminate sentencing, about one-third of the states now use the present offense and prior record to regulate at least some sentencing decisions through determinate or mandatory minimum sentencing statutes or administrative sentencing guidelines (Feld, 1988b). The clearest departure from traditional juvenile court sentencing practices occurred in 1977 when the State of Washington enacted just deserts legislation that sought individual and system accountability, equality, and proportionality through presumptive sentences based on age, present offense, and prior record (Feld, 1981b; Fisher, Fraser & Forst, 1985;

Schneider & Schram, 1983). New Jersey instructs juvenile court judges to consider the offense and criminal history when sentencing juveniles, enumerates statutory "aggravating and mitigating" circumstances, and provides enhanced sentences for serious or repeat offenders (Feld, 1988b). Texas adopted determinate sentencing legislation for juveniles charged with serious offenses in 1987 (Feld, 1988b).

Several states, including Colorado, Georgia, New York, and Ohio, impose mandatory minimum sentences for certain "designated felonies" (Feld, 1988b). Some mandatory minimum sentencing statutes are discretionary and allow the judge to decide whether or not to commit a juvenile to the state's department of corrections (Feld, 1988b). In other instances, a mandatory sentence is nondiscretionary and the court must commit the juvenile for the statutory minimum period. Nondiscretionary mandatory sentences are usually imposed on juveniles charged with serious or violent offenses, or those who have prior delinquency convictions (Feld, 1988b). These therapeutic sentencing laws are addressed to "violent and repeat offenders," "aggravated juvenile offenders," "serious juvenile offenders," or "designated felons." Mandatory confinement ranges from twelve to eighteen months, to age twenty-one, or to the adult term for the same offense (Feld, 1988b). Basing mandatory terms on the offense precludes any individualized consideration of the offender's "real needs."

Administrative Sentencing and Parole Release Guidelines. Several states' departments of corrections have adopted administrative guidelines that use offense criteria to specify proportional mandatory minimum terms and these provide another form of just deserts sentencing. While adult prison and parole authorities have used guidelines for decades, their use for juveniles is more recent. For example, Minnesota's Department of Corrections adopted determinate "length of stay" guidelines based on the present offense and other "risk" factors (Feld, 1988b). The juvenile risk factors are the same as those used in Minnesota's Adult Sentencing Guidelines that are designed to achieve just deserts (Feld, 1988b). Arizona's Department of Corrections uses five offense categories to specify proportional mandatory minimum terms (Arizona Department of Corrections, 1986). Georgia's Division of Youth Services supplements its "designated felony" statute with administrative determinate sentencing guidelines based on the present offense and other "aggravating factors" (Forst, Friedman & Coates, 1985). California juveniles committed to the Youth Authority are released by a Youthful Offender Parole Board that bases parole eligibility on the seriousness of the offense (Feld, 1988b).

Empirical Evaluation of Juvenile Court Sentencing Practices

Juvenile court judges decide what to do with a child, in part, by reference to statutory mandates. However, practical, bureaucratic considerations also influence their discretionary decisions (Bortner, 1982; Cicourel, 1968; Emerson, 1969). Because of the need to look beyond the present offense to "best interests" and due to paternalistic assumptions about the control of children, juvenile court judges enjoy greater discretion than do their adult court counterparts.

The wide frame of relevance associated with individualized justice raises concerns about discretionary decision making and particularly its impact on lower-class and nonwhite youths (Dannefer & Schutt, 1982; Fagan, Slaughter, & Hartstone, 1987; Krisberg et al., 1987; McCarthy & Smith, 1986). When practitioners of individualized justice make discretionary judgments based on social characteristics rather than legal variables, do their decisions result in differential processing and more severe sentencing of minority youths (Fagan et al., 1987; Krisberg et al., 1987; McCarthy & Smith, 1986)? Or, despite the theoretical commitment to individualized justice, are sentences based on offenses and does the disproportionate over representation of minority youths result from real differences in rates of offending by race (Hindelang, 1978; Huizinga & Elliott, 1987; Wolfgang, Figlio & Sellin, 1972)? In short, to what extent do legal factors—present offense and prior record—or social characteristics —race, sex, or social class—influence judges' dispositional decisions?

While evaluations of juvenile dispositions yield contradictory results, two general findings emerge. First, most evaluation research indicates that offense considerations structure decision making: the present offense and prior record account for most of the variation in sentencing that can be explained (Barton, 1976; Clarke & Koch, 1980; Feld, 1989; Horowitz & Wasserman, 1980; McCarthy & Smith, 1986; Phillips & Dinitz, 1982). Second, after controlling for offense variables, individualization is often synonymous with racial disparities in sentencing (Fagan et al., 1987; Krisberg et al., 1987; McCarthy & Smith, 1986; Pope & Feyerherm, 1990a, 1990b).

Practical administrative considerations provide an impetus to base sentences on the offense. The bureaucratic desire to avoid scandal and unfavorable political and media attention certainly can constrain juvenile court dispositions and encourage more formal and restrictive responses to more serious delinquency (Bortner, 1982; Cicourel, 1968; Emerson, 1968; Matza, 1964). As a result, juvenile and adult sentencing practices are more similar in their emphases on present offense and prior record than their statutory language suggests (Greenwood, Lipson, Abrahamse & Zimring, 1983).

While there is a modest relationship between offense variables and dispositions, most of the variance in the sentencing of juveniles remains unexplained (Clarke & Koch, 1980; Horowitz & Wasserman, 1982). Recent statutory changes emphasizing offenses may reflect legislative disquiet with the underlying premises of individualized justice, the idiosyncratic exercises of discretion, and the inequalities that result (Feld, 1987, 1988b). Whatever the reasons, legislation, sentencing guidelines, and actual practices contradict the individualized, offender-oriented sentencing premises of juvenile courts.

Conditions of Juvenile Confinement

Examining the correctional facilities to which young offenders are committed provides another indicator of whether juvenile courts are punishing or treating juveniles. It was the routinely deplorable institutional conditions reported in *Gault* (1967) that motivated the Court to insist upon minimal procedural safeguards for juveniles. While involuntary confinement does not constitute punishment per se, the Court in *Gault* viewed incarceration as a severe penalty, a denial of autonomy, and a status degradation, all of which are elements of punishment.

The juvenile court's rhetorical commitment to rehabilitation has been contradicted since its inception by the reality of custodial institutions. Historical studies of Progressive juvenile correctional programs provide dismal accounts of training schools and other institutions that failed to rehabilitate and that were scarcely distinguishable from their adult penal counterparts (Rothman, 1980; Schlossman, 1977). The juvenile court's lineage of punitive confinement in the name of rehabilitation can be traced to its institutional precursor, the house of refuge (Hawes, 1971; Mennel, 1973; Rothman, 1971).

The inadequacy of juvenile correctional programs is not simply an historical artifact. Contemporary evaluations of juvenile correctional facilities reveal a continuing gap between the rhetoric of rehabilitation and its punitive reality (Bartollas, Miller & Dinitz, 1976; Feld, 1977, 1981a; Lerner, 1986). Research in Massachusetts described institutions in which staff physically abused inmates and were frequently powerless to prevent inmate abuse of other inmates (Feld, 1977, 1981a). Other studies report similarly violent and oppressive institutions supposedly intended to rehabilitate young delinquents (Bartollas et al., 1976). Staff and inmate violence, physical abuse, and degrading make-work tasks are common (Guggenheim, 1978). A recent review of California Youth Authority (CYA) institutions concluded that "a young man . . . cannot pay his debt to society safely. The hard truth is that the CYA staff cannot protect its inmates from being beaten or intimidated by other prisoners" (Lerner, 1986, p. 12). Despite rehabilitative rhetoric, the daily reality for juveniles confined in many so-called treatment facilities is one of violence, predatory behavior, and punitive incarceration.

Coinciding with these post-*Gault* evaluation studies, several lawsuits challenged conditions of confinement, alleging that the institutions violated inmates' "right to treatment" and inflicted "cruel and unusual punishment," and thereby provided another outside view of juvenile correctional facilities (Feld, 1978, 1984). Federal judges found that juveniles routinely were beaten with fraternity paddles, injected with psychotropic drugs for social control purposes, and deprived of minimally adequate care or individualized treatment (*Nelson v. Heyne*, 1974). Other courts found youths confined in dungeon like cells in their underwear, locked in solitary confinement, and subjected to a variety of punitive practices (*Inmates v. Affleck*, 1972). Still others found numerous instances of physical abuse, staff-administered hazing, beating, and teargassing, homosexual assaults, extended solitary confinement, repetitive and degrading make-work, and minimal clinical services (*Morales v. Turman*, 1976). Violence, aggression, and homosexual rape is prevalent in juvenile facilities (Bartollas et al., 1976; Feld, 1977). Unfortunately, these cases are not atypical, as the many decisions documenting inhumane conditions in juvenile institutions and even adult jails where juveniles are also held demonstrate (Krisberg et al., 1986). Rehabilitative euphemisms, such as "providing a structured environment," cannot disguise the punitive reality of juvenile confinement. Although juvenile institutions are not as uniformly bad as adult prisons, neither are they so benign or therapeutic as to justify dispensing with procedural safeguards. Evaluation research provides scant support for the effectiveness of such "rehabilitative" programs (Lab & Whitehead, 1988).

Summary of Changes in Juvenile Court Sentencing Practices

There is a strong nationwide movement, both in theory and in practice, away from therapeutic, individualized dispositions toward punitive, offense-based sentences. In 1970, when the Court decided *McKeiver*, no states used determinate or mandatory minimum sentencing statutes or administrative guidelines. In the mid- to late 1970s several states began to adopt "designated felony" and serious offender sentencing legislation and determinate sentencing guidelines (Feld, 1988b). Since 1980, eleven more states have adopted mandatory minimal, determinate sentences, or administrative guidelines (Feld, 1988b), so that now about one-third of the states use explicitly punitive juvenile sentencing strategies.

These formal changes and actual practices eliminate most of the differences between juvenile and adult sentencing. Basing sentences on the offense and prior record contradicts any therapeutic purpose for juvenile dispositions. Imposing mandatory minimum sentences on the basis of the offense avoids any reference to a youth's "real needs" or "best interests." The revised juvenile court purpose clauses and court decisions eliminate even rhetorical support for rehabilitation. As a result, "the purposes of the juvenile process have become more punitive, its procedures formalistic, adversarial and public, and the consequences of conviction much more harsh" (*Javier A.*, 1984, p. 964). These changes repudiate the original juvenile courts' basic assumptions that juveniles should be treated differently than adults, that juvenile courts operate in a youth's "best interest," and that rehabilitation is an indeterminate process that cannot be limited by fixed-time punishment (Coates, Forst & Fisher, 1985). These changes also contradict the premise of the *McKeiver* Court that juvenile dispositions are rehabilitative and therefore require fewer procedural safeguards.

The shift from rehabilitation to retribution raises questions about the characteristics of juveniles sentenced under these punitive sentencing statutes as opposed to those juveniles who are sentenced more routinely. How do legislative changes affect the lengths of time that such youths serve? What is the relationship between special sentencing legislation and institutional overcrowding? How do punitive sentencing laws and overcrowding affect conditions of institutional confinement? Has the emphasis on the offense as a sentencing criterion also affected the disproportionate minority overrepresentation in public institutions (Krisberg et al., 1985)?

The Procedural Convergence Between Juvenile and Criminal Courts

The shift in sentencing focus from the offender to the offense, from treatment to punishment, raises questions about the quality of procedural justice that *McKeiver* avoided. Since *Gault*, there has been substantial convergence between the formal procedural attributes of juvenile courts and those of criminal courts (Feld, 1984, 1988b). There remains, however, a substantial gulf between theory and reality, between the law on the books and the law in action. Theoretically, juveniles receive procedural formality at their adjudication: triallike hearings to determine legal guilt, the assistance of counsel to confront and cross-examine witnesses, the application of rules of evidence, and the like (*Gault,* 1967). The actual quality of procedural justice, however, is far different. Despite the criminalizing of juvenile court procedures, it remains nearly as true today as two decades ago that "the child receives the worst of both worlds: he gets neither the protections accorded to adults nor the solicitous care and regenerative treatment postulated for children" (*Kent,* 1966, p. 555). Despite increased punitiveness, most states' juvenile codes provide neither special procedural safeguards to protect juveniles from their own immaturity nor the full panoply of adult criminal procedural safeguards. Instead, juvenile courts employ procedures that assure that youths continue to "receive the worst of both worlds," treating juvenile offenders just like adult criminal defendants when formal equality redounds to their disadvantage, and using less-adequate juvenile court safeguards when those deficient procedures redound to the advantage of the state (Feld, 1984).

Jury Trials in Juvenile Court

The right to a jury trial and the assistance of counsel are two critical procedural safeguards when sentences are based on the offense rather than the offender. In denying juveniles a jury trial, the *McKeiver* Court posited virtual parity between the factual accuracy of juvenile and adult adjudications. But juries serve special protective functions to assure factual accuracy and are more likely to acquit than are judges (Kalven & Zeisel, 1966). By dispensing with juries, *McKeiver* rendered it easier to convict a youth appearing before a judge in juvenile court than to convict him or her, on the basis of the same evidence, before a jury of detached citizens in a criminal proceeding (Feld, 1984; Greenwood et al., 1983).

Moreover, *McKeiver* simply ignored the reality that constitutional procedural safeguards also serve to prevent governmental oppression (Feld, 1981b, 1984, 1988b). In *Duncan v. Louisiana* (1968), the Supreme Court held that fundamental fairness in adult criminal proceedings requires a jury to achieve both factual accuracy *and* to protect against governmental oppression. The Court in *Duncan* noted that jury trials protect against a weak or biased judge, inject the community's values into the process, and increase the visibility of justice administration. These protective functions are even more crucial in juvenile courts that labor behind closed doors immune from public scrutiny.

Few of the states that sentence juveniles on the basis of their offenses provide jury trials; several have rejected constitutional challenges. The increased punitiveness of juvenile justice raises a dilemma of constitutional dimensions: "Is it fair, in the constitutional sense, to expose minors to adult sanctions for crimes, without granting them the same due process rights as adults?" (Private Sector Task Force on Juvenile Justice, 1987, p. 7). For juvenile justice operatives, jury trials have symbolic importance out of all proportion to their practical impact, since even in those states where they are available, they are seldom used (Feld, 1988b). As a symbol, the jury requires candor about the punitive reality of juvenile justice, what actually transpires in the name of rehabilitation, and the need to safeguard against even benevolently motivated governmental coercion.

Rehabilitation is an expansive concept that widens the net of social control and lends itself to abuse through self-delusion (Allen, 1964, 1981). Punishment, by contrast, frankly acknowledges that coercion is harmful and requires proportional limits and procedural protections (Cohen, 1978). Is there anything about juveniles or justice that requires different procedures than those for adults? If there is, proponents of the juvenile court should justify with evidence, not just rhetoric, every procedural difference.

The Right to Counsel in Juvenile Court

Procedural justice hinges on access to and the assistance of legal counsel. In *Gault* (1967), the Supreme Court held that juveniles were constitutionally entitled to counsel in delinquency proceedings. *Gault* also held that juveniles enjoy the privilege against self-incrimination and the right to confront and cross-examine their accusers at a hearing. Without the assistance of counsel, these other rights could be negated.

Prior to the *Gault* decision, attorneys appeared in perhaps 5 percent of delinquency cases (Feld, 1989). Shortly after *Gault*, observers reported that juveniles were neither adequately advised of their right to counsel nor had counsel appointed for them (Lefstein, Stapleton & Teitelbaum, 1969). In most hearings in which counsel appeared, they did nothing (Ferster & Courtless, 1972).

In the decades since *Gault*, the promise of counsel remains unrealized. Despite formal changes, the actual delivery of legal services has lagged behind. Recent evaluations indicate that lawyers still appear less often than might be expected. Clarke and Koch (1980) found that only 22.3 and 45.8 percent of juveniles were represented in two sites in North Carolina. Aday (1986) found rates of representation of 26.2 and 38.7 percent in a southeastern state. Only 32 percent of juveniles in a large north-central city were represented (Walter & Ostrander, 1982). Bortner (1982) reported that only 41.8 percent of juveniles in a large, midwestern county's juvenile court had an attorney. Feld (1988a) reported the only statewide data available as well as the only interstate comparisons and found that in three of the six states surveyed, half or less of the juveniles had counsel. In another study, Feld reported that in 1986, the majority of youths in Minnesota did not have counsel and that rates of representation varied by county, ranging from 100 percent in one county to less than 5 percent in several others (Feld, 1984, 1988a, 1989). While juveniles charged with serious offenses are more likely to be represented (Feld, 1988a, 1989), they constitute a small part of most juvenile court dockets. Nearly one-third of the Minnesota youths removed from their homes and more than one-quarter of those confined in institutions were unrepresented; the larger group of youths charged with misdemeanor offenses are most likely to be incarcerated without representation (Feld, 1988a, 1989).

There are a variety of possible explanations for why so many youths are unrepresented: parental reluctance to retain an attorney; inadequate public defender services in rural areas; judicial encouragement of waivers of counsel in order to ease their administrative burdens; cursory and misleading judicial advisories that suggest that waiver is simply a meaningless technicality; continuing judicial hostility to an advocacy role in juvenile court; and judicial predetermination of dispositions and denial of counsel where probation is anticipated (Bortner, 1982; Feld, 1984; Lefstein et al., 1969; Stapleton & Teitelbaum, 1972). Whatever the reasons, most juveniles in most states never see a lawyer, waive their right to counsel without consulting with or appreciating the consequences of relinquishing counsel, and confront the power of the state alone and unaided.

The most common explanation is that juveniles waive their right to counsel. Courts use the adult standard—"knowing, intelligent, and voluntary" under the "totality of the circumstances"—to assess the validity of a juvenile's waiver of a constitutional right (*Fare*, 1979; Feld, 1984, 1989; *Johnson*, 1938). The Supreme Court held that an adult defendant could waive counsel and appear *pro se* in state criminal trials so long as he or she chooses to do so (*Johnson*, 1938; *Faretta*, 1975). The crucial issue for juveniles, as for adults, is whether a waiver can be "knowing, intelligent, and voluntary," particularly if it is made without consulting with counsel. The problem is exacerbated when the juvenile court judges who give the counsel advisories seek a predetermined result, waiver of counsel, that influences the information they conveyed and their interpretation of juveniles' responses.

The "totality of the circumstances" approach to waivers of rights by juveniles has been criticized extensively as an instance of treating juveniles just like adults when formal equality redounds to their disadvantage (Feld, 1984; Grisso, 1980). Juveniles simply are not as competent as adults to waive their constitutional rights in a "knowing and intelligent" manner (Grisso, 1980, 1981). While several states recognize this developmental fact and prohibit either waivers of counsel or incarceration of unrepresented delinquents (Feld, 1989), in most states juveniles waive counsel without consulting with counsel.

The questionable validity of these waivers of counsel also raises collateral issues. Absent a valid waiver, counsel must be appointed as a prerequisite to any sentence restricting liberty (*Scott v. Illinois*, 1979). Despite this doctrine, one-third of the juveniles removed from their homes and more than one-quarter of those confined in Minnesota lacked counsel (Feld, 1988, 1989). Moreover, prior convictions obtained without counsel may not be used to enhance later sentences (*Burgett*, 1967; *Tucker*, 1972; *Baldasar*, 1980), and courts have applied this principle to juvenile prior convictions as well (Feld, 1989). Despite this, juvenile court judges rely upon prior uncounseled convictions to sentence juveniles, to impose mandatory minimum or enhanced sentences, to waive juveniles to criminal court, and to "bootstrap" status offenders into delinquents.

What can be done to assure the delivery of legal services in juvenile courts? What additional reforms are necessary to assure that juvenile court judges observe the formal procedural rights that juveniles theoretically enjoy? What social structural or contextual factors determine the implementation of procedural safeguards? What are the implications of procedural formality for sentencing severity?

The Transformation of the Juvenile Court: Reformed But Not Rehabilitated

The procedural deficiencies of juvenile courts are untenable in an institution that is increasingly and explicitly punitive. Recent changes in juvenile court jurisdiction, sentencing practices, and procedure reflect a basic philosophical ambivalence about the role of the court. As juvenile courts converge both procedurally and substantively with adult criminal courts, is there any reason to maintain a separate juvenile criminal court whose sole distinction is inadequate procedures under which no adult would consent to be tried?

The juvenile court is at a philosophical crossroads that cannot be resolved by simplistic "treatment versus punishment" formulations. In reality, there are no practical or operational differences between the two. Recognizing the punitive reality of juvenile justice carries with it a concomitant obligation to provide appropriate procedural safeguards since "the condition of being a boy does not justify a kangaroo court" (*Gault*, 1967, p. 28).

While providing young offenders with full procedural parity may realize the *McKeiver* Court's fear of sounding the deathknell of the traditional juvenile court, to fail to do so perpetuates injustice. Fair procedures, an opportunity to participate in the dispute resolution, and treating parties with respect for personal dignity, honesty, and consistency are fundamental elements of justice (Melton, 1989). To punish juveniles in the name of treatment, to treat similarly situated offenders dissimilarly, and to deny them basic safeguards fosters a sense of injustice that will thwart the effectiveness of even the best rehabilitative efforts.

After more than two decades of constitutional and legislative reforms, juvenile courts continue to deflect, coopt, ignore, and absorb ameliorative procedural reform with minimal institutional change. Despite its transformation from a welfare agency to a criminal court, the juvenile court remains essentially unreformed. The quality of procedural justice routinely afforded to youths would be intolerable for adult defendants facing incarceration. Public and political concern about drugs and youth crime fosters a "get tough" mentality to repress rather than rehabilitate young offenders. With fiscal constraints, budget deficits, and competing demands from other interests groups, there is little likelihood that treatment services for delinquents will expand. Coupling the explicit emergence of punitive policies in juvenile courts with a continuing public and political unwillingness to commit scarce social resources to the welfare of children in general, much less to those who commit crimes, is there any reason to believe that the contemporary juvenile court can be rehabilitated?

References

Aday, D. P., Jr. (1986). Court structure, defense attorney use, and juvenile court decisions. *Sociological Quarterly, 27*, 107–119.

Allen, F. A. (1964). Legal values and the rehabilitative ideal. In *Borderland of the criminal law*. Chicago: University of Chicago Press.

Allen, F. A. (1981). *The decline of the rehabilitative ideal: Penal policy and social purpose.* New Haven: Yale University Press.

Allinson, R. (1983). *Status offenders and the juvenile justice system.* Hackensack, NJ: National Council on Crime and Delinquency.

American Friends Service Committee. (1971). *Struggle for justice.* New York: Hill and Wang.

Arizona Department of Corrections. (1986). *Length of confinement guidelines for juveniles.* Tucson, AZ: Author.

Bartollas, C., Miller, S. J., & Dinitz, S. (1976). *Juvenile victimization.* New York: Wiley.

Barton, W. (1976). Discretionary decision-making in juvenile justice. *Crime and Delinquency, 22,* 470–480.

Boland, B. (1980). Fighting crime: The problem of adolescents. *Journal of Criminal Law and Criminology, 71,* 94.

Bortner, M. A. (1982). *Inside a juvenile court.* New York: New York University Press.

Bortner, M. A. (1986). Traditional rhetoric, organizational realities: Remand of juveniles to adult court. *Crime and Delinquency, 32,* 53.

Chesney-Lind, M. (1988). Girls and status offenses: Is juvenile justice still sexist? *Criminal Justice Abstracts, 20,* 144–165.

Cicourel, A. V. (1968). *The social organization of juvenile justice.* New York: Wiley.

Clarke, S. H., & Koch, G. G. (1980). Juvenile court: Therapy or crime control, and do lawyers make a difference? *Law and Society Review, 14,* 263–308.

Coates, R., Forst, M., & Fisher, B. (1985). *Institutional commitment and release decision-making for juvenile delinquents: An assessment of determinate and indeterminate approaches—A cross-state analysis.* San Francisco: URSA Institute.

Cohen, F. (1978). Juvenile offenders: Proportionality vs. treatment. *Children's Rights Reporter, 8,* 1–16.

Dannefer, D., & Schutt, R. (1982). Race and juvenile justice processing in court and police agencies. *American Journal of Sociology, 87,* 1113–1132.

Emerson, R. M. (1969). *Judging delinquents.* Chicago: Aldine.

Fagan, J., & Dechenes, E. P. (1990). Determinants of judicial waiver decisions for violent juvenile offenders. *Journal of Criminal Law and Criminology, 81,* 314–347.

Fagan, J., Forst, M., & Vivona, S. (1987). Racial determinants of the judicial transfer decision: Prosecuting violent youth in criminal court. *Crime and Delinquency, 33,* 259.

Fagan, J., Slaughter, E., & Hartstone, E. (1987). Blind justice? The impact of race on the juvenile justice process. *Crime and Delinquency, 33,* 224–258.

Farrington, D. P. (1986). Age and crime. In M. Tonry & N. Morris (Eds.), *Crime and justice: An annual review* (Vol. 7, pps. 189–250). Chicago: University of Chicago Press.

Feld, B. (1977). *Neutralizing inmate violence.* Cambridge, MA: Ballinger.

Feld, B. (1978). Reference of juvenile offenders for adult prosecution: The legislative alternative to asking unanswerable questions? *Minnesota Law Review, 62,* 515–618.

Feld, B. (1981a). A comparative analysis of organizational structure and inmate subcultures in institutions for juvenile offenders. *Crime and Delinquency, 27,* 336–363.

Feld, B. (1981b). Juvenile court legislative reform and the serious young offender: Dismantling the "rehabilitative ideal." *Minnesota Law Review,* 69, 141–242.

Feld, B. (1983). Delinquent careers and criminal policy: Just deserts and the waiver decision. *Criminology, 21,* 195.

Feld, B. (1984). Criminalizing juvenile justice: Rules of procedure for juvenile court. *Minnesota Law Review, 69,* 141–276.

Feld, B. (1987). Juvenile court meets the principle of offense: Legislative changes in juvenile waiver statutes. *Journal of Criminal Law and Criminology, 78,* 471–533.

Feld, B. (1988a). *In re Gault* revisited: A cross-state comparison of the right to counsel in juvenile court. *Crime and Delinquency, 34,* 393–424.

Feld, B. (1988b). Juvenile court meets the principle of offense: Punishment, treatment, and the difference it makes. *Boston University Law Review, 68,* 821–915.

Feld, B. (1989). The right to counsel in juvenile court: An empirical study of when lawyers appear and the difference they make. *Journal of Criminal Law and Criminology, 79,* 1185–1346.

Feld, B. (1990). Bad law makes hard cases: Reflections on teenaged axe-murderers, judicial activism, and legislative default. *Journal of Law and Inequality, 8,* 1–101.

Ferster, E. Z., & Courtless, T. F. (1972). Predispositional data, role of counsel and decisions in a juvenile court. *Law and Society Review, 7,* 195–222.

Fisher, B., Fraser, M., & Forst, M. (1985). *Institutional commitment and release decision-making for juvenile delinquents: An assessment of determinate and indeterminate approaches, Washington State—A case study.* San Francisco: URSA Institute.

Forst, M., Friedman, E., & Coates, R. (1985). *Institutional commitment and release decision-making for juvenile delinquents: An assessment of determinate and indeterminate approaches, Georgia—A case study.* San Francisco: URSA Institute.

Fox, S. J. (1970). Juvenile justice reform: An historical perspective. *Stanford Law Review, 22,* 1187–1239.

Gardner, M. (1982). Punishment and juvenile justice: A conceptual framework for assessing constitutional rights of youthful offenders. *Vanderbilt Law Review, 35,* 791–847.

Georgia Division of Youth Services. (1985). *Policy and procedure manual.* Atlanta, GA: Georgia Department of Human Resources.

Greenberg, D. (1977). *Corrections and punishment.* Beverly Hills, CA: Sage.

Greenwood, P. (1986). Differences in criminal behavior and court responses among juvenile and young adult defendants. In M. Tonry & N. Morris (Eds.), *Crime and justice: An annual review* (Vol. 7, pp. 151–188). Chicago: University of Chicago Press.

Greenwood, P., Abrahamse, A., & Zimring, F. (1984). *Factors affecting sentence severity for young adult offenders.* Santa Monica, CA: Rand.

Greenwood, P., Lipson, A., Abrahamse, A., & Zimring, F. (1983). *Youth crime and juvenile justice in California.* Santa Monica, CA: Rand.

Greenwood, P., Petersilia, J., & Zimring, F. (1980). *Age, crime, and sanctions: The transition from juvenile to adult court.* Santa Monica, CA: Rand.

Grisso, T. (1980). Juveniles' capacities to waive Miranda rights: An empirical analysis. *California Law Review, 68,* 1134–1166.

Grisso, T. (1981). *Juveniles' waiver of rights.* New York: Plenum Press.

Guggenheim, M. (1978). A call to abolish the juvenile justice system. *Children's Rights Reporter, 2,* 7–19.

Hagan, J., & Leon, J. (1977). Rediscovering delinquency: Social history, political ideology and the sociology of law. *American Sociological Review, 42,* 587–598.

Hamparian, D., Estep, L., Muntean, S., Priestino, R., Swisher, R., Wallace, P., & White, J. (1982). *Youth in adult courts: Between two worlds.* Washington, DC: Office of Juvenile Justice and Delinquency Prevention.

Hawes, J. (1971). *Children in urban society.* New York: Oxford University Press.

Hawes, J., & Hiner, N. (1985). *American childhood: A research guide and historical handbook.* Westport, CT: Greenwood Press.

Hindelang, M. (1978). Race and involvement in common law personal crimes. *American Sociological Review, 43,* 93–109.

Horowitz, A., & Wasserman, M. (1980). Some misleading conceptions in sentencing research: An example and reformulation in the juvenile court. *Criminology, 18,* 411–424.

Huizinga, D., & Elliott, D. S. (1987). Juvenile offenders: Prevalence, offender incidence, and arrest rates by race. *Crime and Delinquency, 33,* 206–223.

Institute of Judicial Administration–American Bar Association. (1980). *Juvenile justice standards relating to juvenile delinquency and sanctions.* Cambridge, MA: Ballinger.

Kalven, H., & Zeisel, H. (1966). *The American jury.* Chicago: University of Chicago Press.

Kett, J. F. (1977). *Rites of passage: Adolescence in America 1790 to the present.* New York: Basic Books.

Klein, M. W. (1979). Deinstitutionalization and diversion of juvenile offenders: A litany of impediments. In M. Tonry & N. Morris (Eds.), *Crime and justice: An annual review* (Vol. 1, pp. 145–201). Chicago: University of Chicago Press.

Krisberg, B., Schwartz, I., Fishman, G., Eisikovits, Z., Guttman, E., & Joe, K. (1987). The incarceration of minority youth. *Crime and Delinquency, 33,* 173–205.

Krisberg, B., Schwartz, I., Lisky, P., & Austin, J. (1986). The watershed of juvenile justice reform. *Crime and Delinquency, 32,* 5–38.

Lab, S. P., & Whitehead, J. T. (1988). An analysis of juvenile correctional treatment. *Crime and Delinquency, 34,* 60–83.

Lefstein, N., Stapleton, V., & Teitelbaum, L. (1969). In search of juvenile justice: *Gault* and its implementation. *Law and Society Review, 3,* 491–562.

Lerman, P. (1984). Child welfare, the private sector, and community-based corrections. *Crime and Delinquency, 30,* 5–38.

Lerner, S. (1986). *Bodily harm.* Bolinas, CA: Common Knowledge Press.

Martinson, R. (1974). What works? Questions and answers about prison reform. *Public Interest, 35,* 22–54.

Matza, D. (1964). *Delinquency and drift.* New York: Wiley.

McCarthy, B., & Smith, B. L. (1986). The conceptualization of discrimination in the juvenile justice process: The impact of administrative factors and screening decisions on juvenile court dispositions. *Criminology, 24,* 41–64.

Melton, G. B. (1989). Taking *Gault* seriously: Toward a new juvenile court. *Nebraska Law Review, 68,* 146–181.

Mennel, R. (1973). *Thorns and thistles.* Hanover, NH: University Press of New England.

Minnesota Department of Corrections. (1980). *Juvenile release guidelines.* St. Paul, MN: Author.

Morris, N. (1974). *The future of imprisonment.* Chicago: University of Chicago Press.

Packer, H. L. (1968). *The limits of the criminal sanction.* Stanford, CA: Stanford University Press.

Petersilia, J. (1980). Criminal career research: A review of recent evidence. In M. Tonry & N. Morris (Eds.), *Crime and justice: An annual review* (Vol. 2, pp. 321–379). Chicago: University of Chicago Press.

Petersilia, J., & Turner, S. (1987). Guideline-based justice: Prediction and racial minorities. In M. Tonry & N. Morris (Eds.), *Crime and justice: An annual review* (Vol. 9, pp. 151–218). Chicago: University of Chicago Press.

Phillips, C. D., & Dinitz, S. (1982). Labelling and juvenile court dispositions: Official responses to a cohort of violent juveniles. *Sociological Quarterly, 23,* 267–278.

Platt, A. (1977). *The child savers.* Chicago: University of Chicago Press.

Polk, K. (1984). Juvenile diversion: A look at the record. *Crime and Delinquency, 30,* 648–659.

Pope, C. E., & Feyerherm, W. H. (1990a). Minority status and juvenile justice processing: An assessment of the research literature, Part 1. *Criminal Justice Abstracts, 22,* 327–335.

Pope, C. E. Feyerherm, W. H. (1990b). Minority status and juvenile justice processing: An assessment of the research literature, Part 2. *Criminal Justice Abstracts, 22,* 527–542.

Private Sector Task Force on Juvenile Justice. (1987). *Final report.* San Francisco: National Council on Crime and Delinquency.

Rothman, D. J. (1971). *The discovery of the asylum.* Boston: Little, Brown.

Rothman, D. J. (1980). *Conscience and convenience.* Boston: Little, Brown.

Rubin, H. T. (1985). *Juvenile justice: Policy, practice, and law* (2nd ed.). New York: Random House.

Ryerson, E. (1978). *The best-laid plans.* New York: Hill and Wang.

Schlossman, S. (1977). *Love and the American delinquent.* Chicago: University of Chicago Press.

Schneider, A., & Schram, D. (1983). *A justice philosophy for the juvenile court.* Seattle, WA: Urban Policy Research.

Schwartz, I. M. (1989a). Hospitalization of adolescents for psychiatric and substance abuse treatment. *Journal of Adolescent Health Care, 10,* 1–6.

Schwartz, I. M. (1989b). *(In) Justice for juveniles: Rethinking the best interests of the child.* Lexington, MA: Lexington Books.

Schwartz, I. M., Jackson-Beeck, M., & Anderson, R. (1984). The hidden system of juvenile control. *Crime and Delinquency, 30,* 371–385.

Sechrest, L. B., White, S. O., & Brown, E. D. (1979). *The rehabilitation of criminal offenders.* Washington, DC: National Academy of Sciences.

Stapleton, W.V., & Teitelbaum, L. E. (1972). *In defense of youth.* New York: Russell Sage.

Sussman, A. (1977). Sex-based discrimination and the PINS jurisdiction. In L. E. Teitelbaum & A. R. Gough (Eds.), *Beyond control: Status offenders in the juvenile court* (pp. 179–199). Cambridge, MA: Ballinger.

Sutton, J. R. (1988). *Stubborn children.* Berkeley and Los Angeles: University of California Press.

Teitelbaum, L. E., & Gough, A. R. (Eds.). (1977). *Beyond control: Status offenders in the juvenile court.* Cambridge, MA: Ballinger.

Thomas, C. W., & Bilchik, S. (1985). Prosecuting juveniles in criminal courts: A legal and empirical analysis. *Journal of Criminal Law and Criminology, 76,* 439.

Twentieth Century Fund Task Force on Sentencing Policy toward Young Offenders. (1978). *Confronting youth crime.* New York: Holmes and Meier.

Von Hirsch, A. (1976). *Doing justice.* New York: Hill and Wang.

Von Hirsch, A. (1986). *Past versus future crimes.* New Brunswick, NJ: Rutgers University Press.

Walkover, A. (1984). The infancy defense in the new juvenile court. *University of California at Los Angeles Law Review, 31,* 503–562.

Walter, J. D., & Ostrander, S. A. (1982). An observational study of a juvenile court. *Juvenile and Family Court Journal, 33,* 53–69.

Wiebe, R. H. (1967). *The search for order: 1877–1920.* New York: Hill and Wang.

Weithorn, L. (1988). Mental hospitalization of troublesome youth: An analysis of skyrocketing admission rates. *Stanford Law Review, 40,* 773.

Wolfgang, M., Figlio, R., & Sellin, T. (1972). *Delinquency in a birth cohort.* Chicago: University of Chicago Press.

Zimring, F. (1981). Notes toward a jurisprudence of waiver. In J. C. Hall, D. M. Hamparian, J. M. Pettibone, & J. L. White (Eds.), *Readings in public policy* (pp. 193–205). Columbus, OH: Academy for Contemporary Problems.

Cases

Baldasar v. Illinois, 446 U.S. 222 (1980).

Breed v. Jones, 421 U.S. 519 (1975).

Burgett v. Texas, 389 U.S. 109 (1967).

D.D.H. v. Dostert, 269 S.E.2d 401 (1980).

Duncan v. Louisiana, 391 U.S. 145 (1968).

Fare v. Michael C., 442 U.S. 707 (1979).

Faretta v. California, 422 U.S. 806 (1975).

Inmates of Boy's Training School v. Affleck, 346 F. Supp. 1354 (1972).

In re D.F.B., 430 N.W. 2d. 476 (1988).

In re Gault, 387 U.S. 1 (1967).

In re Javier A., 159 Cal., App.3d 913, 206 Cal Rptr. 386 (1984).

In re Seven Minors, 99 Nev. 427, 664 P.2d 947 (1983).

In re Walker, 191 S.E.2d 702 (1972).

In re Winship, 397 U.S. 358 (1970).

Johnson v. Zerbst, 304 U.S. 458 (1938).

Kent v. United States, 383 U.S. 541 (1966).

Parham v. J.R., 442 U.S. 609 (1979).

McKeiver v. Pennsylvania, 403 U.S. 528 (1971).

Morales v. Turman, 535 F.2d 864 (1976).

Nelson v. Heyne, 491 F.2d 352 (1974).

Scott v. Illinois, 440 U.S. 367 (1979).

Stanford v. Kentucky, 109 S. Ct. 2969 (1989).

State v. Lawley, 91 Wash.2d 654, 591 P.2d 772 (1979).

State v. Schaaf, 109 Wash.2d 1, 743 P.2d 240 (1987).

United States v. Tucker, 404 U.S. 443 (1972).

5

The Rights of Children and the Juvenile Court

Frank A. Orlando and Gary L. Crippen

The Courts and Children

The courts are seen as a safe shelter in our society, a place where each individual's rights are protected. Under our system, Justice Hugo Black wrote a half-century ago, "courts stand against any winds that blow as havens of refuge for those who might otherwise suffer because they are helpless, weak, outnumbered, or because they are non-conforming victims of prejudice and public excitement" (*Chambers v. Florida,* 1940).

But for some members of our society, the promise of judicial protection has not been kept. Unless we blink to avoid seeing the truth, we know the courts have been an untrustworthy refuge for children. Countless words have been spoken and written to declare good will for children and to claim the high judicial purpose of serving the "best interests" of our young. Unfortunately, children continue to be hurt through their contacts with the courts.

Two primary questions need attention. What kind of court system do we have for children? What goes wrong in these courts?

Late in the twentieth century children confront the courts in many ways. Domestic courts determine which parent can meet a child's custodial needs. Commitment courts determine whether children must be placed in an institution for mental health treatment. Juvenile courts intervene in efforts to protect neglected children, often by removing them from their homes. Juvenile courts frequently determine whether to terminate parental rights. Finally, juvenile courts deal with childhood offenses, some of them constituting serious or violent crime, some only misdemeanors or minor delinquencies, and some so-called status offenses, including truancy, disobedience, and other conduct that would not be punished if committed by an adult.

Our focus here will be limited to the juvenile court in its dealings with

89

crime and other prohibited behavior for children. Were we to attempt more, the project would be too large for the purpose of this book. It is true, however, that there are serious problems in other areas of court work with children, especially in the countless number of cases that result in children being involuntarily confined to live in institutions.

Throughout most of this century, all forms of juvenile misconduct have been labeled "delinquency." Juvenile courts were created and charged with the responsibility to deal with delinquent behavior. These specialized courts were established to fulfill a public desire to help troubled children. Premised on the historic notion of *parens patriae* (the power of the king to act as parent), the courts were given broad-ranging powers, but were supposed to be committed to the notion of care and rehabilitation. These courts, it was declared, "should have a scientific understanding of each child," should see that treatment is "adapted to individual needs," and should operate with "a presumption in favor of keeping the child in his own home and his own community, except when adequate investigation shows this not to be in the best interest of the child" (Children's Bureau, U. S. Department of Labor, 1923).

It was expected from the beginning that children would pay a price for the benevolence of the juvenile court. First, because old notions of crime and punishment were being discarded within the juvenile court system, these courts would function without procedures employed in adult criminal cases. As recalled by the United States Supreme Court, "the apparent rigidities, technicalities, and harshness . . . observed in both substantive and procedural criminal law were . . . discarded" (*In re Gault,* 1967).

Second, the juvenile courts were given the authority to take severe steps if deemed necessary. The child could be confined to an institution for therapy or for treatment. The child could be confined to a so-called state training school or housed at least temporarily in detention facilities, including jails. These placements could be continued indefinitely, even from year to year, until the child was old enough to be free of juvenile court jurisdiction. Moreover, nothing in the laws on juvenile courts regulated the internal operation of "training schools," "treatment centers," "children's homes," or "detention centers." As poorhouses and work-houses demonstrated in the century before juvenile courts were formed, such institutions pose the danger of being snake pits for those consigned to them.

A half-century after full implementation of the juvenile court system, the system finally came to the attention of the United States Supreme Court. The court was unequivocal in its indictment of a terrible problem.

Children were paying a severe price for their separate court system in the form of loss of their fundamental rights. Much worse, it appeared that they were not receiving the benefit of promises made about care and rehabilitation. Justice Abe Fortas declared, "that the child receives the worst of both worlds: . . . he gets neither the protection accorded to adults nor the solicitous care and regenerative treatment postulated for children" (*Kent v. United States*, 1966).

Twenty-five years have passed since Justice Fortas and the Supreme Court issued their ringing indictments of the juvenile justice system. During this quarter century, countless efforts have been made to correct the problems of the juvenile court system. Efforts have been made to correct both the abuse of process and the absence of care. The effort for better process was initiated by the Supreme Court itself. The court announced children's entitlements to the right to counsel (*Gault*, 1967), and the right to receive a fair hearing (*Kent*, 1966; *Gault*, 1967; *McKeiver v. Pennsylvania*, 1971).

How could the promise of care be made more credible? Congress addressed this problem in 1974, announcing a national resolve to curb the placement of children in institutions, especially jails and detention centers (Schwartz, 1989; U. S. Department of Justice, 1980). In addition to the efforts of Congress, reformers throughout the country stimulated a movement for deinstitutionalization.[1]

It should be observed that deinstitutionalization was not a new idea, but an effort to legitimize the *parens patriae* promise first declared for the juvenile courts.[2]

What Happened to Reform?

Reform efforts over the past quarter of a century have been disappointing. The rights of children are still in peril in the juvenile court. Many dispositions are still made without due process, and institutionalization has mushroomed. Justice Fortas's words should haunt us. Children continue to receive the worst of two worlds.

Institutionalization

A half-dozen observations should be made about the exploding pattern of placements from the juvenile courts:

1. Juvenile incarceration trends are commonly examined in terms of placements in training schools. The 1984 records show that 66,000 U.S. children received juvenile court dispositions in the form of a commitment

to a public correctional facility, usually a so-called training school (see Schwartz, 1989, pp. 40–46). Twenty-five percent of these commitments were made to secure short-term detention facilities, even though these places had been built and designed solely for use as emergency, short-term places of confinement.

The training school commitment pattern represents only the tip of the iceberg. Tens of thousands of other residential facilities, most of them privately operated, had become available for juvenile court placements. For example, when a legislative body in Minnesota studied the situation in 1983, they found that placements were being made to 225 separate institutions in that state, even though the state had a population of only 4.5 million people and itself maintained two publicly operated training schools (Fine, 1983). This number did not include foster homes for up to four children, nor any facilities for mentally retarded children. In 1981, when training school placements in Minnesota numbered approximately 400, another 2400 children were placed by the courts in other facilities. Another 1000 institutional placements occurred in dependency and neglect proceedings. Using the Minnesota ratio of one to seven for training school commitments (400) as compared with total delinquency-status offense placements (2800), a rough national incidence can be projected. In 1984 66,000 children were committed to training schools. Multiplying this number by seven, we get nearly a half-million total U. S. juvenile court delinquency-status offense placements in 1984.

2. The same trend is reflected in detention practices, the incarceration of young people before a court determines whether they have committed an unlawful act. There have been more than 400,000 secure detention admissions in the United States each year since 1965 (Sarri, 1980; Schwartz, 1989; Schwartz, Fishman, Hatfield, Krisberg, & Eisikovits, 1987; Silberman, 1978). The same records show that predisposition detention has rapidly expanded since 1984; nearly a half-million children were securely detained in 1989.

3. The practice of juvenile courts referring some cases for adult prosecution represents a special problem that cannot be fully explored here (Feld, 1987). Here again, however, records show increasing numbers of cases in which juvenile court jurisdiction is waived. In 1985 American prison admissions included nearly 2500 persons under age eighteen, and nearly one-half of these were in prison for property offenses, mostly burglary and theft (Bureau of Justice Statistics, U. S. Department of Justice, 1990).

4. The iceberg of placements has a dimension much greater than that already discussed. Most placements of children are categorized as "volun-

tary," whether or not the child himself or herself agrees with this label. Many "voluntary" placements are arranged by police, probation officers, or parents as an alternative to further court proceedings. In the 1983 Minnesota study of placements, which showed 3700 court commitments in delinquency, status offense, and neglect cases, the researchers found total placements of over 25,000 children in this single state during the year 1981 (Fine, 1983). But even this indication of an astronomical level of "voluntary" placements excludes still another modern phenomenon, the massive "voluntary" placement of children in hospitals (see Schwartz, 1989, pp. 131–148).

5. Much of the placement explosion in recent years is a reflection of current negative public sentiment regarding youthful offenders. Concerns regarding violent offenders have spilled over to harm the interests of those who have only committed minor delinquencies or status offenses. Negative public sentiment is now built into the juvenile codes of many states, where many legislatures have declared that one of the purposes of the courts is to punish offenders.[3] Remarkably, the official purpose of many juvenile courts no longer reflects their creators' desire to treat and rehabilitate delinquent children. In 1966 Justice Fortas pointed to a juvenile court system that had *neglected* its promise of care. Now that promise has been totally *abandoned* in many states.

6. Finally, one of the myths of reform should be briefly considered. As part of the deinstitutionalization efforts begun during the 1970s, many state laws were amended to carefully distinguish status offenses and petty offenses from more serious delinquent conditions. The purported aim of these amendments was to promote restraint in detentions and dispositions for minor offenders. Ironically, however, many of these "reform" statutes dealing with minor offenses granted juvenile courts the same broad range of powers they had always had. The reform statutes specifically empowered the juvenile courts to make placement dispositions for minor offenses (*Minn. Stat.*, 1990).

This tendency in legislation is in accord with an historic pattern of juvenile court law. Thus, it has been true and remains true that a juvenile placement that will continue for many years can occur as well for a simple shoplifting offense as for a group of armed robberies.

Due Process

Because the juvenile court has more and more become an instrument for confinement of children in institutions, the Supreme Court prescription for due process is increasingly critical. In a free society, confinement should never occur without protection of the individual's fundamental liberties. Notwithstanding the need, there has been remarkably limited success in bringing due process to the juvenile court.

Although children and other U.S. citizens have many rights, we will simplify this complex topic by focusing on three fundamental rights. First, the child should know the stakes in his or her case. In other words, to respond intelligently to the court, the child must be given sufficient information as to the kinds of dispositions the juvenile court is empowered to make. Second, the child is entitled to a hearing on any accusation. Within a hearing setting, of course, many other procedural rights are protected. Also, the child has a right to the assistance of counsel. Counsel is necessary to help a child during the hearing. More important, counsel is required to advise the child on the right to a hearing and the consequences of the case, and to advise whether a hearing should be requested. We will overlook here the ongoing discussion about whether children should also have the right to a jury trial.[4]

What has happened to a child's right to counsel? It is estimated that attorneys appeared in about 5 percent of delinquency proceedings when *Gault* was decided in 1966 (Feld, 1990). Years later, fewer than half of the juveniles who are found delinquent have any assistance of counsel (Feld, 1990). For example, counsel was not present in 48 percent of 10,000 1983 Minnesota delinquency and status offense cases studied in 1984 (Coleman & Guthrie, 1984).

Is counsel routinely provided when children are confined to an institution? Unfortunately, no. In the 1984 Minnesota study, 46 percent of the children placed by the Minnesota juvenile courts received no services of counsel (Coleman & Guthrie, 1984). Even among children placed in correctional facilities, 28 percent never had occasion to meet with an attorney. Moreover, we can take no comfort in knowing that some of the children who were denied counsel were not directly confined to an institution. Children originally placed in the community may later be institutionalized if accused of violating the conditions of their supervision or for being in contempt of court instructions (Feld, 1990). In addition, under modern law, the juvenile's record may prompt incarceration for a later offense (Feld, 1990).

What explains loss of the right to counsel? Very simply, the records show that counsel is offered but technically waived. Instead of assigning counsel, most courts *permit* the child to choose whether to have the services of counsel. This right of the child, as well as the right for a fact hearing, is often waived.

Why do children waive their rights? Why do they proceed without counsel, and give up their right to have a hearing? In great part, the answer lies in the inability of children to understand their rights (Feld, 1990). In addition, children in juvenile court are commonly given an inadequate advisory. An advisory to children must be put in simple terms, but it must be complete enough to help them understand what is at stake, what is involved in the right to have a hearing, and what is involved in the right to counsel. Many advisories are obviously inadequate, or so many children would not agree to waive their rights. The authors are among many who have actually observed inadequate juvenile court advisories, many of them occurring in a fraction of a minute.

A Dangerous System

In sum, the problems Justice Fortas pointed to in 1966 continue today. Neither care nor due process is consistently given.

Many attempts to reform the juvenile justice system will fail because of the very nature of juvenile courts. These courts are specialized and thus controlled by a small number of people in each jurisdiction. Even competent counsel can become intimidated and ineffective in such a system (Feld, 1990).

In addition, the unlimited dispositional powers of the court are sufficient to defeat any discipline or any educational effort that is not enacted as a legislated limit on the kinds of dispositions appropriate for certain cases.

Indicative of local court power over the juvenile system is the disparity of practices between jurisdictions. Placement patterns vary radically from one county to another, and from one state to another. Thus, for example, secure commitments in Massachusetts occur at the rate of 4 per 100,000 people; in Nebraska and Nevada, these placements occur at a rate of more than 280 per 100,000 people (Schwartz, 1989). Likewise, detention practices vary radically. One state has a pattern of detaining 3 out of every 1000 youths, while another state detains 60 out of 1000, twenty times as many (Sarri, 1980; Schwartz, 1989; Schwartz et al., 1987; Silberman, 1978). The same sources indicate that in 1974, in Wisconsin, one in three status offense cases involved secure detention. Across the border in Hennepin County (Minneapolis), Minnesota, more than four out of five (83 percent) of status offenders were detained.

Finally, the same pattern has been observed concerning waiver of counsel. In 1986, in St. Paul, Minnesota, and in three suburban metropolitan counties, 0–7 percent of the children in juvenile court waived counsel

(Feld, 1989). In Minneapolis, 48 percent waived, and in another metropolitan suburb 93 percent waived. Three counties in Minnesota had not a single child in 1986 who did not waive counsel (Feld, 1989).

Given the immense powers of local officials in the juvenile courts, the system is subject to individual personal judgment. Thus, of course, it is subject to judgments both informed and uninformed. It is subject to the will of those who are interested and to those who are disinterested. It is subject to those who are disciplined to determine winners and losers, rather than to solve human problems. It is subject to the will of those who are angry, and even to those who dislike children or certain groups of children.

Finally, an accurate perception of the juvenile court system is hidden by its euphemistic language. Confinement is commonly called "treatment" or "shelter care." A locked place of detention may be called a "group home." Training school confinement blocks are called "cottages." Cells in a detention center are called "bedrooms." Solitary confinement is called "quiet time." This modern double-speak explains many of the problems of the juvenile court, and it defeats reformers who are satisfied with words of promise from those who support its authority.

What should be done?

Remedies for the Juvenile Court System

Abolition

Some who have examined the juvenile court system have concluded that the delinquency-status offense jurisdiction of these courts should be abolished (Guggenheim, 1978). It is sometimes proposed that this jurisdiction be given to the adult criminal justice system, where fundamental rights are better safeguarded.

Efforts made to reform the juvenile courts have been sufficiently frustrated to stimulate an abolition movement. Some critics conclude that the juvenile courts cannot be rehabilitated. As this proposal is being weighed, however, several considerations should be kept in mind:

1. Abolition will destroy the good along with the bad. Many juvenile court operations are staffed by able and sensitive people who have developed remarkably good programs. Due process rights are carefully protected in many courts. Rehabilitation programs are cautiously and effectively employed in many jurisdictions. Do flaws, even serious flaws, in

some parts of the system justify eliminating those other parts that have successfully carried out the original design for these courts?

2. Organization of the courts is governed by state legislatures. Congress can do little to create a policy for abolition. National policymakers can act only on a state-by-state basis. Other reform efforts may be more amenable to determining national policy.

3. Abolition is a more complex process than one might think. So, for example, the simple transfer of delinquent-status offenses jurisdiction to an adult court merely substitutes one judge for another. Abolition requires that substantive and procedural law for children's cases be reshaped to match the law in adult cases. It is particularly important to reformulate dispositional powers in children's cases, so that the courts do not have the freedom to use severe remedies for minor misconduct. In addition, however, adult sentencing practices must be modified to permit use of special institutions designed for the correctional needs of young people.

New Efforts for Reform

Short of abolition, other steps might be taken to protect the rights of children in juvenile courts:

1. Public laws can be passed to mandate appointment of counsel for children accused of misconduct. This single step would eliminate the danger of waivers and the accompanying danger of children who have never had the assistance of counsel receiving severe dispositions.

2. The quality of services of counsel can be upgraded by utilizing statewide public defender programs such as those frequently employed in the adult criminal justice system. These defender systems are traditionally well disciplined and effective in serving clients. They are less subject than private practice attorneys to domination by the officials of local trial courts. A statewide organization can make sure that juvenile court work is not delegated to inexperienced counsel.

3. In the vast majority of states, the juvenile corrections system is a hodgepodge of local programs, all subject to the control of local courts. By contrast, in states such as Massachusetts and Utah, where reforms have already been enacted, nearly all juvenile corrections programs are under the administrative control of a state agency. State control of corrections is accepted as a matter of fact in the adult criminal justice system, and it may be a major step toward needed reform of the juvenile court system.

4. Dispositional powers of the court must be subjected to some meaningful limits. The length of disposition in a misdemeanor case should

not be the same as the length of disposition in a more serious case. The duration of court jurisdiction in a status offense case must be specifically limited. Placements out of the community should be limited to severe cases. Curbs must be placed upon the use of contempt proceedings to enlarge a minor problem into a major crisis for the child.

5. More work must be done to develop uniform in-court advisories on the rights of children. A solid professional effort should be made to guide judges in communicating to children what they need to know about their right to counsel, their right to a hearing, and their understanding of the dispositional powers of the court.

6. Detention practices are difficult to control. An unusual breadth of discretion is needed to decide when detention is required. To control exercise of this discretion, every system must be served by a trustworthy means for assessing the need for detention. This requires proper staffing and the uniform use of good tools for assessment.

7. Study and experimentation should continue on the use of court alternatives, including mediation and diversion practices. It must be remembered, however, that mediation and diversion can also be dangerous for the child. In this process too there must be limits on the severity and length of dispositions employed. In addition, advocates must be employed to guarantee expression of the child's wishes.

Conclusion

Since its inception, the juvenile court has posed a danger to the rights of children. This was strikingly observed a half-century ago by Dean Roscoe Pound of the Harvard Law School:

> Child placement involves administrative authority over one of the most intimate and cherished of human relations. The powers of the Star Chamber were a trifle in comparison with those of our juvenile courts and courts of domestic relations. The latter may bring about a revolution as easily as did the former. It is well known that too often the placing of a child in a home or even in an institution is done casually or perfunctorily or even arbitrarily. Moreover, effective preventive work through these courts requires looking into much more than the bad external conditions of a household, such as poverty or neglect or lack of discipline. Internal conditions, a complex of habits, attitudes, and reactions, may have to be dealt with and this means administrative treatment of the most intimate affairs of life. Even with the most superior personnel, these tribunals call for legal checks. (1937, p. xxvii)

Not surprisingly, several decades later the United States Supreme Court concluded that children were receiving the worst of two worlds, bad care and bad process. It may shock many to learn that we have not eliminated these problems since the Supreme Court indictment in 1966. Children's rights in juvenile court remain in danger.

Given the problems children have experienced in juvenile court, it is no wonder some critics want to abolish the system. If the states do not take steps of that kind, it is vital as an alternative that other constructive actions of reform are implemented.

Notes

1. An outstanding example of the deinstitutionalization movement is provided by the reform of the Massachusetts juvenile justice system beginning in 1972, (see Schwartz, 1989, pp. 51–53).

2. The initial federal standards for juvenile courts, published in 1923, declared a presumption in favor of preserving placements of children in their own home and community. Those standards also declared that children should never be detained in jails or police stations (Children's Bureau, U. S. Department of Labor, 1923, p. 4). Also, the standards declared that "detention should be limited to children for whom it is absolutely necessary" (p. 3).

3. Juvenile court laws are to "promote the public safety . . . by maintaining an integrity of the substantive law prohibiting certain behavior and by developing individual responsibility for lawful behavior" (*Minn. Stat.* SS 260.011, subd. 2[c] [1990]).

4. As juvenile courts abandon the *parens patriae* model, the case grows for extending to children the right to a jury trial. See *McKeiver,* 1971; *Matter of Welfare of D.S.F.,* 416 N.W.2d 772, 775 (1987) (Crippen, J., dissenting).

References

Bureau of Justice Statistics, U. S. Department of Justice (1990). *National corrections reporting program: 1985* (Pub. No. NCJ-123522). Washington, DC:

Children's Bureau, U.S. Department of Labor. (1923). *Juvenile court standards* (Vol. 6, Pub. No. 121). Washington, DC:

Coleman, S. & Guthrie, K. (1984). *Directions: How today's juvenile justice trends have affected policy.* St. Paul: Criminal Justice Statistical Analysis Center, Minnesota State Planning Agency.

Feld, B. (1987). Juvenile court meets the principle of the offense: Legislative changes in juvenile waiver statutes. *Journal of Criminal Law and Criminology, 78,* 471–533.

Feld, B. (1989). The right to counsel in juvenile court: An empirical study of when lawyers appear and the difference they make. *Journal of Criminal Law and Criminology, 79,* pp. 1185–1346.

Feld, B. (1990). The right of counsel in juvenile court: Fulfilling *Gault's* promise. *Youth Law News, 11*(3), 20–23.

Fine, K. (1983). *Out of home placement of children in Minnesota: A research report.* St. Paul: Research Department, Minnesota House of Representatives.

Guggenheim, M. (1978). A call to abolish the juvenile justice system. *Children's Rights Reporter, 2,* 7–19.

Juvenile Justice and Delinquency Prevention Act of 1974 (JJDPA). Pub. L. No. 93–415, 88 Stat. 1109 (1974) (codified at 42 U.S.C. 5633(a)(12)(A)(1974).

Pound, R. (1937). Foreword In P. Young, *Social treatment in probation and delinquency,* p. xxvii. New York and London: McGraw-Hill Book Co., Inc.

Sarri, R. (1980). Status offenders: Their fate in the juvenile justice system. In R. Allison (Ed.), *Status offenders and the juvenile justice system: An anthology* (2nd ed, pp. 61–77). San Francisco: National Council on Crime and Delinquency.

Schwartz, I. M. (1989). *(In) Justice for juveniles.* Lexington, MA: Lexington Books.

Schwartz, I. M., Fishman, G., Hatfield, R., Krisberg, B., & Eisikovits, Z. (1987). Juvenile detention: The hidden closets revisited. *Justice Quarterly, 4*(2), 219–235.

Silberman, C. (1978). *Criminal violence. Criminal Justice,* New York: Random House.

Cases

Chambers v. Florida, 309 U.S. 227, 241 (1940).
In re Gault, 387 U.S. 1, 15 (1967).
Kent v. United States, 383 U.S. 541, 555 (1966).
Gault, 387 U.S. at 34–42 (1967).
Kent, 383 U.S. at 554, 561–563 (1966).
Gault, 387 U.S. at 31–34, 42–59 (1967).
McKeiver v. Pennsylvania, 403 U.S. 528, 545 (1971).
Minn. Stat. S 260.195 (1990) (petty offenders).

6

Prosecutors and Juvenile Justice: New Roles and Perspectives

James Shine and Dwight Price

The nation's local prosecutors will play an increasing role in juvenile justice during this decade and beyond. Only those most knowledgeable about the juvenile justice system fully appreciate the breadth of discretion prosecutors exercise every day in deciding how juvenile delinquency cases should be handled. In many jurisdictions prosecutors decide not only whether a case is legally sufficient but also make the "social" decision about whether legally adequate cases should be transferred to the adult court, diverted, or formally petitioned. Add to this discretion the authority to make plea agreements about charges or dispositional recommendations and it becomes clear that the prosecutor's policies and practices substantially affect the course of many young persons' lives.

The developing trend is for prosecutors to exercise more discretion and to become even more active in juvenile justice decision making. For instance, prosecutors are assuming the case intake function in many jurisdictions where this was previously performed by probation departments. Since *In re Gault* (387 U.S. 1) was decided in 1967, prosecutors have become increasingly involved not only in adjudicatory hearings but also in detention, disposition, and probation hearings.

While some juvenile justice practitioners may be alarmed at the increasing role of prosecutors, many believe that this involvement will promote a superior level of justice both for communities and for individual juveniles. The National District Attorneys Association, a membership organization for prosecutors nationwide, has recently rewritten prosecution standards with respect to juvenile delinquency (NDAA Prosecution Standard 19.2: Juvenile Delinquency).[1] The standards admonish prosecutors to "seek justice while fully and faithfully representing the interests of the state." Prosecutors are challenged to balance their primary concern for the safety and welfare of the community and individual victims with the special interests and needs of the juvenile.

101

Prosecutors are carving out new roles for themselves in juvenile justice. There are approximately 2800 county and city prosecutors nationwide. These prosecutors have tremendous potential influence on the administration of justice at the local level for two reasons. First, they are elected officials (exceptions are Alaska, Delaware, New Jersey, and Rhode Island, states in which prosecutors are appointed by the governor) directly responsible to the public and empowered to shape local criminal justice systems. Second, they exercise wide latitude in deciding how to deal with juveniles arrested by the police. These decisions go to the disposition of both individual juvenile cases and large categories of cases, for example, juvenile sex offenders. To summarize, if prosecutors choose to fully utilize this influence, they can become the "quarterback" within the juvenile system. They can help to promote a fair and just system, one that protects the public but is also concerned with the welfare of each juvenile.

This chapter examines the role of the prosecutor through a discussion and amplification of NDAA Standard 19.2 (hereafter referred to as "the standards.") The standards are the best description available of the potential role of the local prosecutor in juvenile justice. (For the convenience of the reader, Standard 19.2 is reprinted as an appendix to this chapter and referred to throughout by section letter and number [e.g., "Std. B1") refers to Section B, paragraph 1].)

In addition to a discussion of the standards, the authors asked five prosecutors representing a diversity of jurisdictions in terms of both population and geography to comment on the issues presented. Each of these prosecutors is a nationally recognized leader in the field of juvenile justice. Each has made a substantial contribution to improving the administration of justice. The five prosecutors are Gus Sandstrom, district attorney for Pueblo, Colorado, and chairman of the NDAA Juvenile Justice Committee; Scott Harshbarger, attorney general of Massachusetts (formerly district attorney, Middlesex County, Massachusetts); Peter Reinharz, chief, Family Court Division, New York, New York; Craig Corgan, district attorney, Bartlesville, Oklahoma; and Robb Scott, chief, Juvenile Division, Anoka County, Minnesota. The personal perspectives of these prosecutors are interspersed throughout this chapter.

It is important to note that NDAA Standard 19.2 is intended only as an aspirational guide for prosecutors and is not a set of ethical rules or rules of conduct. The standards recognize that different approaches to juvenile prosecution are necessary because of varying state laws and practices, limitations on resources, and institutionalized philosophical differences. The authors cannot emphasize strongly enough their respect for this principle. Prosecutors must remain the final arbiters of policy in their offices. Their independence in performing their duties with direct accountability to the public is a cornerstone of our criminal justice system. The potential roles of prosecutors in juvenile justice described in this chapter are in no sense mandates; they are only outlines of possibilities worthy of consideration by every district attorney.

Rationale for Revised Prosecution Standards

The NDAA's Juvenile Justice Committee undertook a revision of Standard 19.2 beginning in 1987. The standards were originally adopted by the NDAA in 1977. Members of the Juvenile Justice Committee prepared ten drafts over eighteen months before presenting a final revision of Standard 19.2 to the NDAA board of directors. District attorneys on the committee extensively discussed and debated the revisions, helped by input from both assistant prosecutors and juvenile justice practitioners. The committee also carefully examined the Institute of Judicial Administration/American Bar Association (IJA/ABA) Juvenile Justice Standards published in 1980.[2] With respect to juvenile prosecution, the revised Standard 19.2 largely agrees with the IJA/ABA standards on prosecution of juveniles. The board of directors of the National District Attorneys Association approved Standard 19.2 in February 1989.

The revision of Standard 19.2 was undertaken for several reasons. First, the committee believed that the prosecutor has no more important responsibility than to address the problem of juvenile crime. Crimes committed by juveniles are every bit as significant to their victims as are crimes committed by adults. The difference is that with juveniles there is a much greater chance to alter the course of their future behavior. This opportunity can translate directly into a safer community.

District attorney Gus Sandstrom believes that prosecutors can fulfill their responsibility to address juvenile crime by leading the way in restoring public confidence in the juvenile justice system: "Whether correct or not, there is a perception running rampant in this society that juvenile justice operates without meaning, consequence, or purpose. In the 1990s the first issue that must be addressed concerning juvenile prosecution is how to strengthen public confidence that the juvenile justice system will take some action that is meaningful when dealing with juveniles who commit crimes. One change that is needed to make the system more meaningful is a balancing of what is consistently been a treatment mode with an accountability model that demands consequences and responsibility be part of the juvenile justice system."

It is important to note here that the standards embrace a due process model for the juvenile courts. This is consistent with the approach of the

IJA/ABA standards. Prosecutors believe that the juvenile court should, first and foremost, be a court of justice. Unfortunately, the due process model has not been fully implemented in many juvenile courts. One clear indication of this serious lack is the fact that even to this day a substantial number of juveniles in some states appear in court and are even committed to secure confinement without ever having been represented by an attorney.[3] The prosecution standards are designed to improve the administration of justice and to enhance due process protections.

A second reason the Juvenile Justice Committee undertook revisions of the standards was their belief that prosecutors can assume a leadership role in making juvenile justice a priority both within their own offices and in the community at large. The standards call for leadership by prosecutors. Craig Corgan, a district attorney in Oklahoma, states: "Prosecutors must establish juvenile prosecution as a priority in their offices. It must be just as important as other priorities. Prosecutors must be more involved in the juvenile justice system—we must be the leaders and not the followers. Our lack of leadership in the past has greatly contributed to the mess the system is in today."

Finally, the revised standards were designed to guide prosecutors in redefining their role in juvenile justice. The standards are a blueprint for involvement. Gus Sandstrom argues that restored confidence in the juvenile justice system requires new attitudes about juvenile prosecution: "An inappropriate belief exists that prosecutors who deal with juvenile justice are advocates for a 'kiddie-court' concept that provides lenient treatment for those who commit crimes and are under the age of eighteen. That "kiddie-court" concept must be overcome and there must be pride, challenge, and credibility given to those who deal with the most difficult problem faced by America's prosecutors: how to effectively deal with juvenile crime."

The committee rewrote the standards in recognition of the fact that excellence in criminal prosecution demands excellence in all areas, including juvenile justice. In recent years prosecutors have been asked to respond to the formalization of juvenile court procedures that accelerated so rapidly after the Supreme Court rendered its landmark decision in *In re Gault, supra* (1967). Prosecutors have also had to respond to the increasingly violent nature of some juvenile crime. The formalization of juvenile court procedures and the increasingly serious nature of juvenile crime prompted the committee to outline the tools needed by the prosecutor to address these changes. Scott Harshbarger, now attorney general of Massachusetts, summarizes: "Serious juvenile crime should be addressed through 'targeted prosecution programs.' This requires a reallocation of resources and the assignment of more experienced prosecutors to juvenile cases or at least the assignment of a senior prosecutor to provide hands-on supervision of the assistants assigned to the juvenile court. It requires the assignment of victim witness advocates to juvenile cases or again, at a minimum, the implementation of a witness notification procedure. And it requires that the expectations regarding case preparation in juvenile cases be similar to those expected in adult felony cases and that someone in the prosecutor's office be assigned to ensure that such expectations are fulfilled."

This chapter provides an overview of the juvenile justice system from the perspective of the prosecutor. This systemic approach matches the approach of the standards. The chapter begins with a discussion of the nature of the prosecutor's role in juvenile justice and some of the general responsibilities derived from that role. It then turns to the prosecutor's role in several primary functions including: (1) charging, (2) diversion, (3) plea agreements, (4) adjudication, (5) disposition, and (6) postdisposition proceedings.

General Responsibilities of the Local Prosecutor

The primary duty of the prosecutor is to seek justice (Std. A2). The prosecutor represents the interests of the public at large. The safety and welfare of the community must be the prosecutor's primary concern. Peter Reinharz in New York City sees the issue in terms of accountability: "The juvenile justice system must introduce accountability into the dispositional scheme. While youths are often viewed as victims of societal neglect, the juvenile justice system can no longer excuse the behavior of violent offenders. Those who commit violent acts must expect swift and sure punishment."

Prosecution of juveniles, however, is special. Prosecutors should consider the interests and needs of the juvenile to the extent they can do so without compromising their primary concern for the safety and welfare of the community (Std. A2). Scott Harshbarger describes the balancing of these factors as follows: "The consequences imposed on the juvenile, from restitution and community service hours to supervised probation or incarceration, must be predictable, consistently applied, and rigorously enforced. While declining resources may prevent us from custom-designing a disposition for each juvenile offender, we must be sure that the process carries the message that serious juvenile crime will be treated seriously. Assuring accountability in the juvenile justice system can make it strong and effective." The call by some prosecutors for special attention to juvenile cases reflects the philosophy that the safety and welfare of the community is enhanced when juveniles are dissuaded from further criminal activity through counseling, restitution, or more extensive rehabilitative efforts and sanctions. While one could make the same argument about the prosecutor's responsibility with respect to adults, juveniles are special because they are presumably more likely to change their behavior given their young age.

Needless to say, it is often difficult for the prosecutor to pay special attention to the needs of the juvenile without creating a conflict with his or her responsibility to fully represent the public at large. Because of the adversarial nature of our system, any such conflict for the prosecutor must be resolved in favor of fully representing the public. Ideally, what serves the juvenile well also serves the public well.

Many prosecutors believe that the juvenile justice system has emphasized the needs of the juvenile to the detriment of the needs of society. Craig Corgan, an Oklahoma district attorney, comments: "We must have a return to a balance in the system. The policymakers and so-called consultants have a bias against the use of secure confinement. The only answer they see is community treatment. This bias has dismantled our system and given juvenile offenders free rein to create havoc. The need for secure beds is continually held hostage in the name of community treatment. The consultants operating nationally all seem to be advocating for deinstitutionalization and other viewpoints are not considered. We must have a continuum of services, including secure beds. We must bring accountability and respectability back to the system. Change will only happen if prosecutors have the conviction to keep pushing. If we give up, the fight is over, and our viewpoint will never be heard." Peter Reinharz in New York City also sees the system as being out of balance: "The public is quite concerned over the escalating violence among juvenile offenders. Groups of teenagers are seen as threats in our streets and subways. Rowdy youths rob people on trains, in stores, and on the street. Yet the system has not been designed to deal with the increasing number of violent offenses among young criminals."

The Advantages of Full Participation By the Prosecutor

In order to represent the public fully, the prosecutor should be active at all stages of the justice system process (Std. A1). This includes the decision to charge or not charge, as well as hearings for detention, dismissal, entry of pleas, trial, transfer to adult court, disposition, and revocation of probation status. In appearing at each of these hearings, the prosecutor maintains a focus on the safety and welfare of the community at each decision-making level.

Further, full participation by the prosecutor enhances the administration of justice in the juvenile system for three reasons. First, only through full representation by the prosecutor in the juvenile court can the community's interests be adequately served. A legally trained advocate is necessary to offer evidence concerning the underlying delinquent behavior. Further, the prosecutor answers the defense's legal arguments and tactical maneuvers. These functions cannot fully or fairly be assumed by a representative without legal training, or by the presiding juvenile court judge. This approach is generally reflected in the support of prosecutors for a due process model. Scott Harshbarger comments: "It will be important in the 1990s to complete the transition of the juvenile justice system, which began with *In re Gault* in 1967, from a rehabilitative model to a due process model for the adjudicatory phase of juvenile proceedings. There should be a strict adherence to the due process model and to all the procedural guarantees inherent in that model. It will become increasingly important in the absence of both alternative dispositions and secure confinement placements that the process by which a juvenile is held accountable for his actions be perceived as one that is fair and just."

Second, the administration of justice is improved because the prosecutor can serve a key role in promoting fair treatment of the juvenile. For instance, if the legal case against the juvenile is inadequate, the prosecutor is charged with the responsibility of dismissing it (Std. B2). Further, the presence of the prosecutor as an advocate in juvenile court promotes the argument and debate necessary to fairly determine the facts in each case. That presence leads the juvenile court judge to consider the factual and legal merits of each alleged offense and challenges the defense to meet those contentions. In short, an effective prosecutor encourages a rigorous review of the facts involved in each case. This rigorous review increases the chances that both the juvenile and community will be treated fairly.

Third, the administration of justice is improved when the prosecutor plays a role in rehabilitation, treatment, and prevention. Each time a juvenile is redirected from delinquent activity to law-abiding activity, everyone benefits. The juvenile justice system often represents the community's last chance to influence a youth to refrain from criminal activity. Some prosecutors have contributed a great deal in the effort to turn juvenile offenders around. These efforts include establishment of counseling, diversion, and educational programs, law-related education programs, and active involvement in promoting effective treatment programs. Prosecutors involved in prevention and treatment contribute both to the safety and welfare of their communities and to the effective administration of justice. Robb Scott describes the prosecutor's potential role as follows: "If prosecutors recognize and take advantage of their unique role within the juvenile justice system they will have a major impact on the system. The juvenile justice system strives not only to be preventive and rehabilitative, but also to be protective of the public. Police, corrections, defense counsel, educators, child protection workers, medical personnel, and the court itself all interact with the prosecutors in carrying out their respective responsibilities. Active prosecutors with adequate resources will have a major impact on the shaping of public policy toward youth in the 1990s. Effective interplay between those entities involved with the juvenile justice system are needed because each can affect the other. I expect to see in the next ten years more linking of these systems and more exchange of information."

The standards recognize that in some jurisdictions prosecutors are barred by statute from participating in juvenile proceedings. In others, prosecutors are by law or practice not involved in charging or hearings at certain stages. For instance, in many jurisdictions the state attorney general handles all appeals. The standards challenge prosecutors to examine their own system to see whether representation of the community's interest at each particular stage would be better served through the presence and involvement of someone from their office.

Another practical problem for the prosecutor who wishes to participate throughout the justice system process is a lack of resources. Many prosecutors offices are stretched to the limit, thus making it difficult to have a prosecutor involved at all stages of the juvenile process. The standards encourage prosecutors to closely examine their overall resources to determine whether some could be redeployed at the juvenile level. If it is true that the prosecutor can have a great impact at the juvenile level, it is both good policy and good sense to put the resources there.

The standards suggest that, at the least, elected prosecutors should have within their office an identified juvenile unit or an attorney responsible for representing the state in juvenile matters (Std. A3). Scott Harshbarger describes this in terms of "institutionalization" and "professionalization" of the prosecution function in juvenile justice.

The attorneys doing juvenile court work should be experienced, competent, and interested. The standards suggest that juvenile prosecutors should be selected on the basis of their skill and competence, including knowledge of juvenile law, interest in children and youth, education, and experience. Ideally, the juvenile prosecutor should have criminal trial experience and, in addition, receive special training regarding juvenile matters. The standards suggest that the practice of using the juvenile court as a training forum for new attorneys should be reconsidered because of the importance of professionalism in this function. Additionally, the prosecutor for juvenile cases should have adequate staff support to the extent possible given office resources, including secretaries and paralegals, interns, investigators, and victim/witness coordinators (Std. A3). Excellence in the juvenile justice area will result only through a striving for the highest level of professionalism.

Responsibilities of the Prosecutor for the Charging Function

Screening the Facts

The prosecutor must maintain ultimate responsibility for the charging function. This means that the prosecutor should have the exclusive right to screen case facts from the police or other sources to determine whether those facts are legally sufficient for prosecution (Std. B1). While this function has often been delegated by law or by practice to other agencies, it is paramount that the prosecutor have a final decision on whether a case should be charged. There are several reasons for this decision-making power. One primary reason is that charging is a legal decision. When cases are screened for charging, a determination is made as to whether there is sufficient evidence to believe that a crime was committed *and* that the juvenile charged committed it. This is called the *prima facie* case. The standards suggest that a *prima facie* case should only be further processed if it is "legally sufficient" (Std. B2). "Legally sufficient" means that the prosecutor believes that he or she can reasonably substantiate the charges against the juvenile by use of admissible evidence at trial. In other words, the prosecutor has a reasonable chance of "proving" the case. If the facts are not "legally sufficient," the matter should be terminated or returned to the referral source pending further investigation or receipt of additional reports.

The determination as to whether the facts constitute a *prima facie* and legally sufficient case should be made by an attorney. This is what prosecutors are trained to do and this is their responsibility as officials directly accountable to the public. If these determinations are, by law or practice, made initially by an outside agency, it is imperative that the prosecutor have the authority to review and revise them. The standards recommend that these charging decisions are best made through an intake process within the prosecutor's office.

After a determination of legal sufficiency, the next choice to be made is whether a case should be transferred to the adult court, diverted informally, or referred to the juvenile court. This decision has both legal and social implications. It should be made either by an experienced prosecutor who has interest in and experience with juveniles, or by other case screeners under the guidance of a prosecutor. The prosecutor, in exercising this function, should try to accommodate the needs of the juvenile while protecting the safety and welfare of the community.

A prominent role for the prosecutor in screening is desirable to eliminate two major abuses of the juvenile intake process. Juveniles are treated unfairly when they are charged by nonlawyers in cases in which there is insufficient evidence that they committed a crime. All too frequently juveniles are charged without sufficient evidence by well-meaning screeners who only want to get the juvenile "help." In the minds of these screeners, the need for services supersedes the need to have adequate evidence for charging. Although many of these juveniles may well have needs that should be addressed, it is an abuse of process to charge them unless the evidence is there. A lawyer, the prosecutor, should make this determination.

On the other hand, the community is treated unfairly if intake screeners continuously divert a juvenile from the court system despite an extensive background of lawbreaking. In some jurisdictions, juveniles are diverted from prosecution and the court system even after being charged on multiple occasions. This practice does not serve well either the juvenile or the community. Supervision of the screening process by prosecutors should prevent this abuse from occurring.

Prompt Determinations

Another major responsibility of the prosecutor in charging is to see that the determinations of "legal sufficiency" are made promptly. The standards suggest that if a juvenile is being held in custody after arrest, the prosecutor should screen the facts for "legal sufficiency" within twenty-four hours (excluding Sundays and legal holidays) after receipt from the police or other referral source (Std. B4). State law or practice may provide for an even shorter period. If the allegations do not substantiate a legally sufficient basis for proceeding, the matter should be terminated and the juvenile released. The standards then call upon the prosecutor, if the juvenile continues to be held in custody, to determine within seventy-two hours (excluding Sundays and legal holidays) after receiving the facts from the police whether the case should be transferred to the adult court, filed as a formal petition with the juvenile court, or diverted.

For cases in which the juvenile is not held in custody, the standards suggest that the facts should be screened for "legal sufficiency" within seven calendar days of receipt from the police or other referral source, unless state law or practice provides for a shorter period (Std. B5). The decision to transfer, file, or divert, the standards suggest, should be made within ten calendar days after receipt of the report. Again, if the allegations do not substantiate a legally sufficient case, the matter should be promptly terminated.

These time limits in making charging decisions are model ones. The standards recognize that some jurisdictions by law or practice require even more prompt determinations, and that other jurisdictions, due to limitations in resources or other problems, are unable to make such timely decisions. The point is that prompt decisions generally promote confidence in the system and fairness to the victim, the community, and the juveniles. Further, prompt decisions are more likely to further the cause of rehabilitation of the juvenile by providing more immediate attention to his or her conduct and the need to intervene before problems escalate.

The standards also recognize, however, that it is sometimes necessary for the prosecutor to go beyond these time limits. Complicated cases may need additional investigation. A particularly sensitive case may require additional time so that the prosecutor can review a social history or phychological report before making a decision to, for instance, transfer a case to adult court.

The period suggested for review of "legal sufficiency" encompasses only the initial review. A prompt review is meant to uncover deficiencies in a case so that they can be remedied, if possible, through additional investigation. It is worth noting that the time periods must begin to run after law enforcement agencies report the facts to the prosecutor. Delays in law enforcement reporting do not directly affect the time periods unless the prosecutor becomes aware of the facts through an alternate source, for instance, at a detention hearing. Prosecutors should encourage police to present facts promptly. At the same time, they should discourage law enforcement reporting that is incomplete or dependent upon extensive additional investigation unless absolutely necessary. Prosecutors must inform law enforcement agencies that the practice of providing skeletal reports that barely describe probable cause without the background information necessary for charging decisions is unacceptable.

Transfer to Adult Court

Another major decision in charging for the prosecutor is a determination of whether a case should be transferred to the adult court. The standards suggest that the prosecutor should seek transfer to adult court only if the gravity of the current alleged offense or the record of previous delinquent behavior reasonably indicates that the treatment services and dispositional alternatives available in the juvenile court are inadequate for dealing with the youth's delinquent behavior *or* inadequate to protect the safety and welfare of the community (Std. B6). In most states, the juvenile court determines whether a juvenile is to be transferred or not. The juvenile justice system should be utilized to the greatest extent possible given the level of resources available to address the juvenile's behavior. But if the prosecutor determines that the juvenile cannot be rehabilitated within the juvenile system or that the safety and welfare of the community cannot be assured, then it is the prosecutor's duty to use his or her influence with the juvenile court or other appropriate procedures to see that the case is waived to the adult system. Scott Harshbarger believes that transfer to adult court can be minimized: "Assuring accountability in the juvenile justice system can make it strong and effective and, further, eliminate the perceived need for a transfer to adult court in most juvenile cases. While it is necessary to transfer a small group of juveniles to the adult system, it is also true that even the chronic serious juvenile offender can be handled within the juvenile justice system if appropriate prosecutorial attention is focused on the case."

The Role of the Prosecutor in Diversion

The prosecutor or a designee should review legally sufficient cases not appropriate for transfer to adult court to determine whether they should be filed formally with the juvenile court or diverted for treatment, services, or probation. In determining whether to file formally or divert, the prosecutor or a designated case reviewer should investigate to see what disposition best serves the interest of the community and the juvenile (Std. B7). The following factors should be considered: (1) seriousness of the alleged offense; (2) role of the juvenile in that offense; (3) the nature and number of previous cases presented by the police or others against the juvenile; (4) juvenile's age and maturity; (5) availability of an appropriate diversion program; (6) whether the juvenile admits guilt or involvement in the offense charged; and (7) the provision of financial restitution to victims.

Prosecutors differ in their views about whether they should be involved in diverting less serious cases from formal adjudication. The consensus seems to be, however, that because most juveniles are in the process of developing their behavior and values, there is a unique opportunity presented at the juvenile court level to dissuade them from further criminal activity. The prosecutor should seriously consider involvement in this process. Many first-time or minor offenders will never enter the justice system again if their cases are handled properly. Treatment, restitution, or service programs often are viable alternatives to court processing. Prosecutors have an opportunity to be involved either by developing diversion programs based in their offices or through referral to programs outside their offices.

Robb Scott sees effective diversion programs as a necessity: "The prosecutor should take an active role in prevention which can be done in part by linking up with the education system and also by running a diversion program. An effective and efficient diversion program will be one of the only ways a prosecutor will keep up with an increasing workload in the 1990s. A case that goes to court costs three to five times as much as one that goes to diversion. Also, from a numbers standpoint, prosecutors will find that a well-run diversion program will allow them and the judges to give more individual attention to those cases that are filed in court." Peter Reinharz adds: "The juvenile justice system must develop alternatives to incarceration programs for nonviolent offenders. We must develop intensive supervision programs for these youths to prevent the escalation to violent offenses. This means that local government must commit resources to young offenders—to prevent their entry into a life of crime. Once again, schools and communities must be part of the plan—law enforcement cannot proceed alone."

The standards suggest that prosecutors consider the use of diversion programs, and also suggest that if they use them, they should monitor them (Std. C1). Monitoring is necessary to ensure that diversion programs provide appropriate supervision, treatment, restitution to the victim, or services for the juvenile. Prosecutors should maintain a working relationship with all outside agencies providing diversion services to ensure that the agencies are doing their job and that the prosecutor's decision to divert is appropriate.

According to the standards, a case should be diverted only if the juvenile admits guilt for the offense(s) charged in the written diversion contract (Std. C2). If the juvenile does not admit guilt, the case should be filed with the juvenile court. While some are critical of this requirement, the prosecutors who wrote the standards resolved that it was necessary for three reasons. First, juveniles should not be sanctioned unless there is legally sufficient evidence that they committed what would otherwise be a crime if they were an adult. Denial of involvement by the juvenile should weigh heavily in favor of a formal determination of guilt or innocence. Second, many juvenile justice practitioners believe that effective treatment or rehabilitation begins with an acknowledgment of wrongdoing. Third, cases that are diverted with no admission of guilt often cannot be restored if the juvenile fails to meet the conditions agreed upon for diversion. Revival of the case is often not possible as too much time has passed and witnesses are unavailable or evidence is lost. A written admission of involvement provides evidence that the prosecutor may need for use as a confession if the case has to be referred to court upon failure of the diversion process. Only written admissions of involvement in the diversion contract may be used by the prosecutor in any subsequent adjudication. By contrast, the standards hold that oral admissions by the juvenile in interviews by the prosecutor or case screener in the course of investigating an appropriate prosecutorial disposition shall not be used for any purpose by the prosecutor.

Given this requirement for an admission of involvement, the standards delineate a careful process that should be undertaken when a juvenile case is diverted (Std. C3). The diversion contract between the juvenile and the supervising authority should set forth all of the conditions of the informal disposition or diversion, together with an admission of guilt and a waiver of a speedy trial. The diversion contract should be signed by both the juvenile and his or her parent or legal guardian. It is critical that the juvenile and his or her parents or guardian understand the nature of diversion, the effect of an admission of guilt, the waiver of his or her rights, and his or her responsibilities under the diversion contract.

Diversion contracts should, in general, specify duties of both the juvenile and the supervising authority that can be reasonably accomplished in three to six months. If the supervising authority determines that the juvenile has substantially breached his or her diversion contract, the case should be returned to the prosecutor for formal filing of a petition with the juvenile court. On the other hand, if the juvenile successfully complies with the contract duties, the case should be terminated with a favorable report.

Prosecutors recognize that diversion programs are important options in addressing juvenile crime. Good programs help both the juvenile and the community. But prosecutors view participation in diversion as a privilege, not a right. A diversion program should be used only when it "fits the crime" and is appropriate for the particular juvenile. Prosecutors should strive to assure that the programs are worthwhile and that the juveniles referred complete them successfully.

The Role of the Prosecutor in the Adjudicatory Phase

Assumption of Traditional Adversary Role

Prosecutors believe in a formal, adversarial process in the juvenile court with respect to determination of guilt or innocence. The prosecutor has the burden of providing the allegations in the petition beyond a reasonable doubt. The same rules of evidence used in trying criminal cases in the jurisdiction should apply to juvenile court cases involving delinquency petitions. Also, a prosecutor should be under the same duty to disclose exculpatory evidence in juvenile proceedings as he or she would be in adult criminal proceedings.

Speedy Adjudication

When the prosecutor decides to seek a formal adjudication of a complaint against a juvenile, he or she should proceed to an adjudicatory hearing as quickly as possible. This promotes fair treatment for both the victim and the juvenile and serves to make the experience more meaningful for the juvenile. Many juvenile justice professionals believe that a court appearance or a disposition several months after the delinquent act is much less useful than a prompt response. Gus Sandstrom puts it simply: "A timely response to crime by a juvenile may be just as important as the nature of the response itself." Scott Harshbarger adds: "Speedy processing of all juvenile cases is important for two reasons. First, in order to maximize the impact upon the juvenile that he has been caught in a criminal act, that he will be held accountable for what he has done, and that there will be consequences for his actions, it is important that the case be resolved quickly. If the case drags on for too long, the impact of the message is diluted, either because the juvenile has been subsequently arrested for other offenses and 'loses track' of just what it is that he is being prosecuted for or because the juvenile has not engaged in any further delinquent acts and feels that any consequences for the past offense are unfair. Speedy processing is also important because excessive delay is obviously unfair and damaging to victims."

The standards suggest that an adjudicatory hearing should be held within thirty days if the juvenile is held in detention pending trial or within sixty days if the juvenile is arrested and released (Std. E1). The standards also suggest that a dispositional hearing should be held within thirty days after the adjudicatory hearing. The time limits in the standards are only suggested ones. Some jurisdictions may process cases more quickly than this while others may find it impossible to meet these time limits given local law and practice. The standards recognize, for instance, that the defense discovery process in some jurisdictions may require longer time periods. Also, good cause may exist in specific cases to extend the time limits. The point is that cases processed promptly better serve the interests of all those involved.

Plea Agreements

The appropriateness of and the extent to which plea agreements are used in juvenile court are matters of office policy to be determined by the elected or appointed prosecutor. The decision to enter into a plea agreement should be governed by both the interests of the public and those of the juvenile, although the primary concern of the prosecutor should be protection of the public interest as determined in the exercise of traditional prosecutorial discretion (Std. D1). Plea agreements, if appropriate, should be entered into expeditiously in order to protect the juvenile, the victim, and the public.

In entering into a plea agreement, the prosecutor should always take steps to ensure the resulting record is sufficient to reflect the actual nature of the offense. In juvenile courts where a plea to any offense vests full dispositional jurisdiction in the court, there is sometimes a practice of reducing the charge through a plea agreement. For instance, a provable burglary charge is reduced to theft or a sex offense to an assault. For these serious offenses, the standards urge prosecutors to enter only into pleas that reflect the seriousness of the underlying conduct unless there is a problem with the proof. A provable burglary case should result in a court record that reflects commission of a burglary, not just a theft. The court record can then be used as an accurate gauge of prior delinquent behavior if the juvenile is later accused of additional offenses.

A plea agreement with a juvenile should be conducted through defense counsel. Juveniles, and even juveniles and their parents, should not be involved in plea agreements when they are unrepresented by an attorney because of the danger of misunderstanding the nature of the agreement and the grant of the potential consequences. The standards recognize, however, that in some jurisdictions this general rule could result in the availability of "reduced charge" pleas to represented juveniles and not to unrepresented juveniles. A prosecutor must exercise his discretion wisely to avoid any discrimination against unrepresented juveniles.

The Role of the Prosecutor in Disposition and Follow-Up

The standards encourage prosecutors to participate in the dispositional phase (sentencing hearing) of juvenile proceedings because the viewpoint of the community should be represented in this phase just as it is in earlier phases (Std. F1). Prosecutors are urged to make a recommendation to the court after reviewing reports prepared by the probation department and other professionals. The prosecutor's viewpoint can be important because they are knowledgeable about the particular case and should be familiar with appropriate dispositional alternatives.

Robb Scott believes prosecutors should play a role in developing dispositions: "I believe that in the future states will become more involved in developing dispositional guidelines that will take into consideration present offense and prior record with an attempt to provide treatment resources within the guidelines appropriate for the offense and the prior record. While it is arguable whether dispositional guidelines are a good concept, any discussions about them should involve the active participation of the prosecutor."

In recommending a disposition, the prosecutor must bear in mind that community safety or welfare is his or her primary concern. Prosecutors should ensure that the court is aware of the impact of the juvenile's conduct on the victim, if any, and should arrange that restitution be made, if possible.

In recommending a disposition, the prosecutor should consider those dispositions that most closely meet the interests and needs of the juvenile offender so long as the safety of the community is not compromised. This may, on occasion, lead the prosecutor to make a dispositional recommendation that is less restrictive than what the juvenile court judge may contemplate imposing. The theory, as expressed above, is that if a disposition is effective in stopping a juvenile from offending, both the juvenile and the community are served well.

Many prosecutors have limited resources in their offices and it may not be practical to assign attorneys to attend disposition hearings for minor offenses. One possibility in these cases is that the prosecutor submit to the court a written recommendation on disposition. In the case of violent offenders, it seems apparent that the prosecutor should make a dispositional recommendation so that the community's interest is fully expressed.

In addition to making recommendations about specific cases, the prosecutor may wish to view his or her role more expansively. To promote the safety of the community, it may be necessary to advocate for dispositional alternatives and to monitor those that exist. The prosecutor can take a leadership role in the community in assuring there are a wide range of appropriate dispositional alternatives available for youth. Presumably, effective dispositional programs will help cut the crime rate. If the prosecutor discovers that a youth or a class of young people are not receiving the care and treatment envisioned in dispositional decisions, or that the community is not being protected, he should inform the juvenile court of this fact and take steps to ensure that adequate problems exist.

Prosecutors may define their role as playing a part in addressing some of the root causes of juvenile delinquency. Robb Scott comments: "Many of the most difficult cases in juvenile court at the present time are those of youngsters who are multideficit juveniles who should have received services in the social service system prior to their delinquent act. Timely attention to these children requires a reprioritization of services. Society should be providing more services to pregnant mothers and children from birth to age six. I believe that in the next ten years this reprioritization will begin to occur."

Finally, the work of the prosecutor may not be finished at the disposition of the case. The standards encourage prosecutors to follow up on cases to ensure that dispositions are upheld, court-ordered sanctions are administered, and treatment is provided (Std. F1). If possible, the prosecutor should represent the state's interest in hearings concerning revocation of probation, petitions for modifications of dispositions, and—if allowed by state law—appeals. This is consistent with the philosophy that because juvenile cases have an important impact on community safety, they should be monitored just as closely as adult cases are monitored following sentencing.

Need for More Research

Prosecutors who are knowledgeable about juvenile justice agree that research can be an important resource. Many of them find it remarkable that after all of these years of dealing with juveniles committing crimes, we know as little as we do. How can we begin to know how best to use the resources of the prosecutor and the courts without knowing more about the effects of different approaches?

In the interviews with the prosecutors referred to above, several key issues for further research emerged. First, we need to learn more about how to identify repeat offenders at the beginning of their offending, not at the end. Presumably, this knowledge will be better for both the offender and his or her potential victims. Robb Scott summarizes this sentiment: "Younger and younger children are becoming involved in juvenile crime. To be effective, programs must target the young, first-time offender. Research must develop profiles of these youthful offenders, determine behavior patterns, and anticipate their future criminal activities. Methods can then be formulated to redirect their behavior away from criminal activity. What are the constants, if any, that are always present with the young offender? What are the variables?"

Research by some, including Howard Snyder of the National Juvenile Justice Center,[4] suggests that one indication of potential repeat offending can be gauged in part by looking at offense category and the age at the time of offending. Much more needs to be learned about likely repeat offenders—not so that they can be singled out for punishment but instead so they can be singled out for early intervention. Most prosecutors agree that punishment based upon any factor other than offense record is inappropriate. But if there are early interventions that can dissuade juveniles from repeat offending, it is important that those most likely to repeat receive the benefit of those interventions.

A second and related research issue is determining which programs and interventions are most effective. Little is actually known about just what works. This puts prosecutors and others at a loss to decide what to do with certain juveniles and when to best intervene. Good research can help inform these decisions at each potential stage of the remedial process. As Robb Scott points out, researchers should not ignore as a source of information former juvenile offenders. They obviously have a special perspective and insight.

Third, prosecutors are interested in knowing more about how early childhood experiences relate to juvenile delinquency. Do learning disabilities correlate with delinquency? What about the effects of child abuse and neglect? What is the relationship, if any, between drug abuse by mothers while pregnant and later delinquent behavior?

Fourth, more needs to be learned about how immigrant groups are absorbed into local populations. Teenagers in some immigrant groups are not being assimilated into the larger community. Instead, they are forming gangs, some of which are involved in serious crime. We need to learn more about these gangs.

Fifth, there is a trend nationwide to reduce the number of secure placements for juvenile offenders. While many prosecutors might agree that training schools and other secure placements are not a bastion of rehabilitation, nevertheless, there is a need to protect the public from certain violent offenders. The safety of the public must be the prosecutor's key concern. Prosecutors would like to see more research examining this trend to determine whether secure beds in a state can be reduced substantially without putting citizens at risk. Who is making the decision about which juveniles can be safely released? The writers urge prosecutors to be involved in this debate and process.

Conclusion

Prosecutors will play an increasingly important role in juvenile justice in the years to come. Their involvement will promote a due process model that should result in a fairer, more just system for all involved, including the juvenile. Prosecutors will also be increasingly involved in deciding on interventions and treatment options. They bring to this task the responsibility for representing the safety of the community—a key role. Prosecutors, like others, will benefit from research that shows what works in dissuading juveniles from offending. Nothing will go further in protecting the community and promoting the interests of juveniles than good decisions about how and when to effectively intervene. Prosecutors who establish sound policies and practices with respect to juvenile offenders may find they can make no greater contribution to their community.

Appendix: National District Attorneys Association Prosecution Standard 19.2 Juvenile Delinquency

Introduction

Excellence in criminal prosecution demands excellence in all areas—including both adult and juvenile justice. Whether in response to formalization of juvenile court procedures or increased interest in juveniles and the crimes they commit, America's prosecutors are playing a larger role in the juvenile justice system. The important substantive changes in prosecutorial involvement in juvenile delinquency cases prompted NDAA's Juvenile Justice Committee to revise National Prosecution Standard 19.2, Juvenile Delinquency, originally adopted in 1977. The revised Standard is designed to guide prosecutors in redefining their role. Twenty years have passed since the Supreme Court rendered its landmark decision, *In Re Gault*, 387 U.S. 1 (1967). The Standard incorporates many of the lessons learned since then.

The Standard is aimed at promoting justice in juvenile delinquency cases. It emphasizes the prosecutor's duty to provide for the safety and welfare of the community and victims, and at the same time, consider the special interests and needs of juveniles to the extent possible without compromising that primary duty. The Standard accepts the premise that a separate court for most juvenile delinquency cases continues to be an indispensable alternative to the adult court.

Members of the Juvenile Justice Committee prepared ten drafts over eighteen months before the final revision of Standard 19.2 was adopted by the NDAA Board of Directors. Chief prosecutors on the Committee extensively discussed and debated the revisions helped by input from other chief prosecutors, deputy and assistant district attorneys, and juvenile justice practitioners. The Committee also examined carefully the Institute of Judicial Administration/American Bar Association (IJA/ABA) Juvenile Justice Standards published in 1980. With respect to juvenile prosecution, this Standard largely agrees with the IJA/ABA standards on prosecution of juveniles.

The Standard necessarily establishes positions on controversial issues but incorporates the best guidelines the Committee can suggest for prosecutors. It is recognized that different approaches to juvenile prosecution are necessary because of varying state law and practice, limitations on resources, and institutionalized philosophic differences. The Standard is therefore intended to be advisory only. Chief prosecutors remain the final arbiters of policy in their offices, and the commentary to the Standard makes clear this flexibility. At the same time, the Committee believes that the Standard sets forth ideal approaches to the prosecution of juvenile delinquency and is worthy of each chief prosecutor's careful consideration. The Standard can also be used as a model by prosecutors seeking changes in state law and practices.

The Board of Directors of the National District Attorneys Association approved the Standard in February 1989.

A. General Responsibilities of a Prosecutor

1. *Appearance of Prosecutor.* The prosecutor should appear as an attorney for the state in all hearings concerning a juvenile accused of an act that would constitute a crime if he or she were an adult ("a delinquent act"). This includes but is not limited to hearings for: detention, speedy trial, dismissal, entry of pleas, trial, waiver, disposition, revocation of probation

or parole status, and any appeal from or collateral attacks upon the decisions in each of these proceedings.

2. *Primary Duty.* The primary duty of the prosecutor is to seek justice while fully and faithfully representing the interests of the state. While the safety and welfare of the community, including the victim, is their primary concern, prosecutors should consider the special interests and needs of the juvenile to the extent they can do so without compromising that concern.

3. *Personnel and Resources.* Chief prosecutors should devote specific personnel and resources to fulfill their responsibilities with respect to juvenile delinquency proceedings, and all prosecutors' offices should have an identified juvenile unit or attorney responsible for representing the State in juvenile matters. Additionally, the prosecutor for juvenile cases should have adequate staff support to the extent possible given office resources including: clerical and paralegal personnel, interns, investigators, and victim/witness coordinators.

4. *Qualifications of Prosecutor.* Training and experience should be required for juvenile delinquency cases. Chief prosecutors should select prosecutors for juvenile court on the basis of their skill and competence including knowledge of juvenile law, interest in children and youth, education, and experience. While the unit chief, if any, must have criminal trial experience, assistant prosecutors assigned to the unit should also have prior criminal trial experience, assistant prosecutors assigned to the unit should also have prior criminal trial experience, if possible. Entry-level attorneys in the juvenile unit should be as qualified as any entry-level attorney, and receive special training regarding juvenile matters.

5. *Cooperation.* To the extent possible, prosecutors should cooperate with others in the juvenile justice system to promote speedy trials and efficient case processing.

Commentary Section A emphasizes three aspects of the role of the prosecutor. First, the prosecutor is charged to seek justice just as he or she does in adult prosecutions. The prosecutor in the juvenile system, however, is further charged to give special attention to the interest and needs of the accused juvenile to the extent that it does not conflict with the duty to fully and faithfully represent the interests of the state. This call for special attention reflects the philosophy that the safety and welfare of the community is enhanced when juveniles, through counseling, restitution, or more extensive rehabilitative efforts and sanctions, are dissuaded from further criminal activity.

Second, Section A emphasizes the desirability of having the prosecutor appear at all states of the proceedings. In so doing, the prosecutor maintains a focus on the safety and well being of the community at each decision-making level. Further, because the juvenile system is increasingly adversarially based, the prosecutor fulfills an important role in addressing the arguments of other juvenile and social service advocates. The prosecutor's presence guarantees the opportunity to exercise continuous monitoring at each stage and broad discretion to ensure fair and just results.

The Committee recognizes that in some jurisdictions prosecutors are barred by statute from participating at all in juvenile proceedings. In others, prosecutors are by law or practice not involved in hearings or discussions at certain stages. For instance, in many jurisdictions the state attorney general handles all appeals. The Committee suggests that prosecutors examine their systems to see whether representation of the community's interests would be better served through the presence and involvement of someone from their office at each stage of the adjudicatory process. If so, prosecutors may choose to use these standards in advocating for change in existing law or practice.

Finally, this Section emphasizes professionalism in juvenile court work. It provides that attorneys in juvenile court should be experienced, competent, and interested. It suggests that the practice of using the juvenile court as a training forum for new prosecuting attorneys should be reconsidered because continuity of involvement in the system creates professionalism.

B. Responsibilities of the Prosecutor for Charging Function

1. *Right to Screen Cases and File Petitions.* The prosecutor should have the exclusive right to screen facts from the police and other sources to determine whether those facts are legally sufficient for prosecution. If it is determined that the facts are legally sufficient, the prosecutor should determine whether a juvenile is to be transferred to adult court, charged in juvenile court or diverted from formal adjudication.

2. *Definition of Legal Sufficiency.* Legally sufficient cases are those cases in which the prosecutor believes that he or she can reasonably substantiate delinquency charges against the juvenile by admissible evidence at trial. The charging process requires early determination as to whether the facts constitute *prima facie* evidence that a delinquent act was committed and that the juvenile accused committed it. If the facts are not legally sufficient, the matter should be terminated or returned to the referral source pending further investigation or receipt of additional reports.

3. *Prosecutorial Disposition of Legally Sufficient Cases.* The prosecutor or a designee should further review cases determined to be legally sufficient to decide whether the case will be transferred to adult court, filed as a formal petition with the juvenile court, or diverted.

4. *Juveniles Held in Custody.* If the juvenile is being held in custody after arrest or detention, the prosecutor should screen the facts for legal sufficiency within 24 hours (excluding Sundays and legal holidays) after

receipt from the police or other referral sources, unless state law or practice provides for a shorter period. If the allegations do not substantiate a legally sufficient basis for proceeding, the matter should be terminated and the juvenile released. If the juvenile continues to be held in custody based upon legally sufficient facts, the prosecutor should determine within 72 hours (excluding Sundays and legal holidays) after receiving the facts from police and other referral sources whether the case should be transferred to the adult court, filed as a formal petition with the juvenile court, or diverted. State law or practice may provide, however, for a shorter period.

5. *Juveniles Not Held in Custody.* If the juvenile is not held in custody, the facts should be screened for legal sufficiency within seven calendar days from receipt from police or other referral source, unless state law or practice provides for a shorter period. If the allegations do not substantiate a legally sufficient basis for proceeding, the matter should promptly be terminated. If the allegations do substantiate a legally sufficient basis for proceeding, the prosecutor should transfer the case to adult court, file it as a formal petition with the juvenile court, or divert it within ten calendar days after receipt of the report, unless state law or practice provides for a shorter period.

6. *Transfer or Certification to Adult Court.* To the extent that the prosecutor is permitted by law to use discretion to decide whether a juvenile delinquency case should be transferred to the adult court, prosecutors should seek transfer only if the gravity of the current alleged offense or the record of previous delinquent behavior reasonably indicates that the treatment services and dispositional alternatives available in the juvenile court are (1) inadequate for dealing with the youth's delinquent behavior; or (2) inadequate to protect the safety and welfare of the community.

7. *Criteria for Deciding Formal Adjudication Versus Diversion.* The prosecutor or a designee must further review legally sufficient cases not appropriate for transfer to adult court to determine whether they should be filed formally with the juvenile court or diverted for treatment, services or probation. In determining whether to file formally or divert, the prosecutor or designated case reviewer should investigate to decide what disposition best serves the interests of the community and the juvenile, considering the following factors:

a. The seriousness of the alleged offense;

b. The role of the juvenile in that offense;

c. The nature and number of previous cases presented by the police or others against the juvenile, and the disposition of those cases;

d. The juvenile's age and maturity;

e. The availability of appropriate treatment or services potentially available through the juvenile court or through diversion;

f.   Whether the juvenile admits guilt or involvement in the offense charged;

g.   The dangerousness or threat posed by a juvenile to the person or property of others;

h.   The provision of financial restitution to victims; and

i.   Recommendations of the referring agency, victim and advocates for the juvenile.

8. *Qualifications of Case Screeners.* Case screening may be accomplished by the prosecutor or by screeners employed directly by the prosecutor. If case screeners outside the prosecutor's office are employed, the prosecutor should have the right to review charging decisions and to file, modify or dismiss any petition.

Screening for the legal sufficiency of facts related to a criminal incident should be conducted only by a prosecutor. Further screening of legally sufficient cases for prosecutorial disposition (transfer, filing with juvenile court, or diversion) should be conducted by or with advice of screeners knowledgeable about treatment and services for children and youth.

9. *Role of the Prosecutor in Formal Filing.* Formal charging documents for all cases referred to juvenile court should be prepared or reviewed by a prosecutor.

Commentary Section B describes a large role for prosecutors in the charging function. This function has often been delegated by law or by practice to other agencies. While this may be a workable procedure, it is paramount that the prosecutor maintain ultimate responsibility for charging for many reasons. A major function of screening is to determine whether there is sufficient evidence to believe that a crime was committed and that the juvenile charged committed it. A case should only be further processed if it is legally sufficient. "Legally sufficient" means a case in which the prosecutor believes that he can reasonably substantiate the charges against the juvenile by admissible evidence at trial. These determinations should be made by a prosecuting attorney. If these determinations are, by law or practice, made initially by an outside agency, it is imperative that the prosecutor have the authority to review and revise them. The Standards recommend that these decisions are best made through an intake process within the prosecutor's office.

After a determination of legal sufficiency, the next choice to be made is whether the case should be transferred to the adult court, diverted informally, or referred to the juvenile court. This decision has both legal and social implications. It should be made either by an experienced prosecutor who has an interest in juveniles or by other case screeners under the guidance of a prosecutor. The prosecutor, in exercising this function, should try to accommodate the needs of the juvenile while upholding the safety and welfare of the community.

Additionally, at this stage the prosecutor may elect to exercise his or her discretion to dismiss a case that may be technically sufficient but from a policy or economic point of view lacks prosecutorial merit. Continuation of the case may not serve the best interests of justice.

The large role of the prosecutor in screening is intended to eliminate at least two major abuses of the intake process. Juveniles are abused when they are charged by non-lawyers in cases where there is insufficient evidence that they committed a crime. A lawyer, the prosecutor, should make this determination. On the other hand, the community is abused if intake screeners continuously divert a juvenile from the court system despite an extensive background of law-breaking. This Standard seeks to halt these abuses by emphasizing the discretionary role of the prosecutor who has the primary authority to uphold the law and to evaluate what course will best achieve justice for the accused and the community.

Section B also exhorts the prosecutor to make a prompt determination of legal sufficiency and prosecutorial disposition. The time limits suggested are model ones. It is recognized that some jurisdictions by law or practice make even more prompt determinations, and that other jurisdictions, due to limitations in resources or the environment, have been unable to make such timely decisions. The point is that prompt determinations generally promote confidence in the system and fairness to the victim, the community, and the juvenile. Further, prompt decisions are more likely to result in rehabilitation of the juvenile by providing more immediate attention.

The Committee also recognizes that it is sometimes necessary to go beyond these time limits. Complicated cases may need additional investigation. A particularly sensitive case may require additional time so that the prosecutor can review a social history or psychological report before making a decision to, for instance, transfer a case to adult court. These exceptions, in the Committee's view, should not dictate the rule. High volume jurisdictions such as Chicago and Philadelphia have successfully instituted speedy case reviews.

It is important to note that the period described for the review of legal sufficiency encompasses only the initial review. The decision whether to transfer, charge, or divert comes later. This prompt determination is meant to uncover deficiencies in a case, so that they can be remedied, if possible, through additional investigation. If there is insufficient evidence and the deficiencies cannot be remedied, the matter should be terminated promptly and the juvenile, if in detention, should be released.

It is also important to note that the time periods begin to run after law enforcement reports the facts to the prosecutor. Delays in law enforcement reporting do not directly affect these time periods unless the prosecutor becomes aware of the facts through an alternate source, for instance at a detention hearing. Facts presented at a detention hearing commence the time limits. Prosecutors should encourage police to present facts promptly. At the same time they should discourage law enforcement reporting that is incomplete or dependent upon extensive additional investigation unless absolutely necessary. Prosecutors must inform law enforcement that the practice of providing skeletal reports that barely describe probably cause without substantive information necessary for charging decisions is unacceptable.

In many jurisdictions, transfer of juveniles to adult court is controlled by statute or practice. In most states, the juvenile court determines whether a juvenile is to be transferred. This section simply provides guidance for the prosecutor in using his or her discretion to the extent that they participate in this process. The provision reflects the view that the juvenile justice system should be utilized to the greatest extent possible given the level of resources available to address the juvenile's behavior. The provision further suggests that juveniles should not be transferred to the adult system unless and until a determination is made that the juvenile cannot be rehabilitated within the juvenile system or alternatives would be contrary to the safety and welfare of society or the nature of the crime dictates a transfer.

C. Diversion of Legally Sufficient Cases

1. *The Role of the Prosecutor in Diversion.* The prosecutor is responsible for deciding which legally sufficient cases be diverted from formal adjudication. Treatment, restitution, or public service programs developed in his or her office may be utilized or the case can be referred to existing probation or community service agencies. If the probation or service agency decides the case is not appropriate for their services, they must return it immediately to the prosecutor's office. The prosecutor will then make a further determination about an appropriate disposition.

2. *Diversion Requires Admission of Involvement.* A case should be diverted only if the juvenile admits guilt for the offense(s) charged in the written diversion contract. If the juvenile does not admit guilt, the case should be filed with the juvenile court or terminated. Admissions by the juvenile to the prosecutor or case screener in the course of investigating an appropriate prosecutorial disposition shall not be used for any purpose by the prosecutor. Admissions in the juvenile's written diversion contract, however, may be used by the prosecutor in any subsequent adjudication.

3. *Diversion Contract.* All cases diverted require a written diversion contract between the juvenile and the supervising authority. The diversion contract should set forth the conditions of the informal disposition or diversion, together with an admission of guilt and waiver of a speedy trial, and should be executed by both the juvenile and his or her parent or legal guardian. Diversion contracts should, in general, specify duties of the juvenile and the supervising authority that can reasonably be accomplished in three to six months. If the supervising authority determines that a juvenile has substantially breached his diversion contract, the case should be

returned to the prosecutor for formal filing of a petition with the juvenile court. If the juvenile successfully complies with the contract duties, the case should be terminated with a favorable report.

4. *Records of Diversion Contracts and Compliance.* Records of diversion contracts and compliance or noncompliance should be maintained in the prosecutor's office. If screening is conducted outside that office, records should also be maintained in the case screener's office. These records should be used exclusively by the prosecutor or designated case screeners to screen any subsequent case reports with respect to the juvenile. They should be destroyed when the juvenile reaches the age of majority.

5. *Prosecutorial Review of Diversion Programs.* The prosecutor should periodically review diversion programs, both within and outside the district attorney's office, to ensure they provide appropriate supervision, treatment, restitution requirements, or services for the juvenile. The prosecutor should maintain a working relationship with all outside agencies providing diversion services to ensure that the prosecutor's diversion decisions are consistent and appropriate.

Commentary Prosecutors differ in their views about whether they should be involved in diverting less serious cases from formal adjudication. The consensus seems to be, however, that because most juveniles are in the process of developing their behavior and values, there is a unique opportunity presented at the juvenile court level to dissuade them from criminal activity. The prosecutor should seriously consider involvement in this process. Many first-time or minor offenders will never enter the justice system again if their cases are handled properly. Treatment, restitution, or service programs often are viable alternatives to court processing. This section describes the opportunity for prosecutors to be involved either in diversion programs based in their offices or through referral to existing probation or community service agencies.

Diversion pursuant to Section C requires an admission of involvement in the offense. While many are critical of this requirement, the Committee believes it is necessary for three reasons. First, juveniles should not be sanctioned unless there is legally sufficient evidence that they committed what would otherwise be a crime or offense if they were an adult. Denial of involvement by the juvenile should weigh heavily in favor of a formal determination of guilt or innocence. Second, many juvenile justice practitioners believe that effective treatment or rehabilitation begins with an acknowledgment of wrong-doing. Third, cases that are diverted with no admission of guilt often cannot be restored if the juvenile fails to meet the conditions agreed upon for diversion. Revival of the case is often not possible because too much time has passed and witnesses are unavailable or evidence is lost. A written admission of involvement provides evidence that the prosecutor may need if the case has to be referred to court upon failure of the diversion process.

Given this requirement for an admission of involvement, the Section delineates a careful process that should be undertaken when a juvenile case is diverted. It is critical that the juvenile and his parents understand the nature of diversion, the effect of an admission of guilt, the waiver of his rights, and his responsibilities under the diversion contract. In order to ensure that the juvenile and his parents understand this process, the diversion is preceded by execution of a written contract.

D. Uncontested Adjudication Proceedings

Propriety of Plea Agreements. The prosecutor can properly enter into a plea agreement with a defense attorney concerning a filed petition against a juvenile. The decision to enter into a plea agreement should be governed by both the interests of the state and those of the juvenile, although the primary concern of the prosecutor should be protection of the public interest as determined in the exercise of traditional prosecutorial discretion. Plea agreements, if appropriate, should be entered into expeditiously without delaying speedy adjudication and disposition, in order to protect the juvenile, the victim and the state.

Commentary First, Section D reflects the consensus that plea agreements are appropriate in juvenile court to the extent that they are appropriate in the adult court. The appropriateness and extent to which plea agreements are used are matters of office policy to be determined by the chief prosecutor. The prosecutor should always take steps to ensure the resulting record is sufficient to reflect the actual nature of the offense.

In juvenile courts where a plea to any offense vests full dispositional jurisdiction in the court, there is sometimes a practice to reduce the charge through a plea agreement. For instance, a provable burglary charge is reduced to theft or a sex offense to an assault. For at least these serious offenses, the Committee urges prosecutors to only enter into pleas that reflect that seriousness unless there is a problem with proof. A provable burglary case should result in a court record that reflects commission of a burglary, not just theft. The court record can then be used as an accurate gauge of prior delinquent behavior if the juvenile is later accused of additional offenses.

A plea agreement with a juvenile should be conducted through defense counsel. Juveniles, and even juveniles and their parents, should not be involved in plea agreements when they are unrepresented by an attorney because the danger of misunderstanding the nature of the agreement and the potential consequences are so great.

The Committee recognizes that in some jurisdictions this general rule could result in the availability of "reduced charge" pleas to represented juveniles and not to unrepresented juveniles. The rule is not meant to discriminate against unrepresented juveniles and the prosecutor is charged to exercise his discretion wisely to avoid this result.

A plea agreement should be accompanied by a recitation on the court record of sufficient facts to demonstrate a *prima facie* case that the juvenile has committed the acts alleged in the petition to which he or she is pleading guilty. When a confession by the juvenile is introduced, the prosecutor must assure that the record recites corroborative evidence establishing the crime itself. The prosecutor's recitation should be limited to the act(s) to which the juvenile is pleading guilty, except when the juvenile accepts responsibility for financial restitution with respect to dismissed charges. Where restitution is involved for dismissed charges, the court may nevertheless require a recitation to establish the basis for financial liability.

E. The Adjudicatory Phase

1. *Speedy Adjudication.* When the prosecutor decides to seek a formal adjudication of a complaint against a juvenile, he or she should proceed to an adjudicatory hearing as quickly as possible. Detention cases should receive priority treatment. An adjudicatory hearing should be held within 30 days if the juvenile is held in detention pending trial or within 60 days if the juvenile is arrested and released. A dispositional hearing should be held within 30 days after the adjudicatory hearing.

2. *Assumption of Traditional Adversary Role.* At the adjudicatory hearing the prosecutor should assume the traditional adversary position of a prosecutor. The prosecutor should recognize, however, that vulnerable child witnesses should be treated fairly and with sensitivity.

3. *Standard of Proof; Rules of Evidence.* The juvenile prosecutor has the burden of proving the allegations in the petition beyond a reasonable doubt. The same rules of evidence used in trying criminal cases in the jurisdiction should apply to juvenile court cases involving delinquency petitions. The prosecutor is under the same duty to disclose exculpatory evidence in juvenile proceedings as he or she would be in adult criminal proceedings.

4. *Notice to Prosecutor Before Dismissal.* Once a petition has been filed with the juvenile court, it should not be dismissed without providing the prosecutor with notice and an opportunity to be heard.

Commentary The time limits in this section, like those in Section B above, are intended to expedite juvenile cases in order to promote fair treatment to both victim and juvenile, and to make the experience more meaningful for the juvenile. Many juvenile justice professionals believe that a court appearance or a disposition several months after the delinquent act is much less useful than a prompt response. Like the time limits on screening in Section B above, these are suggested limits. Some jurisdictions may process cases more quickly than this while others may find it impossible given local law and practice. The Committee recognizes, for instance, that the defense discovery process in some jurisdictions may require a longer time period. The Committee also recognizes that good cause may exist in specific cases to extend the time period. Prosecutors may find that they can utilize these standards to convince lawmakers or other juvenile justice professionals that changes should be made to ensure prompt case processing and disposition.

Section E envisions a formal, adversarial process with respect to determination of guilt or innocence. This standard, therefore, suggests that the same rules of evidence employed in adult criminal cases in the jurisdiction should be applied to juvenile court cases. Prosecutors should strive in the juvenile court setting to maintain a distinction between a factual determination of innocence or guilt and a determination of disposition. This approach promotes fairness to both the victim and the community, and enhances the integrity of juvenile court findings.

F. Dispositional Phase

1. *Prosecutor Should Take an Active Role.* The prosecutor should take an active role in the dispositional hearing and make a recommendation to the court after reviewing reports prepared by prosecutorial staff, probation department and others.

2. *Victim Impact.* At the dispositional hearing the prosecutor should ensure that the court is aware of the impact of the juvenile's conduct on the victim and should further report to the court any matter concerning restitution and community service.

3. *Prosecutor's Recommendation.* In recommending a disposition, the prosecutor should consider those dispositions that most closely meet the interests and needs of the juvenile offender, bearing in mind that community safety and welfare is his or her primary concern.

4. *Effectiveness of Dispositional Programs.* The chief prosecutor along with the prosecutor in juvenile court should evaluate the effectiveness of dispositional programs used in the jurisdiction, from the standpoint of both the state's and the youth's interests. If the prosecutor discovers that a youth or class of young people are not receiving the care and treatment envisioned in disposition decisions, he or she should inform the court of this fact.

Commentary Section F encourages prosecutors to participate in the dispositional phase because the community should be represented in this phase just as it is or should be in earlier phases. Prosecutors should also offer appropriate alternatives to the Court because they have been involved with the particular juvenile's case. They are familiar with dispositional alternatives that are most appropriate. When a juvenile presents a danger to the safety and welfare of the community, the prosecutor should voice this concern. On the other hand, when appropriate, the prosecutor may offer a dispositional recommendation that is less restrictive than what the juvenile court judge may contemplate imposing. The Committee recognizes that given the scarce resources in many prosecutors' offices, it may not be practical to assign attorneys to attend disposition hearings for minor offenses. One possibility in these cases is that the prosecutor submit to the court a written recommendation on disposition.

This Section also suggests that the prosecutor should take a leadership role in the community in assuring that a wide range of appropriate dispositional alternatives are available for youth adjudicated delinquents. The prosecutor is challenged to assume this leadership role because he is in a unique position to help organize the community and because successful programs should serve to actually reduce crime.

G. Post-Disposition Proceedings

1. *Appeals and Hearings Subsequent to Disposition.* The prosecutor should represent the state's interest in all appeals from decisions rendered by the appropriate court, all hearings concerning revocation of probation, all petitions for modification of disposition, all hearings related to the classification and placement of a juvenile, and all collateral proceedings attacking the orders of that court.

2. *Administration of Sanctions.* If the prosecutor becomes aware that the sanctions imposed by the court are not being administered by an agency to which the court assigned the juvenile, or that the manner in which the sanctions are being carried out is inappropriate, the prosecutor should take all reasonable steps to ensure agency supervisors are informed and appropriate measures are taken. If the situation is not remedied, it is the duty of the prosecutor to report this concern to the agency and, if necessary, to the dispositional court.

Commentary This Section suggests that the work of the prosecutor is not finished at disposition of the case. Instead, the prosecutor is encouraged to follow up on cases to ensure that dispositions are upheld, court ordered sanctions are administered, and treatment is provided. The Committee recognizes that in some states legal restrictions do not allow such follow-up, and that scarce resources prevent follow-up in some offices.

Notes

1. At the time Prosecution Standard 19.2 was revised, the following prosecutors were involved through NDAA's Juvenile Justice Committee:

Gus Sandstrom, Jr., Chairman
District Attorney, Pueblo County
Pueblo, Colorado

David Bludworth
State's Attorney, 15th Judicial Circuit
West Palm Beach, Florida

Ronald Castille
District Attorney, Philadelphia County
Philadelphia, Pennsylvania

Craig Corgan
District Attorney, 11th Judicial District
Bartlesville, Oklahoma

Stephen Goldsmith
Prosecuting Attorney,
19th Judicial Circuit
Indianapolis, Indiana

Scott Harshbarger
District Attorney, Middlesex County
Cambridge, Massachusetts

Alan Rockoff
County Prosecutor, Middlesex County
New Brunswick, New Jersey

Note: Richard Daley, formerly State's Attorney of Cook County, Illinois, and Tom Collins, formerly County Attorney of Maricopa County, Arizona, contributed substantially to the development of Standard 19.2 while serving on the Juvenile Justice Committee.

2. Institute of Judicial Administration-American Bar Association. (1980). *Juvenile justice standards relating to juvenile delinquency and sanctions.* Cambridge, MA: Ballinger.

3. Feld, B. C. (1988). *In re Gault* revisited: A cross-state comparison of the right to counsel in juvenile court. *Crime and Delinquency, 34,* 393–424.

4. Snyder, H. (1989). The juvenile court's response to violent crime. *Update on Statistics,* Office of Juvenile Justice and Delinquency Prevention. Washington, D.C.: U.S. Department of Justice.

Case

In re Gault, 387 U.S. 1 (1967).

7

Interagency Services in Juvenile Justice Systems

Mark Soler

Most services for children and families in the United States are categorical, fragmented, and uncoordinated. Children labeled "delinquent" are tracked toward correctional placements aimed at keeping them within a designated setting and modifying their behavior, with little effort to resolve underlying family problems. Children labeled "abused," "neglected," or "dependent" are removed from their homes and quickly placed in foster care, but rarely receive preventive, family support, or mental health services. Children with mental health needs are placed in secure psychiatric settings and often heavily medicated, with little opportunity for treatment in community-based, family-oriented programs.

This problem is now well recognized. The Select Committee on Children, Youth, and Families, U.S. House of Representatives, has reported that agency administrators and practitioners agree that little has been done to coordinate services among education, health, mental health, developmental disabilities, juvenile justice, and legal systems (Select Committee on Children, Youth, and Families, 1990). Similarly, the American Public Welfare Association's National Commission on Child Welfare and Family Preservation has noted that interagency cooperation between the public child welfare system and public and private agencies is "frequently limited" (National Commission on Child Welfare and Family Preservation, 1990). The Committee for Economic Development, representing a broad array of business leaders and educators, has called for "a comprehensive and coordinated human-investment strategy for child development and education" (Research and Policy Committee of the Committee for Economic Development, 1991). And groups as diverse as the Children's Defense Fund, the National Alliance of Business, the National Association of State Boards of Education, and the National Association of Counties have decried the social welfare system's division of children and family problems into rigid and distinct categories and its inability to craft comprehensive solutions to those problems (Melaville & Blank, 1991).

As a result, cities, counties, and states across the country have sought to develop interagency partnerships to provide services to children and families. Some of these efforts have been limited to modest attempts at cooperation among agencies—for example, by sharing training, by locating intake desks from several agencies at a single site, or by developing joint committees to refer children to existing services. Other efforts have been much more comprehensive, aimed at fundamentally restructuring the way services are provided. Some efforts have been initiated by governmental units, others are supported by foundations, still others involve single, multipurpose, neighborhood-based programs (Lerner, 1990). One of the successful coordination efforts, the Willie M. program in North Carolina, resulted from a civil rights lawsuit. Efforts have been made to forge links between agencies in a variety of areas, including child welfare, mental health, education, health, and juvenile justice.

This widespread interest in interagency services is not surprising. The changing needs of children and families, the stigmatizing effects of the labels placed on children by the various systems, the inefficiencies of those systems as they respond narrowly to the complex problems of children and families, and the continuing budgetary crises at all levels of government have prompted agency administrators and children's advocates alike to search for less destructive, more comprehensive, more cost-effective methods of providing services to children and families at risk.

This headlong rush to the altar of cross-agency efforts, however, raises some important and difficult questions about the nature of social welfare services in our society, the means by which the delivery of those services may be improved, and the reasonableness of expected outcomes from specific interagency efforts. Not all interagency efforts are well planned, carefully executed, or thoroughly evaluated. Some may actually be wasteful. Even with the best interagency programs, there is precious little data available on outcome measures, levels of client satisfaction, or cost effectiveness. For example, a 1984 study of state-level coordination of services for the U.S. Departments of Justice and Health and Human Services concluded, after a survey of the literature:

> When all is said and done, there is little that has been learned definitively about the effectiveness of various coordination approaches or mechanisms in improving the planning and delivery of services.

Available evidence pertains to human services in general, rather than to youth services specifically. Most researchers have concluded that there is no best approach, but that different approaches may be preferred depending on the political and economic contexts, the awareness and commitment of the major actors, the history of past coordination efforts, and the particular task at hand. (O'Connor, Albrecht, Cohen & Newquist-Carroll, 1984, p. 17).

Similarly, a more recent survey of services integration programs for children and families in crisis conducted by the Office of the Inspector General of the U.S. Department of Health and Human Services noted: "We do not claim that these initiatives are the 13 most innovative and effective initiatives in the country. The universe of such initiatives is unknown. Moreover, there is no way objectively to rank the initiatives that are known. We did not independently verify or assess outcomes of the programs" (Kotler et al., 1991, p. 2).

This chapter will discuss interagency services in juvenile justice systems. Unlike the child welfare, mental health, and education systems, all of which are characterized by numerous interagency efforts, there are relatively few such programs for children and youth charged or adjudicated for delinquent offenses. Three are demonstrably effective and widely recognized as exemplary: the Willie M. program for violent and seriously disturbed youth in North Carolina, the case management and family preservation programs instituted by the Department of Juvenile Justice in New York City, and the Ventura County Children's Demonstration Project in California. This chapter will briefly describe each of these programs and note their most important facets.

These three programs, however, are very much the exceptions rather than the rule. Either because of a stated preference for preventive, "front-end" services for children at risk—usually defined as health, education, or social services for infants and young children—or because of political and other pressures to handle the problem of juvenile crime by simply building more secure institutions, few jurisdictions have yet invested much effort in interagency services for the older "back-end" youth in juvenile justice systems. The movement toward interagency services, however, will continue for the foreseeable future, and no systematic evaluation of the effectiveness of existing programs has been done, either in juvenile justice or in other areas. Accordingly, this chapter will look more generally at a number of the critical issues for juvenile justice policy and research that are raised by the movement toward interagency services.

The Willie M. Program

During the 1970s, as the movement toward deinstitutionalization grew in the juvenile justice and mental health areas, North Carolina continued to rely on large warehouselike facilities for its troubled children. There was a glaring absence of community-based programs, particularly for children with serious mental health problems who had been labeled "violent" or "aggressive."

In October 1979, in response to an invitation to bring suit by a juvenile court judge long frustrated by the lack of community placements, a coalition of private attorneys and public interest law offices filed *Willie M. v. Hunt.* This civil rights lawsuit was filed on behalf of four children aged eleven to sixteen who had long histories of delinquent behavior and placement failures, and who needed intensive therapeutic services but had been committed to ineffective institutional placements (state training schools or mental hospitals). The four young plaintiffs represented the whole class of all similarly situated children in the state. The lawsuit alleged that the state's failure to develop appropriate community-based programs violated the children's "right to treatment" under the U.S. Constitution and specific state statutes, as well as federal statutes such as the Education of All Handicapped Children Act (recently renamed the Individuals with Disabilities Education Act, which guarantees eligible children a "free appropriate public education" and "related services," including counseling and psychotherapy, in the least restrictive environment), and §504 of the Rehabilitation Act of 1974 (which prohibits discrimination against the handicapped).

In September 1980 the parties reached a settlement in the case. The state agreed that the plaintiffs had a right to treatment under the U.S. Constitution and federal and state statutes; that treatment was to be individualized and provided in the least restrictive environment possible; and that the treatment provided was to be based on the child's needs, not on the services currently available. If the services needed by the child did not exist, they were to be developed by the state as soon as possible (Soler & Warboys, 1990).

To monitor the settlement, the parties created a five-member "review panel" of experts in mental health, community treatment, and education. Two members of the panel were selected by each side, and the fifth member was selected jointly. The review panel, under the leadership of Dr. James Clements, who had served as monitoring panel in the Willowbrook case, and which involved conditions of confinement in a New York state mental hospital, kept the federal judge apprised of the state's progress

(*New York State Ass'n for Retarded Children, Inc. v. Rockefeller*). Lenore Behar, chief of Child Mental Health Services in the Department of Human Resources' Division of Mental Health/Mental Retardation/ Substance Abuse Services, assumed administrative responsibility for implementation of the settlement. She divided the state into four mental health regions, then subdivided each region into zones, which were usually multicounty areas. Each zone was to contain the complete "system of services" needed by members of the Willie M. class within the zone. The regional mental health hospitals were to provide backup, crisis stabilization, and training.

The concept of "systems of services" came from a report issued a decade earlier by the Joint Commission on Mental Health of Children, *Crisis in Child Mental Health: Challenge for the 1970s* (Joint Commission on Mental Health of Children, 1969). The Joint Commission envisioned a model of coordinated mental health prevention and treatment services, including medical, psychological, nutritional, social, educational, vocational, and legal services. In 1978 this concept was reinforced by a report by the President's Commission on Mental Health (President's Commission on Mental Health, 1978).

There were several necessary components in Behar's plan: a full range of services, from highly restrictive to those approximating normal family living; services provided in the children's own communities, to maximize family involvement and reintegration into their natural environments; linkages among the various components of the system as well as to other children's services systems; flexibility in funding and decision making, to meet the individual needs of the children; a solid management structure; and individualized treatment and educational planning through broadly defined case management (Behar, 1986).

The Joint Commission and President's Commission reports were prescriptive and theoretical: Behar was charged with translating theory into practice when there were no models of successful systems of services in existence. Not surprisingly, there were significant problems in developing systems of services throughout the state and establishing effective fiscal and management structures. Ultimately, however, the program has been extremely successful. Children identified as potentially qualifying for the Willie M. program are screened and evaluated; if eligible, a treatment plan for the child is prepared. A case manager with broad authority to access necessary services is assigned to each child. If needed services are not currently available, they can be developed. Because of the program, there has been a very significant decrease in the use of institutional placements for children, and a corresponding increase in the development of a wide array of community-based placements. The program now commands appropriations from the state legislature totaling almost $30 million annually, and is cited extensively in the professional literature (Gardner, 1989; Knitzer, 1982, 1989).

The Willie M. program broke new ground in providing comprehensive services for violent and severely disturbed children. There were no real-world precedents, and the state eventually reorganized its entire statewide service delivery system for the members of the *Willie M.* class. The case management structure and the management information system which utilizes computerized cost-reimbursement are considered national models, and the entire Willie M. program is a model for other interagency initiatives.

The New York Department of Juvenile Justice

During the late 1970s and early 1980s the New York Department of Juvenile Justice (DJJ) and its secure detention facility, Spofford Detention Center, were often described as disorganized, demoralized, deteriorating, and chaotic. The facility was antiquated and unsafe; children and staff were discouraged and restless; and the department's commissioner was embroiled in debilitating political and professional battles.

In January 1983 Ellen Schall took over as commissioner. Most of the top staff positions were vacant (including all three line divisions and two of the three deputy commissioner positions). Children were running away from the nonsecure detention unit, and a new Aftercare program had few clients. Schall hired Kathleen Feely as deputy commissioner and Rose Washington as director of the Spofford Juvenile Center, and set out to revitalize the agency (Gilmore & Schall, 1986). The results were dramatic, leading to what Dr. Barry Krisberg, president of the National Council on Crime and Delinquency, called the "Spofford Miracle" (Krisberg, 1987). Three years later, Schall and the Department of Juvenile Justice were cited by the Ford Foundation and the Kennedy School of Government at Harvard for having one of the ten most innovative state and local government programs in the United States.

The key to the revitalization was case management (Beilenson, 1987). When a child enters detention, DJJ staff conduct a comprehensive needs assessment that covers medical, dental, mental health, education, and family background. An interdepartmental team then develops an individualized plan for services in Spofford, in nonsecure detention, and, if the child is released home, in Aftercare. In Spofford, a case manager is assigned to each child on the first day of detention. In nonsecure detention and Aftercare, families are often involved in the process of developing the services plan. DJJ then provides service delivery, including casework and recreational services, at nonsecure facilities and Spofford. For children and families who elect to participate in Aftercare upon release from detention, DJJ has an extensive network of referrals to local community agencies that continue working with the child and family. Finally, DJJ monitors all services provided to the child and family. In 1989 DJJ automated its case management system by implementing a computer-based information system known as "Prober" (Department of Juvenile Justice, 1990a).

In February 1989, in Brooklyn Family Court, DJJ initiated a new program, Family Ties, aimed at strengthening families in order to avert court-ordered placement in state institutions. The program is patterned on Homebuilders, the intensive home-based services model developed by the Behavioral Sciences Institute in Tacoma, Washington. Judges refer the cases of adjudicated delinquents who are about to be placed in New York State Division for Youth (DFY) facilities. If the family is eligible and agrees to work toward keeping the child at home, a "family preservationist" works with the family for a period of four to six weeks. Family preservationists have only two cases at a time, spend a minimum of ten to fifteen hours a week with the family in their own environment (home, school, or neighborhood), and are on call twenty-four hours a day, seven days a week. They provide advice, counseling, and crisis intervention work with the children and families to manage stress and set limits on behavior, and address more concrete needs such as employment, education, and child care. At the end of the intervention, if the judge believes that the child and family have made significant progress, the child is placed on probation and DFY placement is averted. To date, approximately 70 percent of families who have participated in Family Ties have avoided institutional placement. DJJ estimates that each DFY placement that is averted saves New York City $35,000 and New York State the same, for a total of $70,000 per child. In fiscal 1991 the program expanded to the Family Courts in the Bronx and Manhattan (Department of Juvenile Justice, 1990b, 1990c).

Like the Willie M. program, DJJ's program is notable for its innovation, sound management and strong leadership. It was the first public juvenile justice agency in the country to provide effective case management for children charged with delinquency offenses, and also the first to provide intensive family preservation services. While other New York City services experienced administrative, staff, and budgetary crises, DJJ was cited as one of the best local government programs in America.

The Ventura County Children's Demonstration Project

Ventura County began efforts to coordinate services in the early 1980s. The focus was on mental health care and the target population was children who were seriously emotionally disturbed. Many of those children were in the county's juvenile justice system. In 1985 the California legislature passed legislation directing Ventura County to develop a model for a "comprehensive, coordinated children's mental health system that can be replicated in other counties" (AB 3920 [Wright]).

Looking at multiple-problem children in the juvenile justice, child welfare, education, and mental health systems who were removed or at risk of removal from their homes, project personnel articulated requirements for effective service delivery that were quite similar to those embodied in Lenore Behar's plan in North Carolina and the DJJ program in New York: access to a comprehensive array of services; treatment in the home, school, or other least restrictive environment; family involvement in all phases of planning and delivery of services; linkages between public agencies and the private sector; effective management and fiscal accountability, with ongoing monitoring of client outcomes and treatment benefits and costs; and provision of services through comprehensive case management. The overall goal was to provide the highest treatment benefit to the child, family, and community at the lowest cost to the public (Ventura County Children's Mental Health Demonstration Project, 1987a, 1987b, 1987c).

For mentally disordered children in the county's juvenile justice system, the project's interdisciplinary screening committee reviews each case and makes a specific recommendation to the probation officer. A court liaison committee (with representatives from the county mental health, corrections, and education agencies) advises the judge on available services. The array of placements is quite broad, from the most restrictive traditional institutional placements (California Youth Authority, county juvenile hall), to a medium-security mental health facility for 120- to 180-day commitments (Colston Youth Center), a short-term low-security work release program (Juvenile Restitution Project), residential group homes, and probation placement at home (with outpatient care, day treatment, or in-home crisis intervention services).

The interagency partnership, and particularly the provision of mental health services, has been quite effective. The project has resulted in reduced commitments to state corrections institutions and private out-of-county facilities; decreases in arrests and days of incarceration; reduced incarceration costs; and reduced recidivism (Ventura County Mental Health Demonstration Project, 1987a, 1987b).

The Ventura County Project is one of the most successful multiagency partnerships in the country. The project was well planned, with clear goals and a specific target population, and implemented with strong sense of common purpose. Results have been carefully documented, and the project has done an outstanding job of communicating its goals and methods to interested public officials, policymakers, and practitioners around the country. The project is now being used as a model for mental health reform for adults and seniors (Jordan & Hernandez, 1990; Ventura County Mental Health, 1989).

Policy and Research Issues

The North Carolina, New York, and Ventura County programs demonstrate (as several commentators have noted) the importance of several aspects of effective coordination programs:

- Establishment of clear goals and a well-defined target population for the provision of services (Bruner, 1991; Knitzer & Yelton, 1990; O'Connor et al., 1984; Soler & Shauffer, 1990)
- An emphasis on working with the entire family, rather than just the identified at-risk child (Kamerman & Kahn, 1989; Melaville & Blank, 1991; Research and Policy Committee of the Committee for Economic Development, 1991; Soler & Shauffer, 1990)
- Development of a broad array of services to meet the different needs of the target population (Agenda for Children Tomorrow, 1990; McGowan, Kahn & Kamerman, 1990; Melaville & Blank, 1991)
- Reliance on case management that includes active brokering for services and advocacy for the child and family (Agenda for Children Tomorrow, 1990; Kamerman & Kahn, 1989; McGown et al., 1990; Kamerman & Kahn, 1989; McGowan et al., 1990; Soler & Shauffer, 1990)
- The importance of leadership in initiating, developing, and implementing the coordination program (Bruner, 1991; Knitzer & Yelton, 1990; Kotler et al., 1991; Melaville & Blank, 1991; O'Connor et al., 1984)

Other characteristics cited as necessary or important for effective interagency coordination include:

- Accessibility of services (Agenda for Children Tomorrow, 1990; McGowan et al., 1990; Soler & Shauffer, 1990)

- Availability of flexible and reliable funding (Bruner, 1991; Kamerman & Kahn, 1989; Kotler et al., 1991; Melaville & Blank, 1991; Research and Policy Committee of the Committee for Economic Development, 1991; Soler & Shauffer, 1990)

- Elimination of categorical funding requirements, confidentiality strictures, and other statutory and regulatory barriers to coordination (Agenda for Children Tomorrow, 1990; Kamerman & Kahn, 1989; Knitzer & Yelton, 1990; Melaville & Blank, 1991)

- Development of processes for facilitating communication among agencies (Bruner, 1991; Knitzer & Yelton, 1990; Kotler et al., 1991; Melaville & Blank, 1991)

- Existence of a mechanism for resolving interagency disputes (Agenda for Children Tomorrow, 1990; O'Connor et al., 1984; Soler & Shauffer, 1990)

- Involvement of the private sector (Agenda for Children Tomorrow, 1990; Bruner, 1991; Soler & Shauffer, 1990)

- Need for enhanced or modified training and other staff supports (Agenda for Children Tomorrow, 1990; Bruner, 1991; Kamerman & Kahn, 1989; Kotler et al., O'Connor et al., 1984; Soler & Shauffer, 1990)

- Facilitation of information collection management and retrieval (Agenda for Children Tomorrow, 1990; Kamerman & Kahn, 1989; McGowan et al., 1990; O'Connor et al., 1984; Soler & Shauffer, 1990)

- Development of meaningful outcome measures (Bruner, 1991; Melaville & Blank, 1991; Research and Policy Committee of the Committee for Economic Development, 1991; Soler & Shauffer, 1990)

- Capacity for innovation (McGowan et al., 1990; Soler & Shauffer, 1990)

Despite the significant amount of current interest in (and writing about) interagency services, there is still little hard data on what works, why it works, and under what circumstances it works: the conclusion of the Department of Justice/Department of Health and Human Services study in 1984, quoted earlier, is hardly less true today.

The absence of definitive information about the effectiveness of various interagency approaches or mechanisms may be cause for more serious concern in the juvenile justice area than in other areas affecting children and families. That is because in other areas there are major initiatives already underway to establish demonstration projects, develop replicable interagency mechanisms, collect relevant data, and conduct meaningful measures of effectiveness.

In the mental health area, for example, there is a history of thoughtful approaches to developing coordinated arrays of services, dating back at least to the Joint Commission on Mental Health of Children report in 1969. In 1982 Jane Knitzer and the Children's Defense Fund documented the country's shocking failure to provide services to seriously emotionally disturbed children (Knitzer, 1982). Congress responded by allocating funds to the National Institutes of Mental Health (NIMH) for an initiative to improve service delivery to that population, and NIMH created the Child and Adolescent Service System Program (CASSP). CASSP was based on a solid conceptual framework (Stroul & Friedman, 1986), and was designed to foster coordinated service delivery. At present there are CASSP-funded programs throughout the United States, and evaluations of individual programs and entire coordinated systems are conducted by the Florida Mental Health Institute of the University of Florida in Tampa and the Regional Research Institute of Portland State University in Oregon (Stroul & Friedman, 1986). In addition to this federally funded effort, individual states are conducting their own interagency efforts (Knitzer, 1989b), and the Robert Wood Johnson Foundation has launched a major multicity initiative to develop interagency services for children with mental health problems.

In the child welfare area, there is also a host of state and local cross-agency programs (Knitzer, 1989a). In addition, the Annie E. Casey Foundation has sponsored a major child welfare reform initiative, and the Edna McConnell Clark Foundation and the Foundation for Child Development have supported specific demonstration projects.

In the education arena, the State of New Jersey initiated the School-Based Youth Services Program in 1988 to provide mental health, family counseling, health, and employment services in schools to at-risk adolescents. The New Jersey Department of Human Resources funds twenty-nine sites in all twenty-one counties, each site located in or near schools to provide students with "one-stop" shopping for services (Kotler et al., 1991). California governor Pete Wilson has championed school-linked services as the centerpiece of his child development and education program, and the Bush administration has included such services as part of its major education reform package. In the private sector, the Annie E. Casey Foundation has sponsored a major five-city initiative under the title

"New Futures," and there are exemplary local programs such as "New Beginnings" in San Diego and the Kentucky Integrated Delivery System ("K.I.D.S.").

But in juvenile justice there is not much action. One of the few initiatives to include juvenile justice services is a pilot program in Iowa to "decategorize" federal, state, and local funding streams in a variety of areas, including foster care, daycare, juvenile detention, state juvenile institutions, state hospital schools, mental health institutes, and county-based juvenile justice services. There is also a collaboration initiative in Contra Costa County, California, to provide comprehensive services to children at imminent risk of out-of-home placement, children in place-ment, families and children at risk, and children and families needing early intervention services. In addition to serving children at risk of placement through the child welfare and mental health systems, this initiative also serves children at risk in the juvenile justice system (Rosewater, 1991). Even the Willie M., New York Department of Juvenile Justice, and Ventura County programs have not developed definitive outcome mea-sures or been subjected to rigorous analysis and scrutiny.

This suggests that there is much to be done in thinking about and developing interagency services for children and youth in juvenile justice systems. Of course, this does not involve writing on a blank slate. The characteristics identified as important for interagency children and family services in general are also important for interagency provision of juvenile justice services in particular. Indeed, those identified characteristics suggest a number of policy and research issues in the juvenile justice area.

First, we need to develop and adhere to a clear and commonly accepted terminology, particularly concerning the type and extent of the relationship among various agencies. Discourse on this issue too often lumps together a variety of interagency mechanisms in a single discussion, or uses different terms interchangeably without recognizing necessary distinctions, subsuming everything under the generic labels "coordination" or "integration." "Colocation," "cooperation," "collaboration," "coordi-nation," and "integration" are not synonyms, but many discussions of interagency services make no distinctions between these or other distinct concepts.

"Colocation" usually refers simply to close physical proximity of services or intake offices. "Cooperation" involves agencies working togeth-er to meet respective organizational goals, but not making any substantial changes in the services they provide or the rules and regulations that govern their activities (Melaville & Blank, 1991). "Coordination" also involves joint activity without modification of individual agency goals, expectations, or responsibilities (Bruner, 1991). "Collaboration" refers to more concerted activity: jointly developing and agreeing on common goals, sharing responsibility and funding for obtaining those goals, and working together to achieve them, using the skills, resources, and expertise of each of the agency partners (Bruner, 1991; Gardner, 1989). "Integration" involves a further blending together of agency staffs, procedures, trainings, administrations, and funding, for the application of multisystemic resources and the implementation of shared goals and objectives (Henggeler & Borduin, 1990; Melton, 1989, 1990). Moreover, the character of interagency efforts may differ, depending upon whether the effort is on the service delivery level or at the system level (Melaville & Blank, 1991).

Second, we need to have clear goals and objectives for interagency efforts for young people accused of or adjudicated for delinquent activity. State juvenile codes provide only the most general statements of goals, using stock phrases such as "the best interests of the child," "protection of self or others," "rehabilitation" (decreasingly), and "protection and safety of the public" (increasingly).

There is no clear consensus in our society on the relative priorities even for these generic goals. It is much more difficult to determine appropriate measures of system goals and objectives. Should traditional one-dimensional measures be used, such as arrest rates, rates of admissions to institutions, or recidivism rates? If so, should arrest rates consider all offenses, or just some subset such as violent crimes? Over what period are recidivism rates meaningful and appropriate? Should more complex measures be used, such as whether total costs of care have been reduced for individual children and for the system? Is it possible to develop objective measures for more inchoate goals, such as "rehabilitation" and "strengthening the family"?

Third, after appropriate goals, objectives, and outcome measures are selected, we need to conduct controlled research to find out whether interagency efforts yield real benefits to children and families. Random-assignment double-blind research, with controlled experimental variables and relevant and objective outcome measures, is difficult to conduct in the area of services delivery to children and families. But it can be done. Controlled research is being conducted in the area of family preservation services (Ensign, 1991), which presents comparable complexities of design. While the difficulties of such research are acknowledged, the results may be quite valuable (Wells & Biegel, 1991).

Fourth, in conducting controlled research, we need to test whether the specific factors identified as characteristics of effective interagency partnerships actually influence the quality of services provided and the benefits ascribed to children and families. For example, everyone agrees that interagency services should be "family-oriented," but we need to adequately define that term, determine appropriate measures of such an orientation, and conduct controlled research to test the relative benefits of such services. Similarly, while there is a consensus that a "broad array of services" is an important part of any comprehensive interagency effort, we need to know which services belong in the array. For youth in the juvenile justice system, are intensive family-based case management services, like DJJ's Family Ties, a necessary part of an effective system? Are group homes required? How critical are mental health services?

Fifth, we need to know more about the specific aspects of case management that make interagency provision of services effective. "Case management" is another of those terms that can be defined in many different ways, from passive, periodic monitoring of the status of children and families in an ongoing system to continuous active advocacy for all needed services, including services that do not currently exist (Kamerman & Kahn, 1989). Is case management in a Willie M. program or Homebuilders sense necessary for effective interagency provision of services? What specific authority (and responsibilities) should a case manager have? Should there be a limit on caseload size for case managers in an interagency system, and if so, what should it be? Should case managers have the ability to contract for services that do not currently exist in the jurisdiction?

Sixth, we need to know more about the cost-effectiveness of interagency provision of services. The start-up costs of interagency efforts, in terms of personnel time and other resources, are substantial. Ventura County, however, has documented substantial savings from its Children's Demonstration Project. Is there a "breaking-in" period, after which we should expect cost savings? Are some services more cost-effective to bring together than others? In addition, financial information is critical for establishing credibility with funding sources, especially public funding. Agency administrators and legislators demand, and are entitled to, information on how tax dollars are best used.

Finally, we need to develop better information management systems that can be used across agency lines. With computer technology advancing at a logarithmic rate, surely it must be possible to create intake forms, computer programs, laptop intake stations, modem-telephone line communications capabilities, spread-sheet financial analyses, and comprehensive reporting formats that can be used by many agencies at once. The Willie M. program, DJJ in New York, and Ventura County have all found their information processing systems to be the core of program management.

These issues are difficult and complex, but they go to the core of effective efforts for children in the juvenile justice system. Only by addressing these issues can we begin to develop successful interagency partnerships for children most in need of comprehensive and coordinated services.

References

Agenda for Children Tomorrow. (1990). Untangling children and family services. In *Three public policy issues in perspective: A report to the mayor* (pp. 11–28). New York: Author.

Behar, L. (1986). A state model for child mental health services: The North Carolina experience. *Children Today, 15,* 16–21.

Beilenson, J. (1987). *Balancing custody and care: A resource book for case management in juvenile detention systems.* New York: Department of Juvenile Justice, City of New York.

Bruner, C. (1991). *Thinking collaborative: Ten questions and answers to help policy makers improve children's services.* Washington, DC: Education and Human Services Consortium.

Department of Juvenile Justice. (1990a). *Case management system for children in detention.* New York: Author.

Department of Juvenile Justice. (1990b). *Family ties.* New York: Author.

Department of Juvenile Justice. (1990c). *Listen to the dreams: Annual report 1990.* New York: Author.

Ensign, K. (1991). *Prevention services in child welfare: An exploratory paper on the evaluation of family support and family preservation programs.* Washington, DC: Office of the Assistant Secretary for Planning and Evaluation, U.S. Department of Health and Human Services.

Gardner, L. C., Jr. (1989). *Leadership in human services: How to articulate and implement a vision to achieve results.* San Francisco: Jossey-Bass.

Gardner, S. (1989, Fall). Failure by fragmentation. *California Tomorrow,* pp. 18–25.

Gilmore, T., & Schall, E. (1986). Use of case management as a revitalizing theme in a juvenile justice agency. *Public Administration Review, 46,* 267–274.

Henggeler, S. W., & Borduin, C. M. (1990). *Family therapy and beyond: A multisystemic approach to treating the behavioral problems of children and adolescents.* Pacific Grove, CA: Brooks/Cole.

Joint Commission on Mental Health of Children. (1969). *Crisis in child mental health: Challenge for the 1970s.* New York: Harper and Row.

Jordan, D. D., & Hernandez, M. (1990). The Ventura Planning Model: A proposal for mental health reform. *Journal of Mental Health Administration, 17,* 26–47.

Kamerman, S. B., & Kahn, A. J. (1989). *Social services for children, youth and families in the United States.* Greenwich, CT: Annie E. Casey Foundation.

Knitzer, J. (1982). *Unclaimed children: The failure of public responsibility to children and adolescents in need of mental health services.* Washington, DC: Children's Defense Fund.

Knitzer, J. (1989a). Children's mental health: The advocacy challenge—"And miles to go before we sleep." In R. M. Friedman, A. J. Duchnowski, & E. L. Henderson (Eds.), *Advocacy on behalf of children with serious emotional problems* (pp. 15–27). Springfield, IL: Thomas.

Knitzer, J. (1989b). *Collaborations between child welfare and mental health: Emerging patterns and challenges.* New York: Bank Street College of Education.

Knitzer, J., & Yelton, S. (1990, Spring). Collaborations between child welfare and mental health. *Public Welfare,* 24–33.

Kotler, E., Rollin, B., Bell, E., Gibbons, R., Lemesh, C., Loeb, D., Mallen J., Pattison, B., Purvis, T., & Folchman, R. (1991). *Services integration for families and children in crisis.* Washington, DC: Department of Health and Human Services.

Krisberg, B. (1987). Foreword In J. Beilenson, *Balancing custody and care: A resource book for case management in juvenile detention systems.* New York: Department of Juvenile Justice, City of New York.

Lerner, S. (1990). *The geography of foster care: Keeping the children in the neighborhood.* New York: Foundation for Child Development.

McGowan, B. G., Kahn, A. J., & Kamerman, S. B. (1990). *Social services for children, youth and families: The New York City Study.* New York: Columbia University School of Social Work.

Melaville, A. I., & Blank, M. J. (1991). *What it takes: Structuring interagency partnerships to connect children and families with comprehensive services.* Washington, DC: Education and Human Services Consortium.

Melton, G. B. (1989). The Jericho principle: Lessons from epidemiological research. In L. Abramczyk (Ed.), *Social work education for working with seriously emotionally disturbed children and adolescents* (pp. 12–25). Columbia, SC: National Association of Deans and Directors of Schools and Social Work.

Melton, G. B. (1990). Realism in psychology and humanism in law: Psycholegal studies in Nebraska. *Nebraska Law Review,* 2, 251–275.

National Commission on Child Welfare and Family Preservation. (1990). *A commitment to change: Interim report.* Washington, DC: American Public Welfare Association.

New York State Association for Retarded Children, Inc. v. Rockefeller, 357 F. Supp. 752 (E.D.N.Y. 1973).

O'Connor, R., Albrecht, N., Cohen, B., & Newquist-Carroll, L. (1984). *New directions in youth services: Experiences with state-level coordination.* Washington, DC: U.S. Government Printing Office.

President's Commission on Mental Health. (1978). *Report to the president.* Washington, DC: U.S. Government Printing Office.

Research and Policy Committee of the Committee for Economic Development. (1991). *The unfinished agenda: A new vision for child development and education.* New York: Committee for Economic Development.

Rosewater, A. (1991). *A new future for Contra Costa's children and their families: A three-year plan.* Available from Contra Costa Social Services Department, 30 Muir Road, Martinez, CA, 94553.

Select Committee on Children, Youth, and Families, U.S. House of Representatives. (1990). *No place to call home: Discarded children in America* (Report No. 101–395). Washington, DC: U.S. Government Printing Office.

Soler, M., & Shauffer, C. (1990). Fighting fragmentation: Coordination of services for children and families. *Nebraska Law Review, 69,* 278–297.

Soler, M., & Warboys, L. (1990). *Services for violent and severely disturbed children: The Willie M. litigation.* New York: Foundation for Child Development.

Stroul, B., & Friedman, R. (1986). *A system of care for severely emotionally disturbed children and youth.* Washington, DC: Georgetown University Child Development Center.

Ventura County Children's Mental Health Services Demonstration Project. (1987a). *Two year report on the Ventura model for interagency children's mental health services.* Ventura County, CA: Department of Mental Health Services.

Ventura County Children's Mental Health Services Demonstration Project. (1987b). *A report and commentary on the Ventura model for children's mental health services.* Ventura County, CA: Department of Mental Health Services.

Ventura County Children's Mental Health Services Demonstration Project. (1987c). *AB 377 report on the Ventura County Children's Mental Health Demonstration Project: A 27-month update and addendum to the two-year report on the Ventura Model for interagency children's mental health services.* Ventura County, CA: Department of Mental Health Services.

Ventura County Mental Health. (1989). *The Ventura Planning Model for mental health services.* Ventura County, CA: Author.

Wells, K., & Biegel, D. E. (1991). *Family preservation services: Research and evaluation.* Newbury Park, CA: Sage.

Willie M. v. Hunt, Civil No. CC-79-0294 M (W.D.N.C.).

8

Public Policy and the Incarceration of Juveniles: Directions for the 1990s

Ira M. Schwartz and Russell Van Vleet

S tate and local policymakers are finding the decade of the 1990s significantly different than any other period in recent memory. Unlike the 1960s, the 1970s, and the 1980s, when there always seemed to be enough money for government services and programs, governors, state legislators, and county executives and board members are now confronting massive budget deficits. It is a situation that appears unlikely to change in the near future (Eckl, Hutchison & Snell, 1991).

The fiscal crisis is forcing elected public officials to make some tough decisions. Deep budget cuts and reductions in public services, even in areas once considered "sacred cows," are being made in states across the country. And, despite widespread anti tax sentiment, tax increases have been enacted in thirty-three states (Eckl et al., 1991). Michigan offers a typical example of the budget squeeze. Its former governor once boasted that, during his tenure, Michigan had become the most punitive state in the Midwest (Blanchard, 1989). With strong legislative backing, he launched one of the most ambitious prison construction programs in the nation. But two of these newly built prisons have never been opened because the state does not have the money to operate them.

As policymakers look for ways to make government services more cost-effective and efficient, they should not overlook opportunities in juvenile detention and correctional programs. These programs are ripe for reform. Moreover, they consume precious resources needed to finance other vital human services.

This chapter explores the potential for reforming youth detention and training school programs. It also discusses some barriers to change and how they can be overcome.

The Economics of Juvenile Detention Centers and Training Schools

In fiscal year 1988 public juvenile detention centers and training schools cost taxpayers more than $1.4 billion to operate. As indicated in Table 8-1, operating costs for these facilities far outstripped the rate of inflation during the 1980s.

National data, while depicting broad trends, tell us nothing about operating costs for these facilities in various states. What data there are suggest enormous disparities in expenditures between jurisdictions. For example, the data in Tables 8-2 and 8-3 rank states by expenditures per eligible youth for fiscal year 1988. Expenditures for training schools ranged from a low of $8 per eligible youth in Florida to a high of $157 in the District of Columbia. Detention center costs ranged from a low of $1 per eligible youth in Arkansas and South Carolina to a high of $183 in the District of Columbia.

Expenditures and Results

Differences in expenditures prompt questions about what various states are getting for their money. For example, are states with higher eligible per-youth expenditures getting better results (e.g., lower recidivism rates, increased public protection, declining rates of juvenile crime, etc.)?

Table 8-1
U.S. Public Detention Centers and Training Schools: Operating Expenditures FY 1982 and FY 1988*

	Detention Centers	
FY 1982	*FY 1988*	*Percent Change*
$385,708,618	$513,866,663	+33%
	Training Schools	
FY 1982	*FY 1988*	*Percent Change*
$721,266, 935	$887,426,973	+23%

Source: Juvenile Detention and Correction Facility Census, 1982–83 and 1988–89. U.S. Bureau of the Census, Current Population Reports, Series p-25, published and unpublished data.

* Cost figures adjusted for the rate of inflation.

Training Schools

Unfortunately, no national studies have examined the relationship between youth detention, training school expenditures, and program outcomes. However, some inferences about training schools can be made from the data presented in Tables 8–2 and 8–3. For example, Massachusetts and Utah rank near the bottom in eligible per-youth expenditures for training schools. Youth correction systems in these states have been evaluated by the National Council on Crime and Delinquency (NCCD) (Austin, Elms, Krisberg & Steele, 1991). The authors concluded that the Massachusetts youth correction system "did not create an excessive [juvenile] crime problem" and that "Massachusetts continues to have one of the lowest rates of juvenile crime in the nation" (Austin et al., 1991, p. 24). The NCCD study found that juveniles placed in the custody of the Massachusetts Department of Youth Services (DYS) "committed far fewer crimes under DYS supervision than before their commitment" (Austin et al., 1991, p. 25). Moreover, "The observed declines in offending in the first year were sustained over the next two years" (Austin et al., 1991, p. 25). From a public policy perspective, the NCCD researchers concluded:

> The Massachusetts approach appropriately balances the concerns of public safety with fiscal considerations. For example, if DYS adopted an incarceration policy similar to that of many states, this would require Massachusetts to spend an additional $11 million per year to build and operate nearly 510 secure beds. At best, this policy might result in a 2 percent reduction in youth arraignments in Massachusetts. The majority of offenses would be property offenses.
>
> (Austin et al., 1991, p. 25)

In the late 1970s, elected public officials in Utah embarked on a policy course designed to restrict the use of incarceration of juvenile offenders. One of the major components of this policy involved closing Utah's only large training school. In its place, policymakers and youth correction officials developed two small thirty-bed and one ten-bed high-security treatment units for violent and chronic offenders. They also developed a wide array of community-based programs for all other delinquent youth committed to the state.

The change in Utah's youth correction policy resulted in a 60 percent decline in the rate of juvenile incarceration between fiscal year 1982 and fiscal year 1988. Also, Utah was one of only twelve states whose institutional operating expenditures actually *declined* during that period

Table 8-2
U.S. Public Juvenile Training Schools & Expenditures per Eligible
Youth, by State[1], 1988

	Total Operating Expenditures[2]	Expenditures per Eligible Youth[3]
D.C.	$8,139,126	$157
Alaska	$6,611,090	$96
Rhode Island	$9,518,063	$95
Wyoming	$5,815,761	$91
Nevada	$7,836,430	$73
California	$180,396,323	$61
New York	$83,556,975	$61
Maine	$7,733,119	$57
Kansas	$15,251,526	$56
Montana	$5,144,909	$55
New Mexico	$9,171,509	$50
Connecticut	$11,826,246	$49
Oregon	$13,906,184	$47
New Hampshire	$5,159,520	$43
Delaware	$2,918,300	$41
Michigan	$37,693,089	$40
Ohio	$50,124,361	$40
Minnesota	$17,798,519	$38
Arizona	$14,122,690	$37
North Carolina	$19,825,604	$37
Louisiana	$16,782,055	$36
Tennessee	$20,205,016	$35
Washington	$17,412,122	$35
North Dakota	$2,556,621	$34
Illinois	$34,652,575	$31
Idaho	$3,887,706	$30
Indiana	$20,179,217	$30
Iowa	$9,584,397	$30
Maryland	$14,699,681	$30
New Jersey	$24,586,000	$30
Wisconsin	$16,619,292	$30
Georgia	$19,629,503	$29
Nebraska	$5,134,865	$29
Arkansas	$8,180,188	$28
Oklahoma	$8,887,672	$28
Virginia	$17,960,915	$28
South Carolina	$9,564,428	$26
Hawaii	$2,897,207	$25
South Dakota	$1,998,264	$25
Colorado	$8,342,282	$24
Kentucky	$10,033,597	$22
Texas	$36,694,223	$21

Table 8-2 continued

	Total Operating Expenditures[2]	Expenditures per Eligible Youth[3]
Pennsylvania	$24,321,454	$19
Mississippi	$6,204,212	$18
Missouri	$7,952,046	$16
Alabama	$7,768,893	$15
Utah	$2,920,869	$11
Massachusetts	$4,303,056	$9
West Virginia	$2,055,945	$9
Florida	$8,863,328	$8
Vermont	nr[4]	nr[4]
Total U.S.	$887,426,973	$35

Sources: Schwartz, Willis & Battle, 1991, pp. 30–31.

Notes: 1. States are in rank order, from the highest to lowest, by expenditure by youth.

2. Expenditures provided for the preceding calendar year, coinciding with the admission year 1988.

3. Calculated based on youth aged ten through the age of maximum original juvenile court jurisdiction, and the total operating expenses for each state and the District of Columbia.

4. Indicates no facilities reporting for indicated state and facility type for the census year.

(Schwartz, Willis & Battle, 1991). The NCCD evaluation of the Utah system concluded that "The recidivism data for [Utah Division of] Youth Corrections offenders strongly indicate that the imposition of appropriate community-based controls on highly active serious and chronic juvenile offenders does not compromise public protection" (Austin, Joe, Krisberg & Steele, 1990, p. 1).

More recently, officials in Maryland initiated steps to reform their youth correction system, resulting in a 36 percent reduction in the rates of juvenile incarceration (Schwartz, Willis & Battle, 1991). One important development was the closing of one of Maryland's two training schools and the reallocation of the bulk of that institution's operating expenditures to financing community-based programs (Butts & Streit, 1988).

Oklahoma reduced its rate of juvenile incarceration by more than 57 percent between fiscal year 1982 and fiscal year 1989. This was accompanied by a 49 percent decline in Oklahoma's institutional operating expenditures, the largest drop of any state during the decade (Schwartz, Willis & Battle, 1991).

Table 8-3
U.S. Public Juvenile Detention Centers: Expenditures per Eligible Youth, by State,[1] 1988

	Total Operating Expenditures[2]	Expenditures per Eligible Youth[3]
D.C.	$9,541,428	$183
Nevada	$7,153,570	$67
Alaska	$3,314,099	$48
California	$133,413,818	$45
Washington	$21,425,633	$43
Michigan	$31,324,060	$33
New Jersey	$23,101,167	$28
Florida	$32,894,454	$28
Vermont	$1,150,000	$26
Virginia	$15,950,812	$25
Georgia	$16,478,449	$24
Illinois	$23,131,724	$21
Ohio	$26,062,556	$21
Arizona	$7,180,555	$19
Delaware	$1,313,085	$18
New York	$23,654,090	$17
Connecticut	$3,985,648	$17
Pennsylvania	$21,026,667	$17
Utah	$4,132,621	$16
Maryland	$7,613,136	$16
Kansas	$3,810,406	$14
Missouri	$6,785,218	$14
Colorado	$4,644,021	$13
Minnesota	$5,976,418	$13
Texas	$22,585,113	$13
Hawaii	$1,339,352	$12
Louisiana	$5,618,515	$12
Oregon	$3,569,945	$12
Alabama	$5,473,193	$11
South Dakota	$907,126	$11
Massachusetts	$5,065,227	$10
Wisconsin	$5,478,885	$10
Indiana	$6,529,488	$10
New Mexico	$1,634,470	$9
North Carolina	$4,723,016	$9
Nebraska	$1,286,603	$7
Oklahoma	$2,265,878	$7
West Virginia	$1,715,284	$7
Kentucky	$2,864,625	$6
New Hampshire	$672,890	$6
Tennessee	$2,960,153	$5
Idaho	$471,043	$4

Table 8–3 continued

	Total Operating Expenditures[2]	Expenditures per Eligible Youth[3]
Iowa	$1,309,595	$4
North Dakota	$289,717	$4
Mississippi	$1,095,853	$3
Arkansas	$401,979	$1
South Carolina	$545,078	$1
Maine	nr[4]	nr[4]
Montana	nr[4]	nr[4]
Rhode Island	nr[4]	nr[4]
Wyoming	nr[4]	nr[4]
Total U.S.	$513,866,663	$20

Sources: Schwartz, Willis & Battle, 1991, pp. 28–29.

Notes: 1. States are in rank order, from the highest to lowest, by expenditure per youth.

2. Expenditures provided for the preceding calendar year, coinciding with the admissions year 1988.

3. Calculated based on the number of youth aged ten through the age of maximum original juvenile court jurisdiction, and the total operating expenditures for each state and the District of Columbia.

4. Indicates no facilities reporting for indicated state and facility type for the census year.

Juvenile Detention Centers

There were nearly 500,000 admissions to juvenile detention centers in 1989. As indicated in Table 8–4, there was slightly more than a 30 percent increase in the rate of admissions nationally during the 1980s. Thirty-five states reported increases in rates of admissions during this period, while only nine reported decreases. Four states reported increases in excess of 100 percent.

Despite the growth in both costs and admissions to juvenile detention centers, this subject has received remarkably little attention from policymakers, juvenile justice professionals, child advocates, and researchers. Juvenile detention centers should be carefully scrutinized because what research there is suggests the numbers of youth confined in these facilities can be substantially reduced without unduly jeopardizing the community (Schwartz, Barton & Orlando, 1991).

For example, in 1988 a project was implemented in Broward County (Ft. Lauderdale), Florida, designed to reduce the number of admissions to secure detention. When the project started, the detention center was under

Table 8-4
U.S. Public Juvenile Detention Centers: Detained Admissions[1] by State,[2] 1982 and 1988

	1982 Detained Admissions Rate[3]	1988 Detained Admissions Rate[3]	Percent change
D.C.	4,566	14,779	223.7%
North Carolina	422	985	133.7%
Alabama	546	1,192	118.4%
Connecticut	540	1,098	103.4%
Arkansas	408	705	73.1%
Arizona	2,061	3,255	58.0%
West Virginia	292	457	56.5%
New Jersey	1,015	1,539	51.6%
Tennessee	1,838	2,754	49.9%
Wisconsin	535	793	48.3%
Maryland	619	900	45.5%
Georgia	1,748	2,445	39.9%
Hawaii	1,941	2,671	37.6%
California	3,025	4,111	35.9%
Oklahoma	697	932	33.8%
Minnesota	947	1,264	33.5%
Iowa	586	772	31.7%
Michigan	983	1,253	27.4%
Texas	1,109	1,411	27.3%
Ohio	2,098	2,654	26.5%
Kansas	937	1,183	26.3%
South Dakota	1,697	2,142	26.3%
Florida	2,598	3,257	25.4%
New York	402	503	25.0%
Indiana	1,306	1,577	20.7%
Missouri	1,617	1,914	18.3%
Pennsylvania	847	994	17.4%
New Mexico	2,687	3,093	15.1%
Nebraska	926	1.062	14.7%
Mississippi	1,019	1,120	9.9%
Nevada	5,887	6,450	9.6%
Illinois	1,258	1,378	9.6%
Colorado	2,176	2,340	7.6%
Delaware	1,221	1,310	7.3%
Kentucky	550	578	5.0%
Virginia	1,583	1,602	1.2%
North Dakota	490	484	−1.2%
Oregon	2,211	2,129	−3.7%
Louisiana	729	670	−8.1%
Washington	3,267	2,974	−9.0%

Table 8–4 continued

	1982 Detained Admissions Rate[3]	1988 Detained Admissions Rate[3]	Percent change
Alaska	986	881	−10.7%
Idaho	594	518	−12.7%
Utah	2,710	2,145	−20.9%
South Carolina	308	243	−21.3%
Massachusetts	848	360	−57.5%
Montana	nr[4]	nr[4]	nr[4]
Maine	nr[4]	nr[4]	nr[4]
Rhode Island	nr[4]	nr[4]	nr[4]
New Hampshire	nr[4]	223	nr[4]
Vermont	nr[4]	473	nr[4]
Wyoming	nr[4]	nr[4]	nr[4]
Total U.S.	1,414	1,846	30.5%

Sources: Schwartz, Willis & Battle, 1991, pp. 14–15.

Notes: 1. Detained youth are those confined prior to their appearance in court or awaiting formal court disposition or placement.

2. States are in rank order by percent change, from highest increase to highest decrease.

3. Rates are based on the numbers of eligible youth per 100,00 aged ten through the age of maximum original juvenile court jurisdiction for each state and the District of Columbia.

4. Indicates that no youth were reported in the relevant category for the years listed above.

litigation because of unconstitutional conditions of confinement and other scandalous practices (Dale & Sanniti, 1991). With a capacity to house 109 juveniles, the average daily population in 1988 was 150.

The project started with an assessment of the detention center population. The assessment revealed that a large proportion of the confined juveniles were accused of minor and petty offenses and did not present a clear and substantial threat to the community (Van Vleet, Butts & Barton, 1988). The assessment served as a catalyst for bringing juvenile justice professionals in the county together to develop criteria for the use of secure detention, plans for upgrading existing community-based alternatives, and plans to create new services. This process resulted in restructuring the detention intake screening process, revitalizing an existing home detention program, creating a day report center operated by the Boys and Girls Clubs, and developing a small six-bed shelter program (Schwartz, Barton & Orlando, 1991).

The detention center population has declined steadily since the project began. Average daily population during the first eight months of 1991 was approximately seventy, almost forty below capacity. Initially, administrators in Florida's Department of Health and Rehabilitative Services (HRS) wanted to add thirty beds to the facility in order to alleviate overcrowding. These plans have been shelved. Also, according to HRS juvenile justice staff in Broward County, significant cost savings have been realized because of reduced expenditures for staff overtime, food, supplies, and so on.

On the day a census was taken in 1989, 50 percent of the juveniles confined in detention centers nationwide were housed in overcrowded facilities (Schwartz, Willis & Battle, 1991). That same census indicated that only about 42 percent of the youth (44 percent of the males and 23 percent of the females) were confined after having been accused of committing a Part 1 offense. These data suggest the experience in Broward County could be replicated in many jurisdictions throughout the country, reducing populations in overcrowded facilities before pressures mount to increase bed capacities.

Barriers to Reform

If local and state juvenile detention and training schools are prime targets for policy and fiscal reforms, why have they been essentially untouched by proponents of fiscal responsibility and cost effectiveness in government services? Why have they escaped the budget cutters' scalpels, particularly during difficult financial times?

Detention center and training school budgets make up a relatively small proportion of overall state and county budgets. As a result, they are often overlooked by officials trying to reconcile large budget deficits. Also, if forced to identify where budget cuts can be made, state and local youth correction administrators will usually identify savings realized primarily from community-based programs as the easiest and least "risky" programs to cut.

Juvenile justice officials advocating "get tough" measures as a strategy for responding to the juvenile crime problem are a potent political force. They often claim detention centers and training schools are essential in the fight against juvenile crime for keeping dangerous and violent young offenders off the streets. They also maintain that reducing the number of juveniles incarcerated by deinstitutionalizing them will jeopardize the community. These arguments are difficult to combat, particularly by budget officials, agency planning and policy analysts, staff aides to governors and county executives, and elected public officials who may not be familiar with the literature in the field or, for that matter, the characteristics and offender profiles of youth incarcerated in their systems. For example, studies completed on juveniles confined in training schools in various states generally reveal a large proportion of incarcerated youth to be nonserious and nonchronic offenders. Many are juveniles who could be managed in the community without compromising public safety and at considerably less cost (Van Vleet & Barton, 1991; Van Vleet & Butts, 1990; Van Vleet, Ortega & Willis, 1991; Van Vleet & Steketee, 1990).

Another barrier to change is that there is little, if any, political capital to be made by reforming detention and training school systems, particularly in comparison to the political benefits likely to accrue from reforming public education, health care, and services to the elderly. Few people seem to really care about institutions for delinquents and the young people who are confined in them. When juvenile institutions do receive the attention of officials it is generally because of scandals, media exposés, and class action lawsuits. Unlike children who are retarded, handicapped, or abused and neglected, juvenile delinquents do not have vocal and influential constituent advocate groups. Also, there is the obvious political risk for any politician who advocates reforms in the methods of dealing with juvenile offenders. He or she risks being labeled "soft on crime," a definite liability during these "get tough" times.

Policy Considerations

Fiscal problems in the states are likely to continue throughout this decade (Gold, 1991). While budget cuts, tax increases, or a combination of the two seem to be emerging as the primary solutions to such problems, policymakers should not lose sight of the opportunities for restructuring and reforming government services.

In particular, policymakers should look carefully at their state and local youth detention and training school systems. They will find these systems to be costly and ineffective in most instances. Policymakers interested in exploring other options and the potential for reform should consider the following:

1. *Commission a study of the juveniles who are incarcerated.* Comprehensive and objective assessments of juveniles confined in some detention centers and training schools have generally shown a large

proportion of the youth to be nonserious and nonchronic offenders, indicating that many, if not most, could be managed in the community without compromising public safety.

2. *Become familiar with the research on alternatives to the use of detention centers and training schools.* There are a number of juvenile justice research and policy institutes, and national associations such as the National Association of Counties, the National Criminal Justice Reference Service, the American Bar Association, the National Conference of State Legislatures, and the National Council on Crime and Delinquency, that provide important research findings, often at little or no cost. In addition, most colleges and universities have faculty with expertise in this area.

3. *Become familiar with experiences in reducing detention center and training school populations in other jurisdictions.* This includes learning about the political implications of trying to reform these systems. For example, training schools are often located in rural and semirural communities and may be one of the largest employers in the area. The downsizing or closing of such a facility could have a major adverse economic impact on the community and is likely to be resisted. Also, facilities where employees are unionized or constitute a significant political force might prove resistant to reform. These problems are not insurmountable and have been successfully addressed in various jurisdictions throughout the country. The experiences of those who have overcome these barriers could prove beneficial to those confronting similar situations.

4. *Explore the potential for redeploying existing resources.* While some additional funds may initially be needed to develop and strengthen alternative services, policymakers should make a concerted effort to try and shift institutional operating expenditures to cover costs for community-based programs.

Careful planning can help workers relocate to other state agencies, retire, or find new employment. Also, although not a common practice in the public sector, a buy-out of existing employees might be welcomed by state workers and prove to be less costly in the long run.

Discussion

The decade of the 1990s will be one of the most challenging periods in the history of our country. There are signs that the United States is rapidly losing its ability to compete in a global economy. Our systems for public education are not living up to expectations. The rates of child poverty are at an all-time high, and the rates of child maltreatment are at alarming levels. For the first time, the current generation of adults do not expect their children to have a better standard of living than they themselves have. Moreover, this is occurring at a time when resources are diminishing.

While the disparity between needs and resources will require large-scale restructuring at the policy level, elected public officials and other decision makers should not lose sight of the potential for overhauling state and local youth detention and correction systems. In fact, the time has probably never been better for making these systems more efficient and effective. The public is rightly concerned about the juvenile crime problem, but the public is also demanding that juvenile crime control funds be used wisely.

References

Austin, J., Elms, W., Krisberg, B., & Steele, P. A. (1991). *Unlocking juvenile corrections: Evaluating the Massachusetts Department of Youth Services.* San Francisco: National Council on Crime and Delinquency.

Austin, J., Joe, K., Krisberg, B., & Steele, P. A. (1990). *The impact of juvenile court sanctions: A court that works.* San Francisco: National Council on Crime and Delinquency.

Blanchard, J. L. (1989, February). *Building the Future: The Michigan Strategy.* (The Governor's Report to the People of Michigan and the Legislature). Lansing: Michigan Department of Management and Budget.

Butts, J. A., & Streit, S. M. (1988). *Youth correction reform: The Maryland and Florida experience.* Ann Arbor: Center for the Study of Youth Policy, University of Michigan.

Dale, M. J., & Sanniti, C. (1991, November) *Litigation as an instrument for change in juvenile detention: A case study.* Paper presented at the annual meeting of the American Society of Criminology, San Francisco, CA.

Eckl, C. L., Hutchison, A. M., & Snell, R. K. (1991). *State budget and tax actions 1991* (Legislative Finance Paper, preliminary data). Denver, CO: National Conference of State Legislatures.

Gold, S. D. (1991, May). *The state fiscal outlook and its implications for children's advocates.* Paper presented at Leadership Conference for the Association of Child Advocates, Racine, WI.

Lerman, P. (1991). Counting youth in trouble in institutions: Bringing the United States up to date. *Crime and Delinquency, 37,* 465–480.

Schwartz, I. M., Barton, W. H., & Orlando, F. (1991). Keeping kids out of secure detention. *Public Welfare,* Spring, 20–26, 46.

Schwartz, I. M., Willis, D. A., & Battle, J. (1991, December). *Juvenile arrest, detention, and incarceration trends: 1979–1989.* Ann Arbor: Center for the Study of Youth Policy, University of Michigan.

Van Vleet, R. K., & Barton, W. H. (1991, April). *A proposed classification system for determining learning center eligibility.* Ann Arbor: Center for the Study of Youth Policy, University of Michigan.

Van Vleet, R. K., & Butts, J. A. (1990, February). *Risk assessment of committed delinquents: Nebraska youth development centers.* Ann Arbor: Center for the Study of Youth Policy, University of Michigan.

Van Vleet, R. K., Butts, J. A., & Barton, W. H. (1988). *An analysis of the Broward County Juvenile Detention Center.* Ann Arbor: Center for the Study of Youth Policy, University of Michigan.

Van Vleet, R. K., Ortega, R. M., & Willis, D. A. (1991). *Secure care in Arizona: Developing and applying criteria for assessment.* Ann Arbor: Center for the Study of Youth Policy, University of Michigan.

Van Vleet, R. K., & Steketee, M. W. (1990, May). *Alternatives for Arkansas juvenile justice: Report and risk assessment, committed delinquents and youthful offenders, Arkansas Youth Service Centers and Tucker Unit, Department of Correction.* Ann Arbor: Center for the Study of Youth Policy, University of Michigan.

U.S. Department of Justice, Bureau of Justice Statistics and Office of Juvenile Justice and Delinquency Prevention. (1984). *Juvenile detention and correctional facility census, 1982–83.* (Computer file). Ann Arbor: MI: Interuniversity Consortium for Political and Social Research (Bureau of the Census, U.S. Department of Commerce).

U.S. Department of Justice, Bureau of Justice Statistics and Office of Juvenile Justice and Delinquency Prevention. (1990). *Juvenile detention and correctional facility census, 1988–89* (Computer file). Ann Arbor, MI: Interuniversity Consortium for Political and Social Research (Bureau of the Census, U.S. Department of Commerce).

9

Special Issues in Juvenile Justice: Gender, Race, and Ethnicity

Katherine Hunt Federle and Meda Chesney-Lind

I n 1974 Congress passed the Juvenile Justice and Delinquency Prevention Act (JJDPA). Hailed as a major impetus to reform, one of the act's
key provisions mandated diversion and deinstitutionalization of juvenile offenders. Ironically, the deinstitutionalization movement may have
spawned a tripartite system of juvenile justice that is racially and
gender-biased. Although white males appear to be the beneficiaries of
deinstitutionalization in the juvenile justice system, girls and children of
color have not experienced the same beneficial degree of alternative
placements in less-secure facilities.

Since girls have long been brought into the juvenile justice system for
noncriminal status offenses, it would be expected that they would be
among the JJDPA's greatest beneficiaries (particularly since the act
specifically sought diversion and deinstitutionalization of youths charged
with these offenses). But, as this chapter will demonstrate, the paternalism
that has long characterized the juvenile justice system is quite resilient. In
addition, there is evidence that instead of being *de*institutionalized, girls
have been *trans*institutionalized into mental health facilities for behaviors
labeled "inappropriate" since the early decades of the juvenile court.
Indeed, sexually and physically abused girls may find their self-protective
behaviors (like running away) criminalized, just as female status offenders
may be placed in child welfare facilities for their "protection."

The impact of the JJDPA on the experiences of young people of color
with the juvenile justice system has also been disappointing. In essence, the
paternalism that historically characterized the juvenile justice system (and
provided the logic for status offenses) was never extended to Afro-
Americans and other minority groups (Rafter, 1990). Instead, while white
boys were being released and girls were being transinstitutionalized,
minority youth were being warehoused in the public system of juvenile
institutions, although many of these children could have benefited from
the efforts to deinstitutionalize that characterized white experiences within

the juvenile justice system. Instead, deinstitutionalization may have inadvertently created bed space in secure facilities that was immediately filled by minority youths placed by a juvenile justice system that is "getting tough" on juvenile crime. Hence, minority youth are overrepresented in public institutions and underrepresented in the mental health system. Similarly, cultural insensitivity may increase child welfare placements for children of color, who experience longer stays and fewer adoptive placements.

In the pages that follow, we contend that three distinct patterns of institutionalization exist: one for girls, another for children of color, and yet a third for nonminority boys. We begin by analyzing the institutional experience of girls in the juvenile justice, mental health, and child welfare systems. The data suggest that deinstitutionalization of girls has had mixed success given the continued reliance on secure placements outside the juvenile justice system. This chapter then addresses the institutionalization of minorities, where a more complex pattern of cumulative bias emerges.

Gender and the Juvenile Justice, Mental Health, and Child Welfare Systems

Girls in the Juvenile Justice System

Since the establishment of the first juvenile court, bias against girls has haunted the juvenile justice system. Virtually all girls who appeared before these early juvenile courts were charged with immorality or waywardness (Chesney-Lind, 1971; Rafter, 1990; Shelden, 1981; Schlossman & Wallach, 1978), and court officials had little hesitation about incarcerating female youth "for their own protection" (Rogers, 1972). For example, in Chicago (where the first family court was founded), one-half of the girl delinquents but only one-fifth of the boy delinquents, were sent to reformatories between 1899–1909. In Milwaukee, during the same period, twice as many girls as boys were committed to training schools (Schlossman & Wallach, 1978, p. 72), and in Memphis, females were twice as likely as males to be committed to training schools between 1900–1917 (Shelden, 1981, p. 70). In Honolulu, during 1929–30 girls were nearly three times more likely to be sentenced to the training school (Chesney-Lind, 1971).

A key question, then, to all those concerned about this pattern is the degree to which it has been altered in recent years. Between 1888 and 1950 the percentage of girls incarcerated in juvenile correctional facilities grew from 19 percent to 34 percent. By 1980, this pattern appeared to have reversed: girls again made up 19 percent of those held in correctional facilities (Cahalan, 1986, p. 130). By 1989, girls accounted for 11.9 percent of all children held in public detention centers and training schools (Allen-Hagen, 1991, p. 4).

The decline in girls' incarceration in public facilities run by the juvenile justice system is directly linked to the deinstitutionalization reforms of the JJDPA. The act stressed the need to divert and deinstitutionalize youth charged with status offenses and provided states with a number of incentives to achieve this goal. Girls were the clear, but indirect, beneficiaries of this reform effort since status offenses have long comprised a far larger percentage of girls' than boys' arrests. In 1989, for example, two status offenses (runaways and curfew violations) comprised 23.3 percent of girls' arrests, but only 7.8 percent of boys' arrests. Over half (56 percent) of those arrested for running away are girls (Federal Bureau of Investigation, 1990, p. 181).

Despite this seemingly positive trend, girls continue to be institutionalized for minor offenses. The rest of this section will review the impact of deinstitutionalization on patterns of girls' and boys' incarceration. Discussions of girls in the mental health and child welfare systems—systems that have, to a degree, replaced the juvenile justice system in the control of wayward girls—follow.

Girls and Status Offenses. Critical to any understanding of the dynamics of gender bias in the juvenile justice and related systems is an appreciation of the gendered nature of delinquency, and particularly of status offenses. These offenses mask but perpetuate the court's historic and now implicit interest in monitoring girls' sexual activities and their obedience to parental authority (Chesney-Lind & Shelden, 1991; Gold, 1971, p. 571). Perhaps for this reason, status offenses still comprise a substantial proportion of all girls' arrests. Nor are all of these girls diverted from formal court processing despite more than a decade of diversion efforts. In 1985, for example, status offenses accounted for 35 percent of all girls' cases in juvenile courts, but only 9.9 percent of boys' cases (Snyder, Finnegan, Nimick, Sickmund, Sullivan, & Tierney, 1989, pp. 11, 31). Viewed another way, 85 percent of those charged with criminal offenses were male, but 43 percent of those charged with status offenses were female (Snyder et al., 1989, pp. 21, 41).

Youth charged with running away are far more likely than youth charged with other status offenses to be detained. In 1985, 34 percent of youth charged with running away from home were securely detained compared to 11 percent of those charged with liquor law violations and 10 percent of those charged with truancy. Detention is almost as common in charges of runaway as it is for more serious forms of delinquency, including offenses against the person, for which 38 percent of youth are detained (Snyder et al., 1989, pp. 33–57). Girls' problems with juvenile justice, then, are an outgrowth of the fact that they are arrested and referred for the sorts of status offenses, like running away from home, that involve high detention rates.

Other research suggests that regional variations also affect the quality of justice that girls experience. These regional variations reflect a pattern labeled by Feld as the interaction of "gender and geography" (Feld, 1991, p. 209; see also Sickmund, 1990). Like other researchers, he found evidence that girls referred to juvenile court in Minnesota were more likely than boys to be detained, particularly for minor and status offenses. But more to the point, he also found evidence that judicial paternalism was less marked in urban courts, which he characterized as more formal and procedural, than in suburban and rural courts. Specifically, he found that in the rural juvenile courts "larger proportions of females are removed from their homes for minor offenses" (Feld, 1991, p. 209). He also noted that these courts tended to deal with the smallest proportion of juveniles charged with serious criminal activity and the largest proportion charged with status offenses (Feld, 1991).

Girls in Institutions. Despite the legislative intentions of the JJDPA, there is considerable evidence that status offenders are still being brought into the system in large numbers, and that this pattern plays a major role in girls' experiences with juvenile justice. There is also evidence that the early gains of the deinstitutionalization movement are being eroded. Between 1975 and 1979 arrests of girls for status offenses declined by 33.6 percent for curfew arrests and 29.5 percent for runaway arrests. Even sharper declines were observed in boys' arrests for status offenses (a 34.5 percent decline in runaway arrests and a 41.4 percent decline in curfew arrests) for the interval 1975–1979 (Federal Bureau of Investigation, 1980, p. 193). Between 1980 and 1989, however, arrests of both girls and boys for these noncriminal offenses began to increase again. Girls' arrests for runaway, for example, increased by 3.34 percent, and female arrests for curfew increased by 17.2 percent (Federal Bureau of Investigation, 1990, p. 177).

More to the point, not all youth arrested for status offenses are diverted from detention and formal processing; indeed, a fair number do end up in detention. Girls made up 13.8 percent of those held in public detention centers on 15 February 1989. On this day, some 2,299 girls were held; sadly, this number represents a 29 percent increase over the number of girls held in detention a decade earlier (Bureau of Justice Statistics, 1989, p. 44).

In 1989 girls were also far more likely than boys to be detained for a status offense (i.e., running away from home, truancy, curfew violation); 15.1 percent of the girls, but only 2.9 percent of the boys, were detained for a status offense (Center for the Study of Youth Policy, 1991). It must be admitted, however, that the percentage of girls detained for status offenses has declined considerably from the period just prior to the passage of the JJDPA. In 1971, for example, 58.6 percent of the girls in detention were being held for status offenses (Schwartz, Steketee & Schneider, 1990). Other figures on public detention, though not quite so recent, show that the decline in detention of status offenders was far sharper for boys than for girls. Between 1975 and 1985, for example, the number of boys detained for status offenses dropped by 36 percent, while the percentage of girls dropped by only 19 percent. Other research has shown another disturbing trend with reference to the detention of status offenders. A thirteen-state study of cases processed in 1985 and 1986 revealed that youth charged with contempt of court were more likely to be detained than youth charged with any other type of offense: 55 percent of these youth were detained. By contrast, 30 percent of youth charged with personal offenses and 21 percent of youth charged with property offenses were detained (Snyder, 1990, p. 4). (See Figure 9–1.)

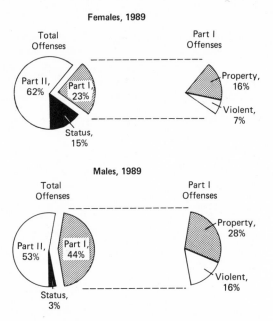

Figure 9–1. U.S. Public Detention Centers One-Day Counts by Offense and Gender

Source: Juvenile Detention and Correctional Census, 1988–1989. Analyzed by Center for the Study of Youth Policy, University of Michigan.

Turning to a consideration of youth in public training schools, Schwartz and his associates at the Center for Study of Youth Policy (1991) found that girls made up 9.6 percent of those in training schools in 1989. The total number of girls in training schools has actually dropped some 11 percent since 1979 (Bureau of Justice Statistics, 1989, p. 45; Center for the Study of Youth Policy, 1991). The offenses for which girls are placed in training schools have also shifted substantially. In 1971 fully 71.2 percent of the girls but only 22.7 percent of the boys in the nation's training schools were incarcerated for status offenses; by 1989, 12.5 percent of the girls, but less than 1 percent of the boys were being held for these offenses. In their analysis, Schwartz and his associates found that girls were being held for less serious offenses than boys. Basically, only one-third (35.3 percent) of the girls but about half of the boys (49.6 percent) were being held for Part 1 offenses; by contrast, over half of the girls were being held for Part 2 offenses (Schwartz et al., 1990, p. 20). (See Figure 9–2.)

In essence, the number of girls held in public facilities, after declining by 40.1 percent in the period between 1974 and 1979, has actually started to rise again (Allen-Hagen, 1991; Flanagan & McGarrell, 1986, p. 517;

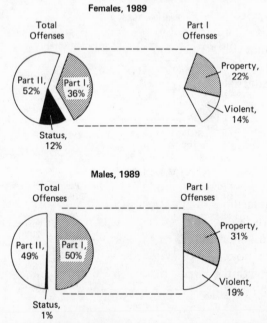

Figure 9–2. U.S. Public Training Schools One-Day Counts by Offense and Gender

Source: Juvenile Detention and Correctional Census, 1988–1989. Analyzed by Center for the Study of Youth Policy, University of Michigan.

Jamieson & Flanagan, 1987, p. 390). A census taken in 1989 showed that there were 56,123 youths held in 1100 public juvenile facilities (a category that includes most detention centers and training schools run by juvenile justice systems) on the day the count was taken, about 6,680 of these youth, or 11.9 percent, were girls. The number of girls held represented a slight increase over 1983, when an average of 6,519 girls were held (Allen-Hagen, 1991). This figure also represents a considerable increase (10 percent) over the number of girls held on any given day in public facilities in 1979.

In general, these figures show that the increase in girls' presence in public juvenile facilities since the late 1970s is largely explained by an increase in the number of girls in public detention centers. The data also seem to indicate that girls are detained and committed for different and less serious offenses than boys.

Much the same pattern can be found when examining youth held in adult jails. In 1989, of the 53,944 juvenile admissions to adult jails, 8,700, or 16.1 percent, of these admissions were girls (Bureau of Justice Statistics, 1990, p. 2). A review of youth found in adult jails in Minnesota during 1985 reveals that girls represented 20 percent of the total population (Schwartz, Harris & Levi, 1988, p. 5). Over one-third of these girls (35.3 percent) were jailed for status offenses, compared to only 13.8 percent of the boys held. By contrast, only 1.6 percent of the girls were incarcerated for violent crimes compared to 3.7 percent of the boys. Most of the males (35.8 percent) were charged with property crimes.

Any slight decline in use of public facilities for girls, however, has likely been offset by the increase in private placements. In 1985 some 10,236 girls, or 30 percent of the total population, were placed in private facilities (Bureau of Justice Statistics, 1989). The number of girls in these facilities had increased by 25.1 percent from 1979 (Flanagan & McGarrell, 1986), although the male population increased by only 16.2 percent (Bureau of Justice Statistics, 1989, p. 43) during the same period. By 1989, over half of all girls held in facilities of any sort were held in private facilities. The vast majority of girls (85 percent) are being held for "nondelinquent" offenses including status offenses, dependency, and neglect, and as "voluntary" admissions; for boys, only slightly over half (57.5 percent) are held for these reasons, with the rest being held for criminal offenses (Jamieson & Flanagan, 1989, p. 596).

Confinement in a private facility, however, does not necessarily indicate a less restrictive placement. A census of both public and private facilities taken during 1985 reveals a sharp increase in the number of private facilities but far less of an increase in the number of public facilities. The majority of public facilities were classified as having an "institutional" environment (high degree of security and lack of direct access by residents to community resources), while most private facilities were classified as having an "open" environment (low degree of security and more direct access to local community resources). However, there has been an increase in the number of private facilities that are institutional rather than open in environment. For example, in 1979 only 18.7 percent of short-term private facilities were institutional; by 1985, the percentage had increased to 25.3 percent. (U.S. Department of Justice, 1989, pp. 40–41).

Moreover, major ethnic differences characterize the populations of girls housed at private and public facilities. In 1987 whites constituted 44 percent of those held in public facilities but 63 percent of those held in private facilities (Jamieson & Flanagan, 1989, p. 595). Between 1979 and 1982 the incarceration rate of white girls increased by 14 percent, while the rate for Hispanic and African-American girls increased by 29 percent. Moreover, the African-American incarceration rate in 1982 was more than double the rate for white girls (Krisberg, Schwartz, Fishman, Eisikovits & Guttman, 1987, p. 16) despite a decline in offense rates for African-American girls (Laub & McDermott, 1985). Deinstitutionalization, therefore, may be working better for white than for nonwhite girls.

Deinstitutionalization and Gender Bias. The sluggish pace of deinstitutionalization efforts in the last decade and the indirect evidence that some status offenders, rather than being released, are simply being shifted to private institutions, suggest a tremendous and high-level resistance to the notion that youth who have not committed any criminal act should not be held in institutions. Court officials, for example, have always been extremely critical of deinstitutionalization (see Schwartz, 1989). A 1978 General Accounting Office (GAO) report concluded that the Law Enforcement Assistance Administration (LEAA), the agency given the task of implementing the JJDPA legislation, was less than enthusiastic about the deinstitutionalization provisions of the act. After reviewing LEAA's efforts to remove status offenders from secure facilities, the GEO report concluded that during certain administrations LEAA had actually "downplayed its importance and to some extent discouraged states from carrying out the Federal requirement" (General Accounting Office, 1978, p. 10). The GAO report found that monitoring systems to assess states' compliance with the law were lax or nonexistent (only nine states had what the GAO thought were complete data), definitions of what constituted detention and correctional facilities were confused (children in jail, for example, were frequently not counted), and LEAA was apparently reluctant to take action against states that had taken federal monies while failing to deinstitutionalize status offenders.

Just how deep the antideinstitutionalization sentiment was among juvenile justice officials became clear during the U.S. House of Representatives hearings on the extension of the act in March 1980. Judge John R. Milligan, representing the National Council of Juvenile and Family Court Judges, argued that the "effect of the Juvenile Justice Act as it now exists is to allow a child ultimately to decide for himself whether he will go to school, whether he will live at home, whether he will continue to run, run, run, away from home, or whether he will even obey orders of your court" (United States House of Representatives, 1980, p. 136). Ultimately, the judges were successful in narrowing the definition of a status offender in the amended act so that any child who had violated a "valid court order" would no longer be covered under the deinstitutionalization provisions (United States Statutes at Large, 1981). This change, which was never publicly debated in Congress, effectively gutted the act. Judges also engaged in other, less-public, efforts to "circumvent" deinstitutionalization by issuing criminal contempt citations to elevate status offenders into law violators, referring or committing status offenders to secure mental health facilities, and developing "semisecure" facilities (Costello & Worthington, 1981–82, p. 42).

The use of the court's contempt power has clearly disadvantaged female status offenders. A recent study in Florida, which reviewed 162,012 cases referred to juvenile justice intake units during the years 1985–87, found that female offenders referred for contempt were more likely than females referred for other delinquent offenses to be petitioned to court, and substantially more likely to be petitioned to court than males referred for contempt (Bishop & Frazier, 1990). Moreover, girls were far more likely than boys to be sentenced to detention. Specifically, the typical female offender in this study had a 4.3 percent probability of incarceration, which increased to 29.95 percent if she were held in contempt; such a pattern was not observed among males in the study. The authors concluded that "the traditional double standard is still operative. Clearly neither the cultural changes associated with the feminist movement nor the legal changes illustrated in the JJDP Act's mandate to deinstitutionalize status offenders have brought about equality under the law for young men and women" (Bishop & Frazier, 1990, p. 22).

Deinstitutionalization or Transinstitutionalization?
Girls and the Mental Health System

Despite considerable resistance, incarceration of young women in public training schools and detention centers across the country fell dramatically after the passage of the JJDPA. But detention rates for girls have been increasing again in recent years. Simultaneously, the placement of girls in private facilities has also been increasing. This suggests that the official response to deinstitutionalization has been to shift girls from public juvenile justice institutions to private mental health facilities. Using records of juveniles institutionalized in mental health and chemical dependency systems in Minnesota, Schwartz, Jackson-Beeck, and Anderson (1984) report an increasing number of youth placed in what they call a "hidden" private juvenile correctional system. These incarcerations, estimated to be about 60 percent female, are considered voluntary because the girls are minors, even though they may object to the placement. The cost of institutionalization is provided by third-party health care insurance plans.

The existence of a procedure considered voluntary, irrespective of the consent of the minor involved, has significant implications for the institutionalization of girls. In 1979 the United States Supreme Court held that a parent's decision to commit a child to a mental health facility over the child's objections did not violate the child's due process rights (*Parham v. J.R.*, 442 U.S. 584 [1979]). Perhaps as a consequence of both the Supreme Court's decision and the partial success of deinstitutionalization within the juvenile justice system, many private hospitals, whose profits are enhanced by filling beds, advise institutional care for "troublesome" youth (Weithorn, 1988, p. 786). The definition of "troublesome" is necessarily vague. Intake criteria at some facilities, for example, suggest "sexual promiscuity" is an example of a "self-defeating" or "self-destructive" behavior necessitating "immediate acute-care hospitalization [as] the only reasonable intervention" (Weithorn, 1988, p. 786).

Given this sort of vague language and the problems that public systems of control have had with sexist interpretations of status offense labels, a number of the examples of egregious abuse of institutionalization involve girls. Some of these cases make the link between status offenses and these incarcerations directly. The case of "Sheila," for example, involved a twelve-year-old girl who was hospitalized in a state psychiatric facility after spending a week in a juvenile detention center on the basis that she was a "child in need of supervision." In another case, "Lisa," a sixteen-year-old girl, was admitted into a private psychiatric hospital because she " 'seduced' older men, drank vodka, skipped school, ran away from home, and disobeyed her divorced mother" (Weithorn, 1988, p. 790). In essence, though the data are far from complete, girls, particularly white girls, are incarcerated in private psychiatric hospitals for the same behaviors that, in previous decades, placed them in public institutions.

Data on admissions to mental health facilities suggest that voluntary commitments may affect girls more than boys. Of these types of commitments, 23.1 percent of girls' admissions were voluntary compared to less than 17 percent of boys' admissions. Obviously, many of these commitments were made without the consent of the minors involved; indeed, the vast majority were not labeled as "self-admitted," but were identified as "referred" admissions (Jamieson & Flanagan, 1989, p. 56). It is estimated that fewer than one-third of all juveniles admitted for inpatient mental health treatment were diagnosed as having severe or acute mental disorders in contrast to between one-half and two-thirds of adults admitted to these sorts of facilities (Weithorn, 1988, pp. 788–789). Despite their lack of major mental disorders, juvenile psychiatric patients remain in the hospital approximately twice as long as adults (Weithorn, 1988, p. 789). Finally, adolescent admissions to psychiatric units of private hospitals have jumped dramatically, increasing fourfold between 1980 and 1984 (Weithorn, 1988, p. 773). There has also been a marked shift in the pattern of juvenile mental health incarceration. In 1971 juvenile admissions to private hospitals accounted for 37 percent of all juvenile admissions, but by 1980 this figure had risen to 61 percent (Weithorn, 1988, p. 783).

Girls in the Child Welfare System

Many girls end up in the juvenile justice and mental health systems because of problems that are actually expressions of difficulties within the family, such as child neglect and physical and sexual abuse. According to a national study of girls in juvenile correctional settings conducted by the American Correctional Association in 1988, a very large proportion (61.2 percent) of these girls had experienced physical abuse, with nearly half reporting that they had been abused eleven times or more. Many girls had reported the abuse, but most said that either nothing had changed (29.9 percent) or that the reporting made things worse (25.3 percent). Nearly as many girls (54.3 percent) had experienced repeated instances of sexual abuse; one-third reported that such abuse had happened between three and ten times, and 27.4% reported that it happened eleven times or more. Again, while most (68.1 percent) reported the abuse, reporting tended to result in no change or to worsen the situation.

Given this history, it should be no surprise that the vast majority of girls (80.7 percent) had run away from home, and, of those that had run away, 39 percent had run ten or more times. Over half (53.8 percent) said they had attempted suicide, and when asked the reason they said it was because they "felt no one cared." What might be called a survival or coping strategy seems to have been criminalized; girls in correctional establishments reported their first arrests were typically for running away from home (20.5 percent) or for larceny theft (25.5 percent). The offenses for which they are currently incarcerated were more varied, but the most significant offenses were probation/parole violation (14.6 percent), aggravated assault (9.5 percent), larceny theft (9.0 percent), and runaway (6.5 percent). The large number of girls incarcerated for probation and parole violations is possibly a measure of new efforts to bootstrap status offenders into delinquents by incarcerating them for these offenses (American Correctional Association, 1990, p. 68).

Given the backgrounds of these girls, early assistance and perhaps placement in noninstitutional settings such as foster homes seem more appropriate than diversion into the juvenile justice system. While this is clearly the case, even these traditional alternatives are fraught with problems. Foster homes, for example, have long been held out as a form of residential treatment that allows young people to grow up in a familylike setting. But at least one study determined that youth placed in such settings were involved in significantly more criminal behavior than youth who were not placed in foster homes (McCord, McCord & Thurber, 1968). Other studies suggest that girls experience a high rate of sexual abuse in foster home placements (Glave, 1987; Prescott, 1981). U.S. Representative George Miller commented that "we are in the situation now where we are underwriting a system of abuse. Amnesty International ought to take a look at these kids" (quoted in Sullivan, 1988, p. B3).

Juvenile justice officials, however, may use child welfare placements to securely detain girls who otherwise would be released from the juvenile justice system. Girls referred to the Division of Youth Services in New Jersey, for example, are often placed in a "structured environment" for "their own good" (Feinman, 1985, p. 50). Feinman's research indicated that girls were more likely than boys to have parents sign a complaint warrant against them. Further, youth "placed" in residential or foster homes have little or no legal protection and may actually spend a longer time in their settings than youth charged with crimes (Feinman, 1985, p. 50). Thus, girls experience two forms of transinstitutionalization: first, girls who are escaping abusive home environments may be placed in juvenile justice facilities; second, female status offenders may be institutionalized by child welfare workers.

Summary

Deinstitutionalization has affected boys and girls differently. There are indications that a "relabeling" of female behaviors has occurred, in part to avoid the mandate of deinstitutionalization, resulting in incarceration of large numbers of girls in facilities that are clearly not meeting their needs for offenses that are far less serious than those committed by male counterparts. Even where progress appears to have been made, as is the case with decreases in commitments of girls to public training schools, the situation requires monitoring. Evidence is mounting that the mental health and child welfare systems are engaging in the same double standard of treatment and justice that once haunted the juvenile justice system. The fact that many commitments to private institutions are still being made, explicitly or implicitly, "for her own protection," is testimony to the durability of the sexual double standard in the incarceration of girls.

Race and Ethnicity and the Juvenile Justice, Mental Health, and Child Welfare Systems

Race and Ethnicity and the Juvenile Justice System

In many ways, the treatment of girls in the juvenile justice system is an experience shared by children of color. Deinstitutionalization did not bring the promised reduction in secure placements for either girls or minorities; rather, these reforms may actually have increased the rates of incarceration experienced by these children. But in other important ways the institutionalization of minorities differs from that of girls. These differences are attributable to underlying but pervasive beliefs, that, in the case of girls, can only be described as paternalism. For children of color, that implicit determinant is racism.

The deinstitutionalization reforms of the JJDPA had little positive impact on the incarceration of minority youth. Of course, few observers expected deinstitutionalization to benefit minority children because, historically, whites have comprised the overwhelming majority of all children arrested for status offenses (see Cahalan, 1986). Even after passage of the act, most children arrested for status offenses continued to be white. In 1978, for example, whites constituted 74.6 percent of curfew and loitering arrests and 85.9 percent of runaway arrests (Hindelang, Gottfredson, & Flanagan, 1981, p. 346). By 1989, although the percentage of white arrests had declined to 72.8 percent for curfew violations and 81.1 percent for running away (Federal Bureau of Investigation, 1990, p. 191), the arrest rate for status offenses was still significantly higher among nonminority youth.

Ironically, the number of minority youths arrested for nondelinquency reasons has actually increased. In 1978 206,518 white children and 28,363 African-American children were arrested for status offense violations (Hindelang et al., 1981, p. 346). By 1989, the number of white children arrested for these offenses declined to 152,385, a 26 percent *decrease* since 1978. During this same period African-American youth arrests rose to 36,147, a 27 percent *increase* (Federal Bureau of Investigation, 1990, p. 191). The most dramatic change, however, occurred in the arrest rates for white runaways, which declined by 29 percent between 1978 and 1989 (Federal Bureau of Investigation, 1990; Hindelang et al., 1981).

Although it has met with mixed success, particularly for girls, the deinstitutionalization movement did reduce the number of children incarcerated for nondelinquency offenses. Between 1977 and 1987 the percentage of youths held in public detention centers for status offenses declined from 1.7 percent to 5.6 percent (Steketee, Willis & Schwartz, 1989, p. 39). In this same period, the number of status offenders in public training schools dropped from 8.8 percent of the total incarcerated population to 2.2 percent (Steketee et al., 1989, p. 39). Of course, if white children (and, more specifically, white boys) have benefitted from deinstitutionalization, then an increase in the percentage of incarcerated minority youth is to be expected. But since the passage of the JJDPA, there has been a significant increase in the number of institutionalized minorities that cannot be explained solely by the deinstitutionalization of white status offenders.

The most dramatic increases in minority populations have been recorded in public juvenile correctional facilities. In 1977 57 percent of all youth in public detention centers were white, 29.9 percent were African-American, 11.2 percent were Hispanic, and 1.7 percent were either Native American or Asian. By 1987, however, the figure for whites had declined to 44.1 percent; minority youths, most of whom were African-American, comprised more than 55 percent of the total population (Steketee et al., 1989, p. 47). A similar shift in the demographic composition of children in public training schools also occurred in this same ten-year period. Minority admissions grew from 46.7 percent in 1977 to 56.3 percent in 1987, an increase attributable to a higher rate of admission for African-American and Hispanic youths. Incredibly, the Hispanic population in training schools actually doubled between 1977 and 1987 (Steketee et al., 1989, p. 48).

The most recent figures for children held in public juvenile facilities indicate that minority admissions continue to outpace those of nonminority youth. In 1989 60 percent of all institutionalized juveniles were minorities, of whom 70 percent were African-American (Allen-Hagen, 1991). Between 1987 and 1989 African-American admissions swelled by 14 percent, Hispanic admissions increased by 10 percent, and other minorities' admissions grew by 5 percent (Allen-Hagen, 1991). During this same period, however, the percentage of white youths in custody actually declined by 5 percent (Allen-Hagen, 1991). The total number of white youth incarcerated in public juvenile facilities also decreased, from 23,375 in 1987 to 22,201 in 1989 (Allen-Hagen, 1991).

These figures are even more dramatic when the number of institution-alized minorities is compared to total ethnic youth populations. Based on 1980 census data for total youth population figures, 154.8 of every 100,000 white males were institutionalized in a public juvenile correctional facility in 1979 (Krisberg et al., 1987, p. 185). For that same period, the rate of institutionalization for Hispanic males was two times greater, and for African-American males it was almost four times greater than the rate for white males (Krisberg et al., 1987, p. 185). By 1982, using population estimates, the institutionalization rate for African-American males had increased an additional 38 percent, whereas the rate for whites had increased by only 18 percent (Krisberg et al., 1987, p. 185). In that same year, Hispanic males also had a much higher rate of institutionalization (480.8 per 100,000) than their white counterparts (183.3 per 100,000) (Krisberg et al., 1987, pp. 185–186).

The institutionalization of minority children in adult jails also differs from that of white youth. In 1984 adult jails reported an average daily juvenile population of 1,482; by 1989, that number had increased to 2,250 (Flanagan & Maguire, 1990, p. 571). Curiously, the racial composition of those children held in adult jails is not reported although this information is requested by the Department of Justice in its annual jail survey (Flanagan & Maguire, 1990, p. 12). At least one study, however, suggests that the experience of minority children in adult jails differs markedly from that of their white counterparts (Schwartz et al., 1988). A survey of jails in the state of Minnesota revealed that minority youth were more likely to be detained for property and violent offenses (Schwartz et al., 1988, p. 142), and were held for longer periods of time than white children (Schwartz et al., 1988, pp. 143–144). Interestingly, a greater proportion of white youths were held for status offenses (Schwartz et al., 1988, p. 142).

Unfortunately, the obvious explanation for the increasing rate of institutionalization among children of color—that minority youth commit more serious delinquent acts than whites—is not supported by the available data. Arrest rates for serious crimes among white and minority youth in the past decade have been quite stable (for the years 1978 through 1989, see Hindelang et al., 1981; Flanagan, van Alstyne & Gottfredson, 1982; Flanagan & McLeod, 1983; Brown, Flanagan & McLeod, 1984; McGarrell & Flanagan, 1985; Flanagan & McGarrell, 1986; Jamieson & Flanagan, 1989; Flanagan & Maguire, 1990). In 1978 white youth accounted for 66.6 percent of all arrests for homicide, forcible rape, robbery, aggravated assault, burglary, theft, arson, and motor vehicle theft. Arrests of African-American youth for these same offenses constituted only 30.4 percent of the total (Hindelang et al., 1981, p. 346). By 1989, although minorities constituted 60 percent of all institutionalized youth in public facilities, the African-American share of these arrests had risen by only 0.1 percent to 30.5 percent (Federal Bureau of Investigation, 1990, p. 191).

Even by isolating the violent crime rate of minority youth, we find no persuasive explanation for the increasing rate of institutionalization among children of color. When only the most serious violent crimes are considered, more African-American youths are arrested than their white counterparts. In 1978 African-American youths were arrested for 52 percent of all murders, forcible rapes, robberies, and aggravated assaults committed by juveniles (Hindelang et al., 1981, p. 346). That rate, however, has remained stable over a ten-year period, increasing only 0.9 percent in 1988 (Jamieson & Flanagan, 1989, p. 431). Arrests of white youth have actually increased in this same ten-year period by 1.1 percent to 45.5 percent (cf. Hindelang et al., 1981, p. 346, with Flanagan & Maguire, 1990, p. 431). Interestingly, only 15 percent of the youth incarcerated in public juvenile facilities in 1989 were held for the most serious violent crimes (Allen-Hagen, 1991).

The Office of Juvenile Justice and Delinquency Prevention (OJJDP) has suggested that the increasing detention of minority youths is attributable to the increase in referrals for drug law violations and the probability that nonwhites are more likely to be detained than their white counterparts (Snyder, 1990). The data do show a dramatic increase in the arrest rate of minority youth for drug-related offenses. In 1978 only 11.9 percent of all drug arrests were attributable to African-American youths (Hindelang et al., 1981, p. 346). By 1989, however, the arrest rate for African-American children had climbed to an astonishing 48.5 percent (Federal Bureau of Investigation, 1990, p. 191). The number of white youths arrested for these offenses sharply declined from 86.2 percent in 1978 (Hindelang et al., 1981, p. 346) to 50.5 percent in 1989 (Federal Bureau of Investigation, 1990, p. 191).

The percentage of juveniles actually institutionalized for drug-related offenses, however, is quite small. Of the 49,322 youths incarcerated in public facilities in 1985, only 2,660, or 7.78 percent, were institutionalized for drug and alcohol offenses (Allen-Hagen, 1991). If only those youths incarcerated for delinquent acts are included, drug and alcohol offenses constitute a mere 5.77 percent of the institutionalized population (Allen-Hagen, 1991). In 1989 drug and alcohol offenders accounted for 11.73

percent (6,586 individuals) of the entire institutionalized population and 12.42 percent of the incarcerated delinquent population (Allen-Hagen, 1991). Notably, the detention data did not differentiate between alcohol and drug offenders, a significant distinction because white youths have accounted for over 90 percent of all alcohol arrests in the last ten years (Hindelang et al., 1981; Federal Bureau of Investigation, 1990).

A stable, but higher, rate of arrest for violent crime, coupled with an increasing arrest rate for drug violations, may justify some slight increase in the incarceration rates for minority youth, but cannot explain why minority populations exceed those of nonminority youth in juvenile facilities. Self-reported delinquency rates reveal no significant differences that would explain the arrest and incarceration rates for minority youth (Huizinga & Elliott, 1987). Several studies, including the previously mentioned OJJDP report, have suggested that institutionalized racism may account for these differences. For example, African-American youths are more likely to be questioned on the street by law enforcement officials (Kowalski & Rickicki, 1982) and to receive differential treatment and processing than that accorded nonminority juveniles (Pope & Feyerham, 1989). African-American youths are detained more often than their white counterparts arrested for similar offenses (Frazier & Cochran, 1986), and these detained youth receive more severe dispositions after adjudication (Bortner & Reed, 1985). In any event, African-American youth receive the most severe dispositions (Marshall & Thomas, 1983). There is a strong suggestion that the cumulative effects of racial bias at various stages of a juvenile proceeding may account for these differences (Pope & Feyerham, 1989).

Despite evidence of racial bias in the treatment of minority youth in the juvenile justice system, many studies have found no suggestion of racial discrimination (Pope & Feyerham, 1989). Historically, many of the studies reporting racial bias have been criticized for their methodological short-comings, while those studies that have found no evidence of racial discrimination have not been subject to the same methodological scrutiny and critique (Pope & Feyerham, 1989). More recent studies have attempted to correct the errors of previous researchers; while some find continuing racial bias, others report inconclusive results (Pope & Feyerham, 1989). Many of those studies that report no effect for race, however, rely on control variables that themselves reflect significant differences between races without addressing their appropriateness. Additionally, those reporting no significant racial effects rely on an analysis of multiple jurisdictions that has a tendency to mask the impact of race in the juvenile justice system (Pope & Feyerham, 1989).

But it is becoming more difficult to ignore the patterns of institutionalization in private juvenile facilities, patterns that strongly suggest racially preferential placement policies. In 1979 21,650 of the children placed in private facilities (75 percent) were white. Admittedly, this figure may be slightly inaccurate because many children of Hispanic origin were included in the white category (Hindelang et al., 1981, p. 481). But the 1979 data do indicate that at least 1,906 of the children institutionalized in private juvenile facilities were Hispanic and 5,843 were African-American (Hindelang et al., 1981, p. 481). Unlike the pattern in public juvenile facilities, however, white non-hispanic youths still comprised a majority (63 percent) of the youths institutionalized in private facilities by 1987 (Flanagan & Maguire, 1990, p. 563). The actual number of white youths institutionalized in private facilities also increased to 24,202 between 1979 and 1987, although the African-American population doubled to 10,182. The Hispanic population remained fairly stable at 2,812 (Flanagan & Maguire, 1990, p. 563).

Clearly, researchers need to determine if racial bias is a significant factor in the arrest, disposition, and placement of minority youths in ever-increasing numbers. Researchers need to pay particular attention to the cumulative effects of racial bias in a process involving multiple decision makers, including law enforcement and correctional officials, because race as a factor may appear significant only as the child moves through the juvenile justice process. Geographic differences and urbanism also may show marked racial effects that may be lost when data is combined across jurisdictions (Pope & Feyerham, 1989). Additionally, little is known about differential treatment of certain minority groups. Most researchers, for example, have focused almost exclusively on the experience of African-American youths in the juvenile justice system but have essentially ignored other minorities, such as Hispanics and Native Americans, for whom race and ethnicity may be significant factors (Pope & Feyerham, 1989).

Data on juvenile populations in public and private facilities strongly suggest that children of color are being warehoused while their white counterparts are benefiting from community and private placements. We therefore need to consider programmatic alternatives and community-based services specifically designed for minority youth. In part, the public sector's increased reliance on the purchase of private services has reduced the funds available for state facilities and programs (Stehno, 1982). Thus, once adjudicated, children of color must be given the same access to private-sector programs, or the state must develop its own community-based alternatives. Juvenile facilities also need to create and develop programs specifically designed to meet the needs of an ever-increasing minority population.

Without more information about racially motivated processing of juveniles, however, legal challenges to the juvenile justice system based on equal protection or due process claims are unlikely to reduce the numbers of minority youth adjudicated in juvenile courts. A minority youth can be tried and adjudicated even though his arrest might have been racially motivated, as long as there was probable cause to support the arrest (*Carroll v. United States,* 267 U.S. 132, [1925]). The absence of probable cause, however, does not require dismissal of that case (*Ker v. Illinois,* 119 U.S. 436, [1886]). Further, a court need not consider discriminatory handling of the juvenile when making the adjudication decision, but simply must ascertain that the government has proven its case beyond a reasonable doubt (*In re Winship,* 397 U.S. 358, [1970]). Within the context of due process, a minority youth has no recourse to set aside the adjudication if he has been accorded certain procedural protections like a fair hearing, counsel, a chance to be heard, and an opportunity to present and examine witnesses (*In re Gault,* 387 U.S. 1 [1967]). The mere fact that the juvenile has been treated differently because of his race prior to the trial will not provide sufficient grounds to set aside the adjudication.

Ironically, the closed nature of the juvenile court prevents a thorough assessment of juvenile proceedings. Some commentators suggest that legal standards are applied differently within the juvenile justice system. A study conducted by the New York State Bar Association in 1984 concluded that an overwhelming number of lawyers failed to provide adequate representation to their clients (Moss, 1987, p. 29). A majority of the attorneys surveyed defined their roles in terms of assisting the courts rather than in zealously defending their clients' legal interests (Moss, 1989, p. 29). Others have suggested that juvenile court judges do not stringently apply the burden of proof required for an adjudication, preferring to keep the youth in the system because they believe that further intervention will assist the child (Guggenheim, 1986, p. 20). Obviously, this type of interventionism works to the disadvantage of minority youth who may be seen to need greater services because of their poverty (Stehno, 1990).

Of course, institutionalization practices and conditions may themselves be challenged in the courts. In the last fifteen years, there has been a virtual "explosion" in civil rights litigation (Soler et al., 1990, pp. 1–2). Many child advocates have found the provisions of the Civil Rights Act and the procedural advantages of class action litigation to be particularly effective when attempting to remedy the conditions and practices of confinement for children (Soler et al., 1990). However, there are many disadvantages to litigation: it is expensive, time-consuming, and uncertain (Soler et al., 1990, pp. 1–5). But at least access to the courts provides an opportunity to correct the racial discrepancies in the institutionalization of juveniles.

Race and Ethnicity and the Child Welfare System

The same patterns of overinstitutionalization in the juvenile justice process emerge in the child welfare system. In 1977 white children comprised 62.2 percent, and minority children 37.9 percent, of all validated reports of child abuse and neglect (American Humane Association, 1977). African-American children were by far the largest minority group in this population, with 19.4 percent of all validated reports (American Humane Association, 1977). By 1985, 65.5 percent of all validated reports of child abuse and neglect involved white children, but, because white children constituted 81 percent of the total youth population in 1985, they were underrepresented in the reporting data (American Humane Association, 1986, pp. 20–21). The percentage of minority children involved declined slightly to 34.5 percent in 1985; however, reports involving African-American children increased slightly to 20.5 percent (American Humane Association, 1986, p. 20).

Although the number of validated reports of child abuse and neglect among children of color has remained constant, minority children are grossly overrepresented in child welfare placements. In 1988 the percentage of minority children in the child welfare system had risen to almost 50 percent, a figure three times greater than that for the total population of minority children (Stehno, 1990, p. 552). In some states and urban areas, minority children constituted a majority of all children in care (Stehno, 1990, p. 552). The data also suggest regional variations that affect patterns of minority involvement with child welfare systems; major urban areas, for example, have a very high percentage of minority children in care (Stehno, 1990, p. 552). The ethnicity of children in child welfare also may depend, in part, on geography. South Dakota reported that 64 percent of all children in care were Native American, while New Mexico indicated that Hispanics constituted 40 percent of children in care (Stehno, 1990, p. 552).

If, then, minority children do not experience greater involvement in child abuse and neglect, but do experience more involvement in the child welfare system itself, differences in processing, care, and treatment of these children may account for the anomaly. There are, in fact, significant differences in the responses of the child welfare system to white versus minority children. For example, the number of African-American children reported as abused or neglected has increased although the number of substantiated reports has not grown (Hogan & Siu, 1988). Most reports of neglect involve African-Americans; between 1976 and 1982 55–65 percent of all reports involving African-American families were for neglect (American Humane Association, 1984). Paradoxically, once the decision to intervene is made, minorities experience harsher assessments and interventions (Close, 1983).

Minority children, however, may not receive the same services and opportunities accorded their white counterparts. For example, minority children have less contact with their social workers and receive fewer comprehensive services (Close, 1983; Olson, 1982). Minority children also wait longer for adoption and are less likely to benefit from adoptive services (Knitzer, Allen & McGowan, 1978). Native American children experience particularly high rates of separation from their parents and more transracial placements because of the paucity of Native American foster and adoptive parents (Knitzer et al., 1978).

Minority children also are more likely to spend substantial periods of time in foster care. A 1980 survey conducted by the Office of Civil Rights found that minority children experience longer placements in different facilities at different locations than their white counterparts (Jenkins et al., 1983). For example, the median time in care for white children was twenty months compared to twenty-five months for Native American, twenty-six months for Hispanic, and thirty-two months for African-American children (Jenkins et al., 1983, p. 43). Of all children who spent five years or more in foster care, 53.5 percent were children of color, while those who spent one year or less in care were predominantly white (Jenkins et al., 1983, p. 43). White children were more likely to receive residential treatment, but they also had more placements out of the county of their residence and in secure facilities (Jenkins et al., 1983, p. 43). Many of these children, however, are delinquents and status offenders (Jenkins et al., 1983) who have been transinstitutionalized.

Ironically, many of the problems experienced by minority children— foster care drift, the unavailability of services, and lack of adoptive placements—were identified historically as fundamental flaws of the child welfare system. However, federal legislation enacted as early as 1974 attempted to redress these ills. In 1974 Congress passed the Child Abuse Prevention and Treatment Act, which provided federal monies for the prevention, identification, and treatment of child abuse and neglect (House Report No. 308, 1973). In 1978 Congress enacted the Child Abuse Prevention and Treatment and Adoption Reform Act to eliminate long-term foster care placements by facilitating interstate adoptions and the permanent placement of children with special needs (Senate Report No.

167, 1977). Concerned with the large and unknown number of children in foster care, Congress also authorized funds for adoption assistance and services (Senate Report No. 167, 1977).

Two years later Congress passed the Adoption Assistance and Child Welfare Act of 1980 to provide incentives for permanency planning (Senate Report No. 336, 1979). The act emphasized the goal that children should remain in or be reunited with their biological families (Senate Report No. 336, 1979) and ordered states to make reasonable efforts to prevent removal or to facilitate reunification (House Conference Report No. 900, 1980). If return to the biological family is not possible, the act required states to find permanent placements and provide adoption assistance payments for adoptive parents (Senate Report No. 336, 1979). States were eligible to receive federal funds after they conducted an inventory of all children in foster care for more than six months, developed statewide foster care information systems, implemented case review procedures, and designed child welfare service programs to promote permanent placements (Senate Welfare Report No. 336, 1979). The act also envisioned the utilization of written case plans, frequent judicial review of placements (House Conference Report No. 900, 1980), and procedural protections to safeguard parental rights (Senate Report No. 336, 1979).

Despite these reforms, minority populations in the child welfare system have continued to increase. Congress, itself alarmed by this trend, passed legislation in 1987 authorizing funds for a minority adoption demonstration program (House Report No. 135, 1987). But many commentators suggest that the disproportionate number of minority youth in the child welfare system is attributable to systemic racial bias (Jenkins et al., 1983; Olson, 1982; Stehno, 1990). Increased reporting and referral of minority families may be due, in part, to cultural and ethnic differences in childrearing behaviors (Small, 1978) and racial biases (Gelles & Lancaster, 1987, p. 22). African-American children, for example, are no more likely to be abused and neglected than are white children but because of their low socioeconomic status, African-Americans are more likely to be brought to the attention of public authorities (Faller & Zeifert, 1981). Others have suggested that the failure to provide minority children with services is attributable to funding decisions and private-sector biases. The increasing use of public monies to purchase services from the private sector, coupled with the low rate of admission among minorities to private programs, has depleted the funding base for public programs, thereby reducing the availability of services to minority children and their families (Stehno, 1982, 1990). Those services that are available are controlled by white-dominated agencies that fail to provide appropriate solutions to the problems faced by minority families (National Center on Child Abuse and Neglect, 1980).

Other commentators have suggested that child abuse and neglect are the products of poverty (Stehno, 1990). Minority children, therefore, are at greater risk because they are more likely to be poor (Stehno, 1990). The percentage of African-American children in poverty grew by 4.7 percent between 1979 and 1986 while the percentage of Hispanics in poverty increased by 33.9 percent (Children's Defense Fund, 1989, p. 248). Homelessness too has been linked to a higher risk of abuse (Children's Defense Fund, 1989, p. 201). At least one study, however, suggests that there is little causal evidence linking poverty and abuse (Gelles & Lancaster, 1987).

Because the problems are widespread, any solution that focuses solely on the child welfare system is unlikely to succeed. However, we do need to determine the impact of race on the decision-making process, with a special emphasis on screening and intake. The failure to find adoptive homes for children of color is particularly troublesome in light of the federal mandate to permanently place children and may suggest the need for preventive services and better in-home care. Service programs for minority children that are ethnically and culturally appropriate must be developed and funded. Legal intervention also may be appropriate and necessary to ensure a racially neutral child welfare system.

Race and Ethnicity and the Mental Health System

Using the mental health system to transinstitutionalize girls and white boys has had a dramatic impact on children of color. Unlike their experiences in the juvenile justice and child welfare systems, minority children may have less contact with the mental health system (Burns, 1990). Between 1975 and 1986, for example, the rate of admission to outpatient services for minority children dropped, while the nonminority rate increased. By 1986, admission of minority children to outpatient treatment was proportional to their rate in the population (Burns, 1990, p. 147). During this same period of time, fewer minorities than nonminorities were admitted to state and county hospitals (Burns, 1990, p. 148).

To some extent, the mental health system has been utilized primarily by white children. In 1975 76 percent of all children receiving outpatient care, and 87 percent of all children in private hospitals, were white (National Institute of Mental Health, 1980). Even in state and county hospitals, whites constituted 68 percent of all juvenile admissions (National Institute of Mental Health, 1980). By 1980, white admissions to private hospitals increased slightly to 88 percent, while minority admissions remained constant (National Institute of Mental Health, 1985). White admissions to state hospitals, however, increased in 1980 to 75 percent while minority admissions declined sharply (National Institute of Mental Health, 1985).

As minority children get older, they are even less likely to receive inpatient psychiatric services. Most of the inpatient psychiatric services from a state or private hospital are provided when minority youth are under ten years of age. For example, minorities constituted 43.8 percent of all admissions for ten year olds to public hospitals and 20.6 percent of admissions for ten year olds to private hospitals in 1980 (National Institute of Mental Health, 1985). After age ten, minority admissions declined in public hospitals to 30.5 percent for children between the ages of ten and fourteen and to 21.3 percent for children aged fourteen to seventeen (National Institute of Mental Health, 1985). The decline is even more dramatic if one looks at private hospitals; only 14.2 percent of children aged ten to fourteen years and 10.4 percent of children aged fifteen to seventeen were minorities (National Institute of Mental Health, 1985).

In some unexpected ways, however, minority children experience overinstitutionalization in the mental health system. When minority admissions are at their highest in public facilities, for example, their length of stay increases significantly. The median length of stay for minority children under ten was ninety-two days in 1980, almost six weeks longer than the median stay for similarly aged white children (National Institute of Mental Health, 1985). The rates of admission to state mental health hospitals in 1980 also suggest an overutilization of these facilities by African-American youth. Based on 1980 census data, 35.2 African-Americans for every 100,000 were admitted to state hospitals compared to 23.7 whites for every 100,000 (National Institute of Mental Health, 1985).

Both the overutilization and the underutilization of mental health services for this population may be attributable to systemic racial bias in the testing and evaluation of minority youth (Thomas & Sillen, 1972; Willie, Kramer & Brown, 1973). For younger children of color who are overrepresented in the public and private mental health facilities, testing biases and cross-racial evaluations may account for the increased use of mental health services. Several studies suggest that testing instruments are invalid for different racial populations because their original validity was determined by using white middle-class test takers (National Institute of Mental Health, 1977). These tests, therefore, fail to take into account cultural differences across heterogenous populations. Mental health practitioners themselves may exhibit bias in their evaluations of minority children or may interpret strategies that are culturally specific and contextually appropriate as flawed coping because they have little or no understanding of the cultural context (Sabshin, Diesenhaus & Wilkerson, 1970).

On the other hand, adolescent minorities may be precluded from using mental health facilities because of long-held misperceptions about normal behaviors in a minority population. Many commentators suggest that psychopathology cuts across racial lines and that deviance can and should be diagnosed in minority populations. One study analyzed the placements of violent youth at a hospital and a juvenile correctional institution and concluded that race was a significant factor in the placement decision (Lewis, Shanok, Cohen, Kligfeld & Frisone, 1980). For example, the study found that violent African-American youth were incarcerated in the juvenile justice system but violent white youth were more frequently hospitalized (Lewis et al., 1980). Whether racial bias operates to overinclude younger minorities but to exclude older children of color is uncertain, but such problems suggest that transinstitutionalization is a growing problem.

Conclusions

The institutionalization practices across the juvenile justice, child welfare, and mental health systems in the United States reveal the existence of three separate tracks for the processing, care, and treatment of girls, minorities, and white boys. For girls, this track is paternalistic; the deinstitutionalization of status offenders has meant the transinstitutionalization of girls in mental health and child welfare facilities. These systems appear to be perpetuating sexist notions about the appropriateness of girls' behavior that is reminiscent of the double standard employed in the earlier days of the juvenile court.

The track experienced by minorities is a racist one. Deinstitutionalization appears to have benefited only white males. The growth of the institutionalized minority population in the juvenile justice system can be explained only in terms of a pervasive, systemic racism. The overutilization of the foster care system itself is the expression of a policy that is intolerant of, and insensitive to, the realities of ethnicity and race. Finally, the curious pattern of institutionalization in the mental health system suggests that white children will be given preferential treatment in the provision of services.

What is needed is a new, more holistic approach to the placement and treatment of children in the juvenile justice, mental health, and child welfare systems. Children, particularly girls and minority youths, seem to be the groups most poorly served by these organizations. Services and placements tend to reflect institutional interests rather than the needs of children, and the urgent problems of these children are often overlooked in the process. Over and above this, these institutions need to be carefully scrutinized so as to ensure that the services they provide are free of sexism and racism. Only then will we be assured of juvenile justice, mental health, and child welfare systems that truly seek the best interest of all youth in the country.

References

Allen-Hagen, B. (1988). *Children in custody: Public juvenile facilities, 1987.* Washington, DC: U.S. Department of Justice.

Allen-Hagen, B. (1991). *Children in custody: 1989.* Washington, DC: Bureau of Justice Statistics, U.S. Department of Justice.

American Correctional Association. (1990). *The female offender: What does the future hold?* Washington, DC: St. Mary's Press.

American Humane Association. (1977). *National analysis of official child neglect and abuse reporting.* Denver: American Humane Association.

American Humane Association. (1984). *Trends in child abuse and neglect: A national perspective.* Denver: American Humane Association.

American Humane Association. (1986). *Highlights of official child neglect and abuse reporting: 1986.* Denver: American Humane Association.

Bishop, D., & Frazier, C. (1990, March). *Gender bias in the juvenile justice system: Implications of the JJDP Act.* Paper presented at the annual meeting of the Academy of Criminal Justice Sciences, Denver, CO.

Bortner, M. A., & Reed, W. L. (1985). The preeminence of process: An example of refocused justice research. *Social Science Quarterly, 66* (2), 413–425.

Brown, E. J., Flanagan, T. J., & McLeod, M. (Eds.). (1984). *Sourcebook of criminal justice statistics: 1983.* Washington, DC: Bureau of Justice Statistics, U.S. Department of Justice.

Bureau of Justice Statistics. (1988). *Survey of youth in custody: 1987.* Washington, DC: U.S. Department of Justice.

Bureau of Justice Statistics. (1989). *Children in custody: 1975–1985.* Washington, DC: U.S. Department of Justice.

Bureau of Justice Statistics. (1990). *Jail Inmates: 1989.* Washington, DC: U.S. Department of Justice.

Burns, B. J. (1990). Mental health service use by adolescents in the 1970s and 1980s. *Journal of the American Academy of Child and Adolescent Psychiatry, 30*(1), 144–150.

Cahalan, M. W. (1986). *Historical corrections statistics in the United States: 1850–1984.* Washington, DC: U.S. Department of Justice.

Carroll v. United States, 267 U.S. 132, (1925).

Center for the Study of Youth Policy. (1991). *Data analysis of the Juvenile Detention and Correctional Facility Census, 1988–89* (Office of Juvenile Justice and Delinquency Prevention, U.S. Department of Justice, Computer file). Ann Arbor, MI: Inter-University Consortium for Political and Social Research (Bureau of the Census, U.S. Department of Commerce).

Chesney-Lind, M. (1971). *Female juvenile delinquency in Hawaii.* Unpublished master's thesis, University of Hawaii at Manoa.

Chesney-Lind, M., & Shelden, R. (1991). *Girls, delinquency, and the juvenile justice system.* Pacific Grove, CA: Brooks/Cole.

Children's Defense Fund. (1989). *A children's defense budget.* Washington, DC: Author.

Close, M. M. (1983). Child welfare and people of color: Denial of equal access. *Social Work Research and Abstracts, 19,* 13–20.

Costello, J. C., & Worthington, N. L. (1981–1982). Incarcerating status offenders: Attempts to circumvent the Juvenile Justice and Delinquency Prevention Act. *Harvard Civil Rights-Civil Liberties Law Review, 16,* 41–81.

Faller, K. C., & Ziefert, M. (1981). Causes of child abuse and neglect. In K. C. Faller & M. Ziefert (Eds.), *Social work with abused and neglected children* New York: Free Press.

Federal Bureau of Investigation. (1980). *Crime in America 1979: Uniform crime reports.* Washington, DC: U.S. Department of Justice.

Federal Bureau of Investigation. (1990). *Crime in America 1989: Uniform crime reports.* Washington, DC: U.S. Department of Justice.

Feinman, C. (1985). Criminal codes, criminal justice and female offenders: New Jersey as a case study. In I. L. Moyer (Ed.), *The changing roles of women in the criminal justice system* (pp. 41–53). Prospect Heights, IL: Waveland.

Feld, B. C. (1991). Justice by geography: Urban, suburban, and rural variations in juvenile justice administration. *Journal of Criminal Law and Criminology, 82,* 156–210.

Flanagan, T. J., & Jamieson, K. M. (Eds.). (1988). *Sourcebook of criminal justice statistics: 1987.* Washington, DC: Bureau of Justice Statistics, U.S. Department of Justice.

Flanagan, T. J., & Maguire, K. (1990). *Sourcebook of criminal justice statistics: 1989.* Washington, DC: U.S. Department of Justice.

Flanagan, T. J., & McGarrell, E. F. (Eds.). (1986). *Sourcebook of criminal justice statistics: 1985.* Washington, DC: Bureau of Justice Statistics, U.S. Department of Justice.

Flanagan, T. J., & McLeod, M. (Eds.). (1983). *Sourcebook of criminal justice statistics: 1982.* Washington, DC: Bureau of Justice Statistics, U.S. Department of Justice.

Flanagan, T. J., van Alstyne, D. J., & Gottfredson, M. R. (Eds.). (1982). *Sourcebook of criminal justice statistics: 1981.* Washington, DC: Bureau of Justice Statistics, U.S. Department of Justice.

Frazier, C. E., & Chochran, J. C. (1986). Detention of juveniles: Its effects on subsequent juvenile court processing decisions. *Youth and Society, 17*(3), 286–305.

Gelles, R., & Lancaster, J. (Eds.). (1987). *Child abuse and neglect: Biosocial dimensions.* New York: Aldine De Gruyter.

General Accounting Office. (1978). *Removing status offenders from secure facilities: Federal leadership and guidance are needed.* Washington, DC: Author.

Glave, J. (1987, Feb. 8). Police say girl sexually abused in three homes. *Philadelphia Inquirer,* p. 26-A.

Gold, S. (1971). Equal protection for juvenile girls in need of supervision in New York State. *New York Law Forum, 17,* 570–591.

Guggenheim, M. (1986). Conducting a bench trial. *Criminal Justice, 1,* 20–22.

Hindelang, M. J., Gottfredson, M. R., & Flanagan, T. J. (Eds.). (1981). *Sourcebook of criminal justice statistics: 1980.* Washington, DC: Bureau of Justice Statistics, U.S. Department of Justice.

Hogan, P., & Siu, S. F. (1988). Minority children and the child welfare system: An historical perspective. *Social Work, 33,* 493–498.

House Conference Report No. 900. (1980). In *United States Code Congressional and Administrative News* 1980 (3), 1561–1588. St. Paul, MN: West.

House Report No. 308. (1973). In *United States Code Congressional and Administrative News* 1974 (2), 2763–2772. St. Paul, MN: West.

House Report No. 135, (1987). In *United States Code Congressional and Administrative News* 1980 (3), 1448–1561. St. Paul, MN: West.

Huizinga, D., & Elliott, D. (1987). Juvenile offenders: Prevalence, offender incidence and arrest rates by race. *Crime and Delinquency, 33,* 206–233.

In re Gault, 387 U.S. 1 (1967).

In re Winship, 397 U.S. 358 (1970).

Jamieson, K. M., & Flanagan, T. J. (Eds.). (1987). *Sourcebook of criminal justice statistics: 1986.* Washington, DC: Bureau of Justice Statistics, U.S. Department of Justice.

Jamieson, K. M., & Flanagan, T. J. (Eds.). (1989). *Sourcebook of criminal justice statistics: 1988.* Washington, DC: Bureau of Justice Statistics, U.S. Department of Justice.

Jenkins, S., Diamond, B., Flanzraich, J., Gibson, J., Hendricks, J., & Marshood, N. (1983). Ethnic differentials in foster care placements. *Social Work Research and Abstracts, 19,* 41–45.

Ker v. Illinois, 119 U.S. 436 (1886).

Knitzer, M., Allen, L., & McGowan, B. (1978). *Children without homes.* Washington, DC: Children's Defense Fund.

Kowalski, G. S., & Rickicki, J. P. (1982). Determinants of juvenile postadjudication dispositions. *Journal of Research in Crime and Delinquency, 19,* 66–83.

Krisberg, B., Schwartz, I. M., Fishman, G., Eisikovits, Z., & Guttman, E. (1987). *The incarceration of minority youth.* Minneapolis, MN: Hubert Humphrey Institute of Public Affairs.

Laub, J., & McDermott, M. J. (1985). An analysis of serious crime by young black women. *Criminology, 23,* 81–98.

Lewis, D., Shanok, S., Cohen, R., Kligfeld, M., & Frisone, G. (1980). Race bias in the diagnosis and disposition of violent adolescents. *American Journal of Psychiatry, 137,* 1211–1216.

Marshall, I. H., & Thomas, C. W. (1983). Discretionary decision-making and the juvenile court. *Juvenile and Family Court Journal, 34,* 47–60.

McCord, J., McCord, W., & Thurber, E. (1968). The effect of foster home placement in the prevention of adult anti-social behavior. In J. R. Stratton & R. Terry (Eds.), *Prevention of delinquency* (pp. 178–183). New York: Macmillan.

McGarrell, E. F., & Flanagan, T. J. (Eds.). (1985). *Sourcebook of criminal justice statistics: 1984.* Washington, DC: Bureau of Justice Statistics, U.S. Department of Justice.

Moss, D. (1987). *In re Gault* Now 20, But . . . *American Bar Association Journal, 73,* 29.

Mushlin, M. B., Levitt, L., & Anderson, L. (1986). Court-ordered foster family care reform: A case study. *Child Welfare, 65,* 141–154.

National Center on Child Abuse and Neglect. (1980). *1978 National Conference on Child Abuse and Neglect.* Washington, DC: U.S. Department of Health and Human Services.

National Institute of Mental Health. (1977). *Psychological tests and minorities.* Washington, DC: U.S. Department of Health, Education and Welfare.

National Institute of Mental Health. (1980). *Hispanic Americans and mental health services: A comparison of Hispanic, black, and white admissions to selected mental health facilities, 1975.* Washington, DC: U.S. Department of Health and Human Services.

National Institute of Mental Health. (1985). *Mental health, United States, 1985.* Washington, DC: U.S. Department of Health and Human Services.

Olsen, L. (1982). Predicting the permanency status of children in foster care. *Social Work Research and Abstracts, 18,* 9–20.

Parham v. J. R., 442 U.S. 584 (1979).

Pope, C. E., & Feyerham, W. M. (1989, November). *Minority status and juvenile processing: An assessment of the research literature.* Paper presented at the annual meeting of the American Society of Criminology, Reno, NV.

Prescott, P. S. (1981). *The child savers.* New York: Knopf.

Rafter, N. H. (1990). *Partial justice: Women, prisons and social control.* New Brunswick, NJ: Transaction Books.

Rogers, K. (1972). "For her own protection . . .": Conditions of incarceration for female juvenile offenders in the State of Connecticut. *Law and Society, 7,* 223–246.

Sabshin, M., Diesenhaus, H., & Wilkerson, R. (1970). Dimensions of institutional racism in psychiatry. *American Journal of Psychiatry, 127,* 787–793.

Schlossman, S., & Wallach, S. (1978). The crime of precocious sexuality: Female delinquency in the progressive era. *Harvard Educational Review, 48,* 65–94.

Schwartz, I. M. (1989). *(In) Justice for juveniles: Rethinking the best interests of the child.* Lexington, MA: Lexington Books.

Schwartz, I. M., Harris, L., & Levi, L. (1988). The jailing of juveniles in Minnesota: A case study. *Crime and Delinquency, 34,* 133–149.

Schwartz, I. M., Jackson-Beeck, M., & Anderson, R. (1984). The "hidden" system of juvenile control. *Crime and Delinquency, 30,* 371–385.

Schwartz, I. M., Steketee, M., & Schneider, V. (1990). Federal juvenile justice policy and the incarceration of girls. *Crime and Delinquency, 36,* 503–520.

Senate Report No. 167. (1977). In *United States Code Congressional and Administrative News,* 1978(3), 557–612. St. Paul, MN: West.

Senate Report No. 336. (1979). In *United States Code Congressional and Administrative News* 1980(3), 1448–1561. St. Paul, MN: West.

Shelden, R. (1981). Sex discrimination in the juvenile justice system: Memphis, Tennessee, 1900–1971. In M. Q. Warren (Ed.), *Comparing male and female offenders* (pp. 55–72). Beverly Hills, CA: Sage.

Sickmund, M. (1990). *Runaways in juvenile courts.* Washington, DC: U.S. Department of Justice.

Small, Willie. (1978). The neglect of black children. In *Child abuse, neglect and the family within a cultural context* (pp. 14–15). Washington, DC: National Center on Child Abuse and Neglect, U.S. Department of Health and Human Services.

Snyder, H. (1990). *OJJDP update on statistics: Growth in minority detentions attributed to drug law violators.* Washington, DC: U.S. Department of Justice.

Snyder, H. N., Finnegan, T. A., Nimick, E. H., Sickmund, M. H., Sullivan, D. P., & Tierney, N. J. (1989). *Juvenile court statistics.* Pittsburgh: National Center for Juvenile Justice.

Soler, M., Shotton, A., Bell, J., Jameson, E., Shauffer, C., & Warboys, L. (1990). *Representing the child client.* New York: Matthew Bender.

Stehno, S. M. (1982). Differential treatment of minority children in service systems. *Social Work, 27*(1), 39–45.

Stehno, S. M. (1990). The elusive continuum of child welfare services: Implications for minority children and youths. *Child Welfare, 69,* 551–562.

Steketee, M., Willis, D., & Schwartz, I. M. (1989). *Juvenile justice trends: 1977–1987.* Ann Arbor: Center for the Study of Youth Policy, University of Michigan.

Subcommittee on Human Resources of the Committee on Education and Labor, U.S. House of Representatives. (1980). *Juvenile justice amendments of 1980.* Washington, DC: U.S. Government Printing Office.

Sullivan, C. (1988, Sept. 27). America's troubled children: The harm in foster care. *Christian Science Monitor,* pp. BI–B8.

Thomas, A., & Sillen, S. (1972). *Racism and psychiatry.* New York: Brunner/Mazel.

U.S. Statutes at Large. Ninety-Sixth Congress, 2nd sess. (1980). *Public Law 96-272—June 17, 1980*. Washington, DC: U.S. Government Printing Office.

Weithorn, L. A. (1988). Mental hospitalization of troublesome youth: An analysis of skyrocketing admission rates. *Stanford Law Review, 40,* 773–838.

Willie, C. V., Kramer, B. M., & Brown, B. S. (Eds.). (1973). *Racism and mental health*. Pittsburgh, PA: University of Pittsburgh Press.

10

The Private Sector in Juvenile Corrections

Yitzhak Bakal and Harvey Lowell

Between 1835 and 1970 large institutions—commonly known as training schools—were seen as the primary solution to the problem of juvenile delinquency in this country. The argument over whether they were successful has long been settled; most scholars, even most members of the general public, now agree that these large institutions were a failure.

Recognized as brutal, violent, costly, ineffective, and often racist, training schools created graduates who now swell the populations of adult correctional institutions and figure prominently in the ranks of those who have committed heinous and violent crimes. The institutions themselves, along with their counterparts specializing in mental health and mental retardation, have been discredited as having represented the worst of all possible choices as a method to deal with a social problem.

Yet in a much more subtle way, the failure of large institutions and the gargantuan social service systems that spawned them are coming to symbolize a doctrine that is more in keeping with the current tenor of the times than the simple notion that large institutions are bad. The failure of large institution-based systems dovetails perfectly with the currently powerful popular view that the state itself is a source of waste and incompetence. In today's political atmosphere government can seemingly do nothing right. Large institutions are viewed as inherently "bad." Even if they were good at doing what they were supposed to do, people believe, state governments would be inept at best, corrupt at worst. In this view, the less government has to do with the business of governing on a day-to-day basis, the better. The shared perception is that all government is too bureaucratic, that the civil service and unions are too powerful to allow reforms or cost-cutting measures that clash with their vested interests, and that the entire public system is too large to move swiftly when confronted with a problem.

196

This growing attitude taps into the deep distrust of government that has always been a part of the American political spectrum, and manifests the conservative desire to limit the role of "big government" in favor of increased involvement by the private sector. "Private enterprise" can get the job done in more efficient and cost-effective ways than government can, or so says the conventional wisdom.

Reform and the Private Sector

The past two decades have seen tremendous changes in youth corrections. It is no accident that the majority of these reform efforts have allocated to the private sector many functions that used to belong exclusively to the state. The private sector was the preeminent tool for engineering the transition from the training schools to community-based programs.

In Massachusetts, the site of the first major reform effort, dozens of private, nonprofit providers were encouraged to develop alternative programs and services in order to shift direct services from state operations. In Pennsylvania, a private organization was created not only to contract with private entities for service, but to establish liaison and effective communications with juvenile court judges. In Utah, private organizations sprang up to offer services the state was not equipped to provide (Bakal & Polsky, 1973; Blackmore, Brown & Krisberg, 1988).

Private providers in these highly charged political arenas compensated for the shortcomings of state systems. Where state systems were rigid, slow moving, and difficult to change, the private sector was flexible, quick, and open to change. In situations where the old system continued to run at the same time a new one was being established, a new infrastructure composed of private providers was itself an extra resource, a new constituency for reform.

Only a few states have attempted large-scale reform without extensive involvement by the private sector. Missouri, for example, was one of the few states where contracting out to new groups was not important because its system was open and cooperative. Yet in every state in which conflict characterized reform efforts new players were drawn into the game; these new players were generally private, not-for-profit providers of human services.

The private sector was both countenanced by and responsible for the revolution that has taken place in community-based care. This chapter explores the opportunities and the risks posed by increasing reliance on the private sector in accomplishing juvenile justice goals.

The Growth of the Private Sector

The overall composition of the juvenile justice system in the United States is changing. A system once almost entirely reliant on public facilities and institutions has evolved into a network of private facilities and programs that service a significant proportion of total admissions. According to Shichor and Bartollas,

> From 1975 to 1984, admissions to public juvenile facilities decreased from 641,189 to 527,754, a decline of 18%. But during this same time period, admissions to private juvenile facilities increased from 56,708 to 101,007, an increase of 78%. The number of private juvenile facilities also increased from 1,277 in 1975 to 1,996 in 1985, an increase of 19%. (1990, p. 290)

Other studies report that while the costs of public and private services are comparable, private-sector services can be significantly less expensive on average (Krisberg, Austin, Joe & Steele, 1987; Krisberg, Austin & Steele, 1989; Lowell & Bullington, 1981). Both inmates and staff give better ratings to private services and programs in areas including inmate living conditions, internal security and control, enhancement of social adjustment and rehabilitation, and management issues. Escape rates are lower, fewer inmate disturbances occur, and staff and inmates report themselves more comfortable at private facilities (Urban Institute, 1989).

One of the enduring ironies of the growth of privatization is that a truly conservative concept is working to promote what were once considered to be radical reforms. Privatization has entered the mainstream of juvenile justice and correctional thinking as much as a result of the desire to reduce the size and scope of government as of a recognition that the radical reforms of the past were not so radical after all. Whatever the reason for its acceptance, it is reasonable to assume that the trend toward increased use of the private sector in the juvenile justice arena will continue.

Advantages of Private-Sector Services

It is evident that the private sector serves at least three major functions in the administration of juvenile justice systems. The first of these relates to the processes of reform in juvenile justice: making systems more effective, more efficient, and more humane. Second, the private sector plays a role in the mundane, day-to-day management of the systems that employ private services extensively. Third, the private sector is often used by astute juvenile justice administrators to counterbalance other formidable forces in their systems, including the state bureaucracy, the civil service, and the unions.

Flexibility

One of the most important and underestimated characteristics of the private sector is that it is a free-market environment. The competition within this environment, the possibility for doing profitable business, brings out an entrepreneurial spirit among private providers. In order to maintain a sound fiscal foundation, the private provider must be flexible in responding to the business environment. This means that private providers are usually very willing to try out new program models, to act quickly to establish new programs, and to discover and implement interesting contracting mechanisms.

From the standpoint of the juvenile corrections administrator, the flexibility inherent in the private-provider community offers the administrator the possibility to contract out for services, and, by doing so, to alter day-to-day operations of the system in ways that do not necessarily require legislative approval.

In Massachusetts, then-commissioner of the Department of Youth Services, Jerome Miller and his staff used federal funds to create a wide variety of smaller community-based programs. They used the surplus bed space in state-run institutions created by these programs to close the state's training schools by administrative directive. In Pennsylvania, Miller created a private nonprofit entity, the Center for Community Alternatives, to spearhead the effort to remove four hundred juveniles from the State Correctional Institution at Camp Hill. In Maryland, Linda D'Amario Rossi, secretary of the Juvenile Services Administration, used old and new providers to accelerate the closing of the state's training schools (Butts & Streit, 1988). These are only a few examples of ways in which the flexibility of private entities can be used to circumvent or to supplement existing operations.

Political Leverage

Each provider brings its own resources to bear on the reform and the contracting process. With their own constituencies and political allies, private providers often have the ability to cut through bureaucratic red tape in unconventional ways. In every state influential providers or groups of providers have intervened in the political process—as does any other interest group—to further their own agendas. As a result, the provider community itself can mobilize a variety of interested parties—clients, boards of trustees, political allies, public media—in support of efforts to reform the existing system.

A Structure for Innovation

Perhaps the best way of illustrating the manner in which a network of private providers offers the possibility, even the likelihood, for innovation is to contrast such a network with a typical state system. State systems are usually rigid and hierarchical. Decisions about everyday operations, to say nothing of new initiatives, cannot be made at low- or even middle-management levels, but must relate to policies developed somewhere further up the "chain of command." In state-run systems, policies governing the operations of one facility are exactly the same as policies governing the operations of another facility. Even when some diversity of programs is built into the system, there are limited centers of power, authority, and decision making. The structure of state-run systems demands a high degree of obedience from participants, and their willingness to subordinate individual decision making to a hierarchical structure. Therefore, it is a virtual certainty that all programs of the same general type will be run in much the same way. The range of acceptable decisions is limited because the number of people (or entities) that can make decisions is limited. In this model, operational decisions become policy decisions, and policy decisions tend to be uniform across the state. In other words, all participants within the purview of one decision-making entity will do business practically the same way.

In contrast, the private provider community by its very nature has many centers of power and decision-making authority. Each provider organization is responsible to its own board of directors, trustees, or shareholders; each has the capacity to make its own independent decisions. By participating in contracts with private providers, the state is essentially sharing responsibility and authority with those providers. As a result, for any one program type it may tap into as many different program philosophies and operating styles as it has providers. In this way, the state can benefit from both true depth and diversity; not only are there different levels of programming, but within each level there are different approaches.

Grass-roots ideas emerging from the interaction between private-sector programs and their communities have a chance to flourish in a way that cannot be matched in state systems. For example, the staff of the

Northeastern Family Institute's Shelter Care program, a detention unit, noted that many of the youth they served had drug problems. They realized that the rest of the system was suffering from an extreme scarcity of drug-awareness options. Out of this recognition grew the KIDS Care program, which both offers youth a drug-awareness program and trains them to give public presentations to groups sponsored by schools, community organizations, and law enforcement agencies. This low-cost, effective, community drug-awareness approach now benefits the entire juvenile justice system. It could not have flourished under a state aegis.

Upgraded Staffing

The existence of an extended provider network changes the staffing dynamics within the juvenile justice system in a number of ways. Such a network greatly expands the career ladder and the set of options available to state staff. For example, state-run institutions are typically low on the totem poles of program quality and staff prestige. Both the public and state workers themselves perceive private providers as more professional. In states where both systems operate, however, it is not uncommon for leading direct service providers to step into high-level state jobs, and even more common for staff at state-run programs to move up into available slots in the private sector. This process of two-way crossover in staffing increases the public's respect for state-run programs and raises morale among state workers in these programs.

Using staff members with expertise from the private sector further fuels the change process. Public agency personnel who have professional experience in the private sector have brought a broadened view and a greater degree of professionalism and legitimacy to the public sector.

A Break with the Past

The public perception of state-run institutions and programs has changed radically over past decades. Once perceived as a benefit to the populations they served and society at large, today they are typically criticized for being repositories for job-seekers in the patronage system or for maintaining a counterproductive civil service system. State bureaucracy, coupled with stultifying civil service rules and union regulations, has become a hindrance to reform, working against improvements in care instead of supporting them. These intrinsic attributes of state social service structures not only work against change, they are increasingly seen as an obstacle to change and a waste of tax monies.

Contracting out many of the state service delivery functions utterly changes the system and the public perception of it. In Massachusetts, the process of contracting out for state-run services came under blistering attack from vested interests in the patronage system, the legislature, and the unions. Nevertheless, and in part because the system of state-run institutions had been so discredited, a better system based on the purchase of private services outlasted the controversy.

Indeed, it is interesting to note one of the lasting legacies of the juvenile justice reform effort in Massachusetts. This purchase-of-service model was first used on a large scale in the juvenile justice arena, but it soon became the method by which Massachusetts reformed its antiquated systems of mental health and mental retardation institutions, and encouraged diversity in its child welfare system. While each of these state systems still operates some of its own programs, contracted services now provide the bulk of the services, and virtually all of the available community-based services.

Public Visibility

A system of community-based programs is highly visible to public scrutiny because such programs operate within local communities. Large state-run facilities usually operate in isolated, secluded, or restricted locations, far from shopping, schools, or the interested gaze of community members. This is the traditional location of institutions whose primary purposes were to remove their clientele from the corrupting influences of urban environments and to remove from the larger society those of its members deemed sufficiently deviant to warrant institutionalization.

In a community-based, privatized system, local communities generally have more input into how and under what conditions facilities operate. Private not-for-profit organization have boards of directors that often include community members. The smart operator of community-based programs will recruit a local advisory board composed of prominent citizens, join the local Chamber of Commerce or neighborhood association, and participate in neighborhood volunteer activities. In short, privatization stimulates the use of the community as a resource, and can be used to teach the community that it has a vital interest in local program success. This community support can translate into support at budget time, increased community acceptance of other agency programs, and a source of volunteers and job opportunities for program participants.

In a state-run system, local communities have no voice, and are usually excluded from daily operation and decision making.

Efficiency Improvements

State-run systems are notoriously sluggish. Each step of every process seems to have been designed to make sure that no one will have to bear responsibility for the consequences of any decision. To be fair, this is not an indictment of state government, but rather a characteristic of large bureaucracies in general. The Pennsylvania case offers an instructive example. The Center for Community Alternatives, a private, not-for-profit organization, was created in 1975 to remove all four hundred juveniles from a Pennsylvania state prison for adults. The state's attorney general had determined that no new placements of juveniles into the State Correctional Facility at Camp Hill could be made after 15 August of that year. The state had just five months to establish new programs and services to replace the medium-security prison as a placement option. It was widely recognized that acting within its usual framework, the state would take years, not months, to accomplish such a task.

By 15 August, the Center for Community Alternatives had set up a number of placement agencies, established working relationships with all county courts, and had begun to handle not only new admissions, but discharges of juveniles from the prison. Within eighteen months, all but seven of the juveniles—whose cases were tied up in litigation—had been removed from the prison in favor of alternative placement plans in the community.

Many other kinds of efficiency measures are possible in privatized systems. For example, a private institute has recently participated in two efforts to establish similar kinds of group residences for people diagnosed as mentally ill. One process—from the design phase through the completion of construction—was handled wholly by the state; the other was bid out by the state to the private sector. After innumerable delays, redesigns, and cost overruns, the state-operated process took more than five years to complete. The private process was completed in six months at a fraction of the cost.

To the extent that privatization also means the downsizing or elimination of large institutions, it is possible to realize large savings by ending the cost of upkeep of the physical plant, and sale of buildings and land can even result in major monetary gains for the state.

Clarifying the Role of the State

With some notable exceptions, most states are not really good at providing direct services for delinquent youth. Moreover, a fundamental conflict of interest emerges when the state pursues the goals of providing services, while simultaneously setting and enforcing the standards for those services. These two functions cannot peacefully coexist when the juvenile justice system is under extreme pressure from increasing juvenile crime rates, or from more frequent judicial commitments to state facilities.

Under these circumstances the state often waives its own standards or licensing regulations. In Delaware, which is presently undertaking a reform of its juvenile justice system, the population of the state training school for delinquent youth was eighty at the time of this writing. The problem is that Delaware's licensing regulations—in compliance with the American Correctional Association Standards for this facility—state that the facility should not hold more than forty children at any one time. In a state system a situation such as this ultimately leads to cries for expansion, which is costly and is not likely to be quickly accomplished. The public system has a built-in incentive to add on more of the same type of beds because this is what the state currently operates, is familiar with, and thinks is the only suitable option. Moreover, construction means jobs, and happy job-holders (and future voters). This type of expansion involves construction costs (currently estimated at more than $100,000 per bed) and operating costs of $40–50,000 per bed year.

The incentive in a more privatized system is to develop a set of smaller, less-intensive, and far cheaper alternatives for those youth currently within the system who have "served their time," or who would not present a significant risk in community programs. These options include everything from group residences to nonresidential tracking and advocacy programs (Bakal and Polsky, 1979).

Entrepreneurship and Innovation

The ethos of the new breed of provider combines idealism with an entrepreneurial spirit. Successful providers cannot just be interested in helping youth if they want to continue to provide services; they must be concerned with competing in a relatively open, free-market environment. They must be innovative in the way they design, continually reassess, and redesign their program models; they must be effective managers to use their limited resources intelligently; and they must be entrepreneurs to ensure that their organizations can continue to provide effective programs in a highly competitive business environment.

The role of the fiercely independent entrepreneurs who have created and continue to create very innovative programs in many different states cannot be underestimated. These founders were and are individuals who want to chart a new direction. The opportunity to contract for services allowed new figures to bring their expertise and ideas into the field.

Innovative management techniques are now applied by many private-sector service providers. Associated Marine Institutes (AMI), for example, is a respected not-for-profit provider of twenty-four programs for delinquent youth in seven different states. It makes strong use of an incentive model for both clients and staff. The AMI model is an innovative one. In what are essentially unlocked day programs, AMI uses boats and the sea as a way to keep its charges interested and involved. AMI gives them the opportunity to work on, to navigate, and to pilot watercraft. Not coincidentally, strong incentives like the chance to pilot a boat are designed to keep the hard-to-reach youth AMI typically serves from walking away from the program. At the same time, clients are motivated to learn to read in order to read an engine repair manual, to do math in order to navigate, and so on (Lerner, 1990). There are built-in academic requirements for each step of the process.

The system of rewards and enhancement for clients is paralleled by a system designed to keep staff enthusiastic about the program. Fiscal incentives are provided to staff in the form of performance-related bonuses tied to specific goals for program performance. The better the program does, the bigger the staff bonuses. These kinds of techniques help retain good staff, thus perpetuating a more effective program over time.

The willingness to implement innovative program models, and to make those models work through equally innovative management measures, are the factors that have enabled a growing number of nonprofit providers to expand from a strong base in one state to a regional or national market. For example, AMI, which began in Florida, now has programs in Texas, Louisiana, South Carolina, Delaware, Virginia, and Maryland. Northeastern Family Institute, which sprang up in Massachusetts, now operates in Vermont, New Hampshire, Rhode Island, and Maryland.

From the innovative nature of the AMI model, to the diversity of client population and normative programs that is the hallmark of NFI, these and many other for-profit and not-for-profit private organizations are expanding as they refine their corporate approaches (Barton, Butts, Stromberg, & Weaver, 1989). As a result, state agency administrators often have the freedom to pick from among a variety of program proposals submitted by providers with experience in the field, and the depth of knowledge and corporate talent to make sure their programs are successful. The abundance of solid choices is itself a factor that will maintain the momentum toward increased involvement of the private sector in juvenile justice systems nationwide.

The Future of the Private Sector: Dangers and Opportunities

Dangers

While privatization has offered tremendous advantages, the proliferation of private community-based services in juvenile justice was bound to create its own set of problems. Time provides an indispensable perspective for analyzing the flaws in this system, and for proposing modifications to turn inherent dangers into opportunities.

The Private Sector as an Opponent of Change. While the private sector has acquitted itself well in its work in juvenile justice, there is nothing inherently good or beneficial in an entrenched and intransigent private sector. The private sector can be as self-interested and as obstinate as its state-run, institution-based predecessor. The history of efforts to reform and privatize juvenile corrections are rife with examples.

In the early 1970s, the efforts of the director of the Illinois Department of Children and Family Services, Jerome Miller, to reduce the number of delinquent youth being sent out of the state were opposed by the powerful, particularly the church-led, private sector in the state at the time. Large private-sector agencies felt threatened. For many years, they had exercised the right to refuse to accept youth they felt would be too difficult to manage in their established programs. Bringing back these youngsters— often aggressive, minority youth—implied a significant reduction in the ability of these agencies to choose with whom they wanted to work. Miller credits these groups as having been his most implacable opposition in Illinois, and feels that their activities ultimately resulted in his dismissal.

The Maryland example is equally instructive. D'Amario-Rossi, Secretary of the Juvenile Services Administration, led an effort to place delinquent youth out of the discredited, overcrowded, and brutal Montrose Training School. She found it extremely difficult to convince the existing network of private providers in Maryland to accommodate these more aggressive, tougher youth. They resisted her appeals to increase capacity and to develop new programs for youth from Montrose. Her proposal would have forced them to upgrade their capabilities and would have limited the ability of the private sector to control the kinds of youth with whom they would work by "skimming the cream" from the top of the system. Through trepidation and inaction rather than active opposition, the private sector in Maryland became an impediment to change.

D'Amario-Rossi's solution was to bring in outside private organizations. These organizations were all willing and able to offer services to difficult youth. Locating powerful competition for already operating private-sector organizations creates anxiety and a strong incentive to change in order to survive.

A Dual System. In circumstances like those just described the private sector is interested in maintaining the status quo, rather than working in the interests of the system. Seeking to work only with a select group of referrals is bound to "widen the net" for delinquents, bringing more youth into the system and further diluting resources available to it. Keeping "safe" youth longer than is necessary diminishes the ability of the system to cope with its increasing capacity. The net effect is the creation of a dual system, where the most difficult, the toughest, and the least desirable are still handled in more institutionalized, publicly operated settings, while others are being served in community-based private programs. In such systems, providers are adopting the narrowest possible view of their mission to further the goals of their own organizations. In fact, they are sidestepping accountability for larger system functioning. Systemic accountability is easy to dodge because it is scattered throughout the expanded private system or because it falls upon the more visible shoulders of state administrators.

The Threat of Stagnation. It is natural for a maturing privatized system to manifest some of the rigidity, inflexibility, and self-interestedness of the old public system. If its improvements are to stand the test of time, the private sector needs to struggle to retain its sense of mission. If the private sector restricts itself to certain kinds of youth, it is not very different from the older state system that provided primarily custodial services.

Such a system stifles creativity and innovation. If providers are interested only in preserving their existing models, or working only with those youth who readily fit them, much of the creative potential made possible by privatization can be lost.

The Danger of State Control. It is also true that complete acquiescence to system demands leads to stagnation as assuredly as does defending provider prerogatives to the exclusion of system needs. The countervailing pressure to the private-sector assertion of its privileges is the tendency of state bureaucracy to subsume the provider community, and to remake it in its own image. One example can be found in the juvenile justice purchase of service system in Massachusetts, the oldest and arguably the most extensive in the nation.

In Massachusetts one can find a pattern of overregulation that is astonishing. I cannot go into great detail here, but I wish to point out that the number of different regulatory requirements administered by different agencies has proliferated madly. The primary tool of control has become line-item budgeting, which allows the state to micromanage contracts without regard to program performance or outcomes. The flexibility that the state has in changing contracts means that private providers are more vulnerable than state-run programs that have extensive infrastructures and political linkages to state government. The classic example is in the field of mental health, where funding did not follow clients out of the hospital and into community programs. The net result has been widespread homelessness among this group of people.

Line-Item Micromismanagement. It is also possible in purchase-of-service systems for politicians and bureaucrats to cut funding while insisting on the same level of services, or to withdraw funding and substantially or even totally cut programs. In Massachusetts, for example, state agencies have used their tight budget controls as a way to coerce programs into operating in ways that they think appropriate. Round after round of incremental budget cuts have occurred over the past three years even though the programs are expected to serve the same numbers of clients. This tendency accelerated during Governor Dukakis's failed run for president. All new initiatives were halted, and all possible efforts were made to quietly recover funds from operating programs. A significant loss of program quality was the end result. In this environment, providers do what they can to avoid these controls.

The Profit Controversy. One aspect of privatization is often framed in moral and ethical terms. Opponents question the delegation of correctional functions of the state to businesses operating for a fee and a profit. On the one hand, the assumption is that profit-making enterprises are prone to economize, reducing quality of care through their need to create profits out of limited resources. Profit-making enterprises, the argument goes, bring with them corporate and shareholder interests that are inherently— or at least potentially—antithetical to client-care concerns.

Not-for-profit private agencies do not have this conflict. By the same token, however, they do operate in a business environment. The terms "not-for-profit" or "nonprofit" are unfortunate in that they have given rise to the durable misconception that tax-exempt agencies do not require profits. It is true that tax-exempt agencies have no owners in the usual sense, and hence do not pay dividends to profit-motivated investors. However, nonprofit providers are in fact businesses, subject to the same economic, fiscal, and marketplace realities as commercial business. All enterprises, tax-paying and tax-exempt, must accumulate capital for such essential purposes as financing lags in collection of accounts receivable, acquiring and replacing fixed assets, financing growth, providing a reserve for unforeseen contingencies, and conducting new program development. As a result, they are all subject to similar pressures, even though the interests at stake and the way they handle those pressures may be different.

The fact is that there are good and bad programs run by representatives of both the profit and the nonprofit private sectors. The argument that one or another leads naturally to better quality services is not necessarily valid. The main variables in distinguishing between them are not directly related to the quality of services alone, but rather to other attributes of both sectors.

There is a place for both nonprofits and for-profit businesses in privatized systems. On the plus side, the distinguishing advantage of the nonprofit sector is its tendency to adopt, support, and enhance systemwide reforms. The for-profit sector is a valuable asset for its access to and capacity to develop capital, a commodity sorely lacking in the field. Using the for-profit sector can also engage a previously uninvolved segment of society in dealing with intractable social problems. Both sectors can be flexible, efficient, and cost-effective, and both can run good programs.

On the negative side, the nonprofit sector can become timid and narrow in its perspective if survival is at issue. It can also fall prey to the same problems that plague state operations. The for-profit sector, without commitment to a mission of deinstitutionalization, can work within any system, as it does within the framework of adult corrections in many jurisdictions. The danger is that the for-profit sector can subvert reform if the price is right, and so must be monitored carefully.

Addressing this issue means abandoning the ethical/moral nature of the argument, focusing instead on operational criteria and performance measures. In this way, juvenile justice administrators will be able to compare program efforts of both sectors, determine how well they work in terms of outcome, and whether they advance the reform goals for the system as a whole.

Opportunities

In one form or another, all of the dangers cited above are endemic in juvenile justice systems adopting privatization as an end product. Each of them provides its own opportunity and represents a chance to continue to modify and readjust the system in order to improve services and administration. In a general way, the great opportunity offered to system administrators and providers alike is to institutionalize a process of evaluation and change. The following is meant as a list of opportunities to revise and improve the way in which our systems are working.

Improve Administrative Flexibility. Juvenile justice administrators should examine all of their options and be willing to seek solutions that break the mold of their existing structures. In Maryland, Linda D'Amario Rossi was able to change overall system functioning by bringing in new players and motivating the old ones. Solutions to other particularly sticky problems within each administration can result from flexible approaches and the willingness to innovate, for the scope of options is wider in privatized systems.

Implement Diversity. The development of the private sector allowed for a diverse set of programs to focus on the individual needs of youth while meeting the requirements of public safety. At the same time, the "dual-system" phenomena perpetuates bifurcated care; small private settings can also furnish options for those difficult clients who remain in more institutional settings. Pursuing this approach accomplishes two desirable goals at once: making providers more responsible for overall system operations and freeing up funds tied into institutional fixed costs.

Define State and Provider Roles. States are increasingly defining themselves as "buyers" rather than as "givers" of service. The state must first define itself as a buyer who sets policy, encourages competition, and demands a high standard from those with whom it contracts. Then state staff can better manage their often unmanageable responsibilities and address their roles as liaison to the courts and the public in more effective ways. The conflict and duplication between referral sources and the agencies providing services is thus greatly reduced.

This approach permits efficient and streamlined state operations. At the same time, it allows state juvenile justice administrators both to determine priorities and to hold providers accountable for their services.

Develop Independent Systems Program Assessment. One of the most important elements in a well-run system of services purchased from the private sector is an effective way for the state to monitor the programs for which it contracts. Unfortunately, in most jurisdictions, effective programs for monitoring the efforts of state facilities have never existed; state systems have rarely been held accountable for either the results of their efforts or the practices they used to obtain them.

Diverse programs in different locations means that both the youth and the organizations responsible for serving them are located in different places, have different philosophies and treatment strategies, and have different boards of directors. In such circumstances, the state must have a mechanism in place for obtaining accurate information about which programs are functioning well and which are not functioning well.

Each system making use of purchased services should incorporate a program audit unit. The unit should be composed of, and the audits carried out by, people who are expert in service delivery, and who can judge the totality of a program in relation to legitimate performance expectations. These expectations should be outlined in the contract between the state and the provider, and specific costs should be tied, as much as possible, to identified program goals and objectives. This mechanism should be independent of the organizational units that contract for services, and should report directly to top administration.

Unify Case Management. Case management is the way in which the state and its providers interrelate. Its current form dilutes and distorts accountability. While juvenile correctional administrators are charged with the responsibility for making the system work, they have lost some of their control over the use of resources within the system.

Case management can be made more effective by using it to enlist providers in sharing responsibility for system operation. One possibility for unifying case management is to contract for small continuums of service—from secure treatment to aftercare—to be run by individual providers. These providers would also have responsibility for case management within their network of services. Accountability for the youth and for the functioning of the minisystem is built into this model (see "No-Rejection" Policies, below).

A second option is to create networks of different providers who operate different services, and to turn over case management to the network itself. While this approach is not as effective in terms of pinpointing accountability, it can foster cooperation within the network and is more feasible for systems that are substantially privatized. A variant of this model is currently operating in Massachusetts in the child welfare area.

"No-Rejection" Policies. Except for cases in which psychiatric hospitalization is required, a unified case management system should be open to all referrals. This no-rejection policy is an excellent way to reorient the state and providers to a joint responsibility for the entire system.

When it is discovered that a youth cannot be served at the initial referral, a plan for needed services can be developed after thirty days, and the person can then be moved to a more appropriate setting. This provides the larger system with the breathing room needed to place a difficult client, to satisfy community demands, and to develop an alternate program. The toughest youth in the system can be accepted (assuming that the right services have been developed). The "worst" cases can take top priority in this approach.

Conclusion

Hierarchical, centralized bureaucracies simply do not fuction well in the rapidly changing, information-rich, knowledge intensive society and economy of the 1990s. They are like luxury ocean liners in an age of supersonic jets: big, cumbersome, expensive, and extremely difficult to turn around. Gradually, new kinds of public institutions are taking their place. Our voluntary, nonprofit organizations are alive with new initiatives. (Osborne & Gaebler, 1992, p. 12).

Freeing policy managers to shop around for the most effective and efficient service providers helps them squeeze more bang out of every buck. It allows them to use *competition* between service providers. It preserves maximum *flexibility* to respond to changing circumstances. And it helps them insist on *accountability* for quality performance. (*Ibid,* p. 33).

There is a pervasive and growing dissatisfaction with government in our society. Government operations are inept and ineffective, and are badly in need of basic reform. At the same time, economic downturns and revenue shortfalls argue strongly for economy and for trimming the size of government. This situation bestows a formidable momentum on efforts to privatize the juvenile justice field. As more units of government struggle to do more with less, the private sector will capture ever-greater shares of interest and attention. As more leaders of government become fiscal conservatives, they will increasingly seek to supplant government functioning with private-sector initiatives. This trend is inevitable, and is already picking up steam. It presents the very real dangers of excluding some from services, putting others on the streets without support, or warehousing many in large institutions. The challenge of the coming decade is to use the opportunities created by this situation to accomplish significant system reform resulting in a unified system with the right mix of services. The result will be a better and more cost-effective system of delinquency services.

References

Bakal, Y. (Ed.), (1973). *Closing correctional institutions.* Lexington, MA: Lexington Books.

Bakal, Y., & Polsky, H. W. (1979). *Reforming corrections for juvenile offenders.* Lexington, MA: Lexington Books.

Barton, W. H., Butts, J. A., Stromberg, C. R., & Weaver, R. S. (1989). *Programs for serious and violent juvenile offenders.* Ann Arbor: Center for the Study of Youth Policy, University of Michigan.

Blackmore, J., Brown, M., & Krisberg, B. (1988). *Juvenile justice reform: The bellwether states.* Ann Arbor: Center for the Study of Youth Policy, University of Michigan.

Bullington, B., Sprowls, J., Katkin, D., & Lowell, H. (1986). The politics of policy: Deinstitutionalization in Massachusetts 1970–1985. *Law and Policy, 8*(4), 507–524.

Butts, J. A., & Streit, S. M. (1988). *Youth correction reform: The Maryland and Florida experience.* Ann Arbor: Center for the Study of Youth Policy, University of Michigan.

Krisberg, B. (1989, December). Juvenile justice: A critical examination.

Krisberg, B., Austin, J., Joe, K., & Steele, P. (1987). The impact of juvenile court sanctions. San Francisco: National Council on Crime and Delinquency.

Krisberg, B., Austin, J., & Steele, P. (1989). *Unlocking juvenile corrections: Evaluating the Massachusetts Department of Youth Services.* San Francisco: National Council on Crime and Delinquency.

Lerner, S. (1990). *The good news about juvenile justice.* Bolinas, CA: Common Knowledge Press.

Lowell, H., & Bullington, B. (1981). *Rediscovering juvenile justice: The cost of getting tough.* Hackensack, NJ: National Council on Crime and Delinquency.

Office of Juvenile Justice and Delinquency Prevention, U.S. Department of Justice. (1988). A private-sector corrections program for juveniles: Paint Creek Youth Center. Washington, DC: U.S. Government Printing Office, (1979).

Osborne, D., & Gaebler, T. (1992). Reinventing government: How the entrepreneural spirit is transforming the public sector. Reading, MA: Addison Wesley.

Shichor, D., & Bartollas, C. (1990). Private and public juvenile placements: Is there a difference? *Crime and Delinquency, 36*(2), 286–299.

Urban Institute (1989). *Comparison of privately and publicly operated corrections facilities in Kentucky and Massachusetts.* Washington, DC: U.S. National Institute of Justice.

11

Juvenile Crime-Fighting Policies: What the Public Really Wants

Ira M. Schwartz

In 1988 state lawmakers in Michigan enacted a package of eighteen juvenile-crime-fighting bills. The laws provided for stiffer penalties for juvenile law violators and made it easier to try young people in the adult courts and have them sentenced to adult prisons (MCLA Sec. 712A.2 et. seq. as amended 1988; Schwartz, Abbey & Barton, 1990). Legislators, both liberal and conservative, and juvenile justice professionals who supported these bills claimed they reflected public demand to crack down on juvenile criminals.

This scenario was and is not unique to Michigan. Punitive juvenile justice policies have been enacted in other states (Schwartz, 1989); again, they were largely justified on the basis that this is what the public wants. Interestingly, although elected public officials and juvenile justice professionals often claim to be speaking for the "community," their perspectives are usually not based on a systematic study of public opinion.

This chapter reports and discusses selected findings from the first comprehensive public opinion survey on public attitudes toward juvenile crime (Alcser, Connor & Heeringa, 1991). The findings should prove helpful to those who are really interested in knowing what adult citizens and taxpayers really think about the juvenile crime problem and, more importantly, what they feel should be done about it.

Methodology

The national public opinion survey of attitudes toward juvenile crime was conducted during August and September 1991 by the Survey Research Center at the University of Michigan's Institute for Social Research. The sample consisted of one thousand randomly selected adults, aged eighteen and over, living in randomly selected households throughout the contiguous United States who were interviewed by telephone. The questionnaire for this survey was developed by William H. Barton, Kirsten Alscer, and

Ira M. Schwartz (see Appendix). It was adapted from a questionnaire used in a survey of adults from the state of Michigan (Breslow, Connor & Heeringa, 1990).

Findings

Perceptions and Fears about Juvenile Crime

The survey included a number of questions about the public's perception and personal concerns regarding serious juvenile crime. For example, respondents were asked whether they felt that the amount of serious juvenile crime had increased or decreased in their state and in their neighborhood during the past three years. Eighty-two percent of the respondents felt that the amount of serious juvenile crime had increased in their state. Sixty-two percent felt that crime had increased a lot, while only 20 percent felt that it had increased a little.

In addition, a large number of respondents indicated that they were concerned about becoming the victim of a serious crime. Seventy-eight percent indicated that they were concerned about becoming the victim of a serious violent crime; 40 percent reported that they were very concerned; and another 38 percent indicated that they were somewhat concerned. Twenty-two percent reported that they were not very concerned or not at all concerned about this possibility. Eighty-one percent expressed concern about being the victim of a serious property crime; 36 percent said that they were very concerned; and 45 percent indicated that they were somewhat concerned. Only 19 percent reported that they were not very concerned or not at all concerned about this issue.

Interestingly, only 27 percent of the respondents believed that the amount of serious juvenile crime had increased in the neighborhood in which they lived. Sixty-three percent felt that there had been no increase, and 11 percent thought that crime had declined. Also, 57 percent of the respondents indicated that they would not be afraid to walk alone at night in any area within one mile of where they lived because of fear of being victimized; the other 43 percent felt that they would be afraid.

The Juvenile Court and Due Process

Laws recently enacted in many states have redefined the purpose(s) of the juvenile court. In general, these laws emphasize the idea that juvenile courts should include punishment as their major, if not their primary, purpose (Feld, 1988). This represents a departure from juvenile court's historical mission of providing treatment and rehabilitation to delinquent youth (Feld, 1988).

In light of this ongoing redefinition of the role of juvenile court, the interviewees were asked whether they thought the main purpose of juvenile court should be to treat and rehabilitate young offenders (youth ages ten through seventeen) or to punish them. Of the 981 people who answered this question, 78 percent felt that the primary purpose should be to treat and rehabilitate juveniles, while only 12 percent felt that it should be to punish them. Ten percent indicated that it should serve both purposes equally.

However, when these same interviewees were asked questions about how juveniles who commit serious property, drug-related, and violent offenses should be treated, their responses were quite different. Ninety-seven percent felt that juveniles who commit serious property crimes or who are found guilty of selling large amounts of drugs should be punished. Ninety-nine percent felt that juveniles who commit serious violent crimes should be punished. Also, approximately half of the respondents felt that juveniles who commit serious property crimes should be tried in the adult courts. Sixty-two percent favored trying juveniles in the adult courts for selling large amounts of drugs and 68 percent wanted juveniles who commit serious violent crimes tried in the adult courts.

While there is support for trying juveniles who commit serious crimes, particularly felonies, in the adult courts, the public does not favor giving juveniles the same sentences as adults *or* sentencing juveniles to adult prisons. Sixty-two percent of the respondents did not feel that juveniles should receive the same sentences as adults. Sixty-three percent did not want juveniles sent to adult prisons for serious property crimes and 68 percent did not want juveniles imprisoned with adults for selling large amounts of drugs. Fifty-five percent did not feel that juveniles should be sent to prison for serious violent crimes.

Although the public wants juveniles who commit serious crimes tried in the adult courts and punished for their misdeeds, they still want them to be treated and rehabilitated. Depending upon the type of crime, between 88–95 percent of the respondents want juveniles who commit serious property, drug-related, and violent crimes treated and rehabilitated if at all possible.

The interviewees were told, "In the adult court system, persons accused of a crime have the right to 'due process.' This includes the right to an attorney, the right to be told what one is charged with, and the right to be present for court proceedings" (Appendix questionnaire, p. 4). They were then asked whether they agreed or disagreed with the following statement: "Juveniles who are accused of a crime should receive the same due process as adults" (Questionnaire, p. 4).

Of the 985 respondents, 57 percent indicated that they *strongly* agreed with the statement, and another 25 percent indicated that they agreed with it. Ten percent disagreed with the statement, and 6 percent *strongly* disagreed with it. The rest had no opinion.

Training Schools and Community-Based Programs

The incarceration of juveniles continues to be one of the most hotly debated youth corrections issues. Despite the demonstration by some states (Florida, Kentucky, Maryland, Massachusetts, Missouri, Oklahoma, and Utah) that the number of juveniles requiring confinement to ensure public safety is relatively small, many jurisdictions continue to rely heavily on the use of training schools.

In light of this controversy and its implications for public policy, questions were included in the survey about this issue. The interviewees were told:

> There are two different approaches that states use to deal with juvenile offenders. Some states send many of their juvenile offenders to residential juvenile correctional institutions, that is, *training schools.* In contrast, other states use training schools *only* for juveniles who have committed serious violent crimes or *many* serious property crimes and they use *community-based programs* for the rest. These programs include very close supervision of offenders; repayment to the victim or the community; special education or job training; treatment and counselling services; and special foster homes or small group homes. (Appendix questionnaire, p. 10)

They were then asked: "If you were to choose between these two approaches, which one would you favor? Would you favor training schools for many types of juvenile offenders *or* community-based programs for all but the most violent or serious juvenile offenders"? (Questionnaire, p. 10). Of the 984 respondents to this question, 71 percent indicated that they favored a system that largely relied on community-based services. Only 29 percent said that they favored the training school approach.

In order to get more of the public's thinking on this subject, the interviewees were asked to give their opinions about the deterrent value and effectiveness of training schools. The respondents were nearly equally divided about whether committing juveniles to training schools serves as a deterrent to other youth. Fifty-one percent felt that sending juveniles to training schools is a deterrent to others, while 45 percent felt that it was

Table 11-1
Effectiveness of Training Schools

Serving time in training schools makes juvenile offenders:	
	Percent[1]
1. much more likely	4%
2. somewhat more likely	6%
3. about as likely	34%
4. somewhat less likely	44%
5. much less likely	11%
to commit crimes again?	

Source: Center for the Study of Youth Policy, University of Michigan.
[1] Percentages are rounded.

not. Also, the public does not seem to be of one mind about the effectiveness of these institutions. As indicated in Table 11-1, 55 percent of the respondents felt serving time in training schools prevents juvenile offenders from committing crimes in the future. Forty-four percent thought otherwise. However, the bulk of the respondents (78 percent) did not appear to have a strong opinion about the effectiveness of training schools. They indicated that juveniles who served time in these facilities were about as likely, or only somewhat less likely, to commit offenses after they were released.

Juvenile Court Dispositions and Drug-Related Offenses

The interviewees were asked their opinions about the dispositions they felt juveniles should receive who were found guilty of serious property, serious violent, and drug-related offenses. The data presented in Figures 11-1, 11-2, 11-3, 11-4, and 11-5 reflect preferred dispositions for juveniles found guilty for the first and second times for these offenses.

In many jurisdictions, drug-related offenses account for a significant number of arrests and referrals to juvenile court. Because of the concern about these offenses, a number of specific questions were included in the survey on this topic. For example, interviewees were asked if they thought "drug *use* by juveniles aged 10 through 17 should be considered a *health* problem or a *criminal* problem" (Appendix questionnaire, p. 15). Forty-six percent felt that drug use should be treated as a health problem, 34 percent felt that it should be handled as a criminal problem, and 20 percent felt that it should be handled as both a health and a criminal problem. Also, the overwhelming majority (69 percent) indicated that

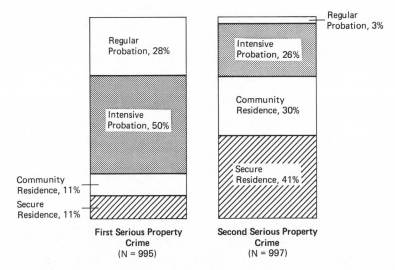

Figure 11–1. Preferred Response to Property Crimes

Source: Center for the Study of Youth Policy, University of Michigan, National Survey of Juvenile Crime.

juveniles found guilty of *using* drugs should be treated differently than those found guilty of *selling* drugs. This finding is consistent with the public's views presented earlier about dispositions for drug-related offenses.

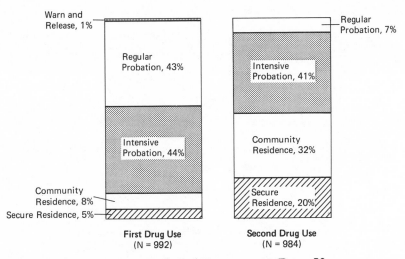

Figure 11–2. Preferred Response to Drug Use

Source: Center for the Study of Youth Policy, University of Michigan.

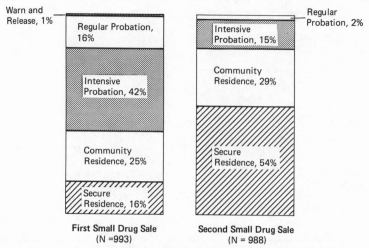

Figure 11–3. Preferred Response to Small Drug Sales

Source: Center for the Study of Youth Policy, University of Michigan.

Attitudes about How Juvenile Crime Control Funds Should Be Spent

Interviewees were asked to give their opinions about how state juvenile crime budget funds should be spent. Table 11–2 lists the relevant items included in the survey and the proportion of respondents who indicated it was *very important* to spend monies on them.

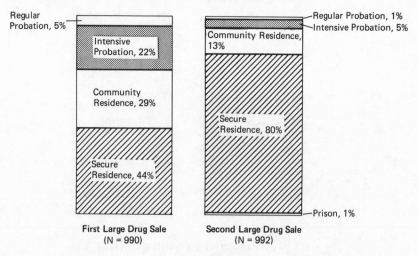

Figure 11–4. Preferred Response to Large Drug Sales

Source: Center for the Study of Youth Policy, University of Michigan.

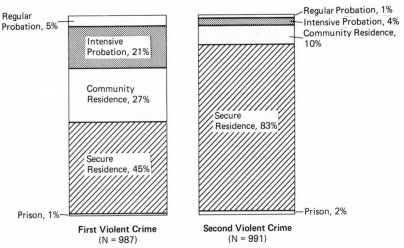

Figure 11–5. Preferred Response to Violent Crimes

Source: Center for the Study of Youth Policy, University of Michigan.

Age of Juvenile Court Jurisdiction

State laws differ concerning the age at which a young person should be tried in adult courts. For example, the upper age of juvenile court jurisdiction ends at sixteen in four states (Connecticut, New York, North Carolina, and Vermont), at seventeen in eight states (Georgia, Illinois, Louisiana, Massachusetts, Michigan, Missouri, South Carolina, and Texas), at eighteen in thirty-eight states (Alabama, Alaska, Arizona, Arkansas, California, Colorado, Delaware, District of Columbia, Florida, Hawaii, Idaho, Indiana, Iowa, Kansas, Kentucky, Maine, Maryland, Minnesota, Mississippi, Montana, Nebraska, Nevada, New Hampshire, New Jersey, New Mexico, North Dakota, Ohio, Oklahoma, Oregon, Pennsylvania, Rhode Island, South Dakota, Tennessee, Utah, Virginia, Washington, West Virginia, Wisconsin), and at nineteen in one state (Wyoming).

Debates often occur in state legislatures about changing the age of juvenile court jurisdiction. The debates usually focus on whether the age of juvenile court jurisdiction should be lowered and are usually triggered by a particularly heinous crime or crimes committed by juveniles. These debates rarely result in lowering the overall age of juvenile court jurisdiction. They do, however, often result in changes in state laws that eliminate specific offenses from the jurisdiction of the juvenile court, allow juveniles who commit a certain kind of offense at a certain age to be prosecuted in the adult courts, and give prosecutors more discretion to

Table 11-2
How State Juvenile Crime Control Funds Should Be Spent

Item	Importance
1. Programs where young offenders can repay their victims or the community	81%
2. Job training and youth employment opportunities for young offenders	70%
3. Community-based programs emphasizing education	69%
4. Community-based counseling	57%
5. Very close supervision while the young person lives at home or in the community	47%
6. Special foster homes and small group homes	36%
7. Building more training schools	36%

Source: Center for the Study of Youth Policy, University of Michigan.

decide in which court to try juveniles (Champion & Mays, 1991; Feld, 1987; Schwartz, 1989).

The survey contained only one question on this subject. The question was, "At what age do you think a person accused of a crime should be brought before an *adult criminal court* rather than a juvenile court?" (Questionnaire, p. 4). Their responses are reflected in Table 11–3.

Discussion

The results of this survey provide much food for thought. While they raise many issues that need to be explored further, they also disclose important, policy-relevant information. For example, the public does not appear to be nearly as punitive and demanding of retribution toward juvenile offenders as many politicians and, in some instances, juvenile justice officials have made them out to be. When politicians and others claim to be speaking for the community, they may well be representing a much smaller group than is typically thought to be the case.

The public does not support the current movement to abandon the historical mission and purpose of the juvenile court. By an overwhelming

Table 11-3
Age at Which Juveniles Should Be Prosecuted as Adults

Less Than 15	15	16	17	18	Greater Than 18
7%	9%	27%	22%	31%	4%

Source: Center for the Study of Youth Policy, University of Michigan.

majority, the respondents to this survey want the juvenile court to retain its emphasis on treatment and rehabilitation, an emphasis contrary to current public policy in a growing number of states. Also, the public supports providing young people with the same due process protections accorded adults. Like the U.S. Supreme Court that handed down the landmark *Gault* decision in 1967, the public does not believe juvenile court should be a "kangaroo" court (*In re Gault*, 1967). They believe it should be a court of justice, compassion, and hope.

However, the public also feels that juveniles who are accused of serious property, drug-related, and violent crimes should be tried in the adult courts. This finding, coupled with the public's willingness to give juveniles the same due process and procedural guarantees accorded adults, raises serious questions about the juvenile court and the public's perception of it. For example, does the public feel that the juvenile courts can handle juvenile felony cases effectively? Also, does the public feel that the juvenile courts are the appropriate place to handle serious cases of juvenile delinquency? More important, if the public does not want serious juvenile offenses handled in the juvenile courts, should there even be a separate juvenile court to handle delinquency and delinquency-related matters? If juvenile felony cases were handled in the adult courts, the only delinquency and delinquency-related issues left for the juvenile courts would be misdemeanors (minor and petty offenses) and status offenses (running away from home, habitual truancy, and being beyond the control of one's parents). Surely, juvenile justice and child welfare officials could develop some less formal and, perhaps, less costly approaches to dealing with these behaviors.

The findings also reveal that if given the choice, the public would support enlightened youth correction policies. For example, by a wide margin, the public would embrace a youth correction system that restricted the use of training schools and incarceration to juveniles who are serious violent and chronic offenders. Only about half of the respondents to this survey believe that training schools have a deterrent effect or are effective in preventing juveniles from committing crimes in the future. This finding can hardly be pointed to as an endorsement of these institutions by the public at large.

In addition to supporting a community-based system, the public wants their juvenile crime-fighting dollars targeted toward these kinds of services. They want their tax dollars invested in programs where young offenders can repay victims and the communities, receive job training and employment opportunities, have access to community-based educational programs, and receive counseling services and intensive community-based supervision. Training schools and other types of residential services were ranked *last* to receive tax dollars.

The public feels strongly that drug *users* should be treated differently than drug *sellers*. They also feel that juveniles who sell small amounts of drugs should receive less-severe dispositions than those found guilty of selling large amounts of drugs. Moreover, a sizeable proportion of the respondents indicated that drug use by juveniles should be considered a health problem or a combination health/criminal problem as compared to being just a criminal issue. This finding suggests that greater investments should be made in substance-abuse treatment services. These are services in short supply in most jurisdictions throughout the country.

In general, the public does not support the idea of sentencing juveniles to adult prisons. However, the fact that only about 55 percent of the respondents indicated that they did not want juveniles who commit serious violent crimes imprisoned suggests that the public may be losing patience with this population and are close to giving up on the juvenile correctional system as an option for them. This is an issue that needs to be carefully addressed by elected public officials, juvenile justice professionals, and child advocates.

Not surprisingly, the findings indicate that the public is very concerned about the juvenile crime problem. They believe that the volume of serious juvenile crime is increasing in their states, and they are fearful about the prospects of being victimized. However, a large majority of the respondents do not believe that the volume of serious juvenile crime is increasing in their own neighborhood. They even feel that it is generally safe to walk alone at night in their own neighborhood. While these responses are encouraging, they should probably be looked at more closely. For example, the results might be somewhat different depending upon the respondents' particular neighborhoods.

Conclusions

Juvenile justice policy is usually made in an emotionally charged atmosphere. Debates are often devoid of data and hard facts needed for making sound decisions. Decisions are usually made by elected public officials and juvenile justice professionals who are out of touch with public opinion.

This chapter contains selected findings from the first national public opinion survey on public attitudes about juvenile crime. The findings raise serious questions about whether policymakers and juvenile justice officials are, in fact, accurately reflecting what the public really wants. For example, the findings of this survey suggest that the public's views about the juvenile crime problem and what should be done about it are relatively enlightened, compassionate, and probably more cost-effective than existing policies or policies being enacted in most states.

The facts that public opinion favors providing juveniles the same due process protections as adults and adjudicating juveniles who commit serious crimes (felonies) in the adult court have important implications for the future of the juvenile court. This is an issue that clearly needs to be put on the public agenda and addressed carefully by policymakers, legal scholars, and juvenile justice and child welfare professionals.

Appendix: National Juvenile Crime Study Questionnaire

Variable #

V1   Case ID

V6   Sample Type
1. RDD
2. LIST

V31   Total Calls Counter
01–47

V38   Length of Interview in Minutes
013–059

V48   Respondent Sex
1. MALE
2. FEMALE

V49   Respondent Age
18–89
98. DON'T KNOW
99. NOT ASCERTAINED

V65   Sex of Informant
1. MALE
2. FEMALE

V66–70   Sex of Other Adults in Household (up to 5 other persons)
1. MALE
2. FEMALE
0. NO MENTION; NO FURTHER MENTION

V76   Age of Informant
        18–89
        98. DON'T KNOW
        99. NOT ASCERTAINED

V77–81 Age of Other Adults in Household (up to 5 other persons)
        18–93
        98. DON'T KNOW
        00. NO MENTION; NO FURTHER MENTION

V94   Interview Start Date (Month/Day)
        801–924

V95   Interview End Date (Month/Day)
        801–924

V151   A1a. We'll be talking about *juveniles,* aged 10 through 17, who have broken the law.

A special court, called juvenile court, deals with these young people. There are different opinions about what should be the purpose of the juvenile court system.

Do you think the *main* purpose of the juvenile court system should be to *treat and rehabilitate young* offenders or to *punish* them?

    1. TREAT AND REHABILITATE
    2. PUNISH
    3. BOTH EQUAL
    4. GET THEM OFF THE STREETS [ACCEPT ONLY AFTER PROBING]
    8. DON'T KNOW
    9. NOT ASCERTAINED

V152   A1b. In most states, the *juvenile court* deals with offenders aged 17 and younger, while *adult criminal courts* deal with older offenders. In some states, the upper age limit for juvenile court involvement is 16 or 15.

At what age do you think a person accused of a crime should be brought before an *adult criminal court* rather than a juvenile court?

    1–21. ENTER AGE
    97. NO SEPARATE JUVENILE COURT [IF VOLUNTEERED]
    98. DON'T KNOW
    99. NOT ASCERTAINED

V153   A2a,b.   In the *adult* court system, persons accused of a
V154   crime have the right to "due process". This includes the right to an attorney, the right to be told what one is charged with, and the right to be present for court proceedings.

Please tell me whether you *strongly agree, somewhat agree, neither agree nor disagree, somewhat disagree,* or *strongly disagree* with the following statements:

Juveniles who are accused of a crime should receive the same due process as adults.

A juvenile who is convicted of a crime should receive the *same* sentence as an adult, *no matter what the crime.*

1. STRONGLY AGREE
2. SOMEWHAT AGREE
3. NEITHER AGREE NOR DISAGREE
4. SOMEWHAT DISAGREE
5. STRONGLY DISAGREE
8. DON'T KNOW
9. NOT ASCERTAINED

V155   A3.   "Training schools" are residential correctional institutions for the confinement of juvenile offenders. Would you *strongly agree, somewhat agree, neither agree nor disagree, somewhat disagree,* or *strongly disagree* that sending juvenile offenders to training schools discourages *other* young people from committing crimes?

1. STRONGLY AGREE
2. SOMEWHAT AGREE
3. NEITHER AGREE NOR DISAGREE
4. SOMEWHAT DISAGREE
5. STRONGLY DISAGREE
8. DON'T KNOW
9. NOT ASCERTAINED

V156   A4.   Would you say that serving time in training schools makes juvenile offenders *more likely, less likely,* or *about as likely* to commit crimes again?

1. MORE LIKELY
2. LESS LIKELY
3. ABOUT AS LIKELY
8. DON'T KNOW
9. NOT ASCERTAINED

V157   A4a. Would you say it makes them *much more likely* or *somewhat more likely* to commit crimes again?

      1. MUCH MORE LIKELY
      2. SOMEWHAT MORE LIKELY
      8. DON'T KNOW
      9. NOT ASCERTAINED
      0. NOT APPLICABLE—V156=2,3,8,9

V158   A4b. Would you say it makes them *much less likely* or *somewhat less likely* to commit crimes again?

      1. MUCH LESS LIKELY
      2. SOMEWHAT LESS LIKELY
      8. DON'T KNOW
      9. NOT ASCERTAINED
      0. NOT APPLICABLE—V156=1,3,8,9

V159   Built strength of likelihood—serving time in training schools.

      1. MUCH MORE LIKELY
      2. SOMEWHAT MORE LIKELY
      3. ABOUT AS LIKELY
      4. SOMEWHAT LESS LIKELY
      5. MUCH LESS LIKELY
      9. NOT ASCERTAINED

V160   A5. *In the last 3 years,* would you say the amount of serious crime committed *in your state* by people aged 10 through 17 has *increased, stayed about the same,* or *decreased?*

      1. INCREASED
      2. STAYED THE SAME
      3. DECREASED
      7. HAVE NOT LIVED HERE FOR 3 YEARS [ACCEPT ONLY AFTER PROBING]
      8. DON'T KNOW
      9. NOT ASCERTAINED

V161   A5a. Would you say it has increased *a lot* or *a little?*

      1. INCREASED A LOT
      2. INCREASED A LITTLE
      8. DON'T KNOW
      9. NOT ASCERTAINED
      0. NOT APPLICABLE—V160 = 2,3,7–9

V162   A5b. Would you say it has decreased *a lot* or *a little?*

      1. DECREASED A LOT

2. DECREASED A LITTLE
0. NOT APPLICABLE—V160 = 1,3,7–9

V163 Built strength of change—amount of serious crime in the last 3 years in your state.

1. INCREASED A LOT
2. INCREASED A LITTLE
3. STAYED THE SAME
4. DECREASED A LITTLE
5. DECREASED A LOT
9. NOT ASCERTAINED

V164 A6. And what about in your own *neighborhood*? Would you say that *in the last 3 years* the amount of serious crime committed *in your neighborhood* by people aged 10 through 17 has *increased, stayed about the same,* or *decreased?*

1. INCREASED
2. STAYED THE SAME
3. DECREASED
7. HAVE NOT LIVED HERE FOR 3 YEARS [ACCEPT ONLY AFTER PROBING]
8. DON'T KNOW
9. NOT ASCERTAINED

V165 A6a. Would you say it has increased a *lot* or a *little?*

1. INCREASED A LOT
2. INCREASED A LITTLE
8. DON'T KNOW
0. NOT APPLICABLE—V164 = 2,3,7–9

V166 A6b. Would you say it has decreased a *lot* or a *little?*

1. DECREASED A LOT
2. DECREASED A LITTLE
9. NOT ASCERTAINED
0. NOT APPLICABLE—V164 = 1,3,7–9

V167 Built strength of change—amount of serious crime in your neighborhood in last 3 years.

1. INCREASED A LOT
2. INCREASED A LITTLE
3. STAYED THE SAME
4. DECREASED A LITTLE
5. DECREASED A LOT
9. NOT ASCERTAINED

V168   A7a,b.   Please tell me whether you *strongly agree,*
V169 ·   *somewhat agree, neither agree nor disagree,*
                        somewhat disagree, or *strongly disagree* with the
                        following statements:

                        Increasing employment opportunities for juveniles
                        could prevent a lot of serious crimes.

                        Most court punishments fit the crime fairly well
                        regardless of the offender's race or income level.

                        1. STRONGLY AGREE
                        2. SOMEWHAT AGREE
                        3. NEITHER AGREE NOR DISAGREE
                        4. SOMEWHAT DISAGREE
                        5. STRONGLY DISAGREE
                        8. DON'T KNOW

V180   B1.   There are two different approaches that states use
                to deal with juvenile offenders. Some states send
                many of their juvenile offenders to residential
                juvenile correctional institutions, that is, **training
                schools.** In contrast, other states use training
                schools *only* for juveniles who have committed
                serious violent crimes or *many* serious property
                crimes and they use **community–based
                programs** for the rest. These programs include
                very close supervision of offenders; repayment to
                the victim or the community; special education or
                job training; treatment and counseling services; and
                special foster homes or small group homes.

                If you were to choose between these two
                approaches, which one would you favor? Would
                you favor training schools for many types of
                juvenile offenders *or* community-based programs
                for all but the most violent or serious juvenile
                offenders?

                1. TRAINING SCHOOLS
                5. COMMUNITY-BASED PROGRAMS
                8. DON'T KNOW
                9. NOT ASCERTAINED

V181   B2,B3a.   People have many different ideas about how their
V182   state's juvenile crime budget should be divided.
                  After I read each item, please tell me how
                  important you think it would be to spend money
                  from that budget on that item.

What about spending money on special foster homes or small group homes for juvenile offenders? Would you say it would be *very important, somewhat important, not very important,* or not at all *important* to **spend money** on this?

What about spending money on community-based counseling to juveniles who break the law? (Would you say it would be very important, somewhat, not very, or not at all important to **spend money** on this?)

1. VERY IMPORTANT
2. SOMEWHAT IMPORTANT
3. NOT VERY IMPORTANT
4. NOT AT ALL IMPORTANT
8. DON'T KNOW
9. NOT ASCERTAINED

V183   B3b.   What about spending money on community programs that emphasize education to juveniles who break the law? (Would you say it would be very important, somewhat, not very, or not at all important to **spend money** on this?)

1. VERY IMPORTANT
2. SOMEWHAT IMPORTANT
3. NOT VERY IMPORTANT
4. NOT AT ALL IMPORTANT
8. DON'T KNOW
9. NOT ASCERTAINED

V184
V185   B4,5.   How about spending money on programs where young offenders can work to repay their victims or the community? (Would you say it would be very important, somewhat, not very, or not at all important to **spend money** on this?)

What about spending money on very close supervision while the young offender remains in the community? (Would you say it would be very important, somewhat, not very, or not at all important to **spend money** on this?)

1. VERY IMPORTANT
2. SOMEWHAT IMPORTANT
3. NOT VERY IMPORTANT

4. NOT AT ALL IMPORTANT
8. DON'T KNOW
9. NOT ASCERTAINED

V186
V187   B6,7.   What about spending money on job training and youth employment opportunities to young offenders? (Would you say it would be very important, somewhat, not very, or not at all important to **spend money** on this?)

And, how about spending money on building more training schools for the confinement of juvenile offenders? (Would you say it would be very important, somewhat, not very, or not at all important to **spend money** on this?)

1. VERY IMPORTANT
2. SOMEWHAT IMPORTANT
3. NOT VERY IMPORTANT
4. NOT AT ALL IMPORTANT
8. DON'T KNOW
9. NOT ASCERTAINED

C0.   There are several different responses that the juvenile court system can use when dealing juvenile offenders. These responses can be broken down into *four* basic categories:

One. Regular probation, where the juvenile is placed on a **regular case load** and visited once or twice a month.

Two. Highly structured probation, where the juvenile is placed on a **special case load** with a small number of other youths and is supervised closely in the community with more **frequent visits** by a specially-trained probation officer.

Three. Residential placement, where the juvenile is moved away from his or her home and must live in a **residential facility,** such as a **group home.**

Four. Secure placement in an institution, where the juvenile must live in a structured, **very secure facility.**

V200   C1a.   The next questions are about juveniles aged 10 through 17 who commit *serious "property crimes"* such as burglary and auto theft.

Keeping in mind the four ways of responding to juvenile offenses, please tell me what you think would be the appropriate way to deal with juveniles who are found guilty of a *serious* property crime for the *first* time? Would you say it should be regular probation, highly structured probation, residential placement, or secure placement in an institution?

1. REGULAR PROBATION
2. HIGHLY STRUCTURED PROBATION
3. RESIDENTIAL PLACEMENT
4. SECURE PLACEMENT IN AN INSTITUTION
5. WARN AND RELEASE [IF VOLUNTEERED]
6. PLACEMENT IN AN ADULT PRISON [IF VOLUNTEERED]
8. DON'T KNOW
9. NOT ASCERTAINED

V201   C1b.   And, what about juveniles who are found guilty of a *serious* property crime for the *second* time? (Would you say the appropriate way to deal with this should be regular probation, highly structured probation, residential placement, or secure placement in an institution?)

1. REGULAR PROBATION
2. HIGHLY STRUCTURED PROBATION
3. RESIDENTIAL PLACEMENT
4. SECURE PLACEMENT IN AN INSTITUTION
5. WARN AND RELEASE [IF VOLUNTEERED]
6. PLACEMENT IN AN ADULT PRISON [IF VOLUNTEERED]
8. DON'T KNOW
9. NOT ASCERTAINED

V202   C2a,b. We have touched on the overall purpose of the
V203   juvenile court system. Now we want to get your views on how to handle particular types of offenses.

Please tell me whether you *strongly agree, somewhat agree, neither agree nor disagree, somewhat disagree,* or *strongly disagree* with the following statements:

Juveniles who commit these *serious* property crimes should be *punished.*

A juvenile who is charged with a *serious* property crime should be tried as an adult.

1. STRONGLY AGREE
2. SOMEWHAT AGREE
3. NEITHER AGREE NOR DISAGREE
4. SOMEWHAT DISAGREE
5. STRONGLY DISAGREE
8. DON'T KNOW
9. NOT ASCERTAINED

V204
V205

C2c,d. (Please tell me whether you *strongly agree, somewhat agree, neither agree nor disagree, somewhat disagree,* or *strongly disagree* with the following statements:)

Juveniles should be sent to adult prisons for committing *serious* property crimes.

Juveniles who commit *serious* property crimes should be *treated and rehabilitated.*

1. STRONGLY AGREE
2. SOMEWHAT AGREE
3. NEITHER AGREE NOR DISAGREE
4. SOMEWHAT DISAGREE
5. STRONGLY DISAGREE
8. DON'T KNOW
9. NOT ASCERTAINED

V209

D1. The next questions are about young people and illegal drugs. Do you think drug *use* by juveniles aged 10 through 17 should be considered a *health* problem or a *criminal* problem?

1. HEALTH PROBLEM
2. CRIMINAL PROBLEM
3. BOTH HEALTH AND CRIMINAL (IF VOLUNTEERED)
8. DON'T KNOW
9. NOT ASCERTAINED

V210

D2. Do you think juveniles who *use* illegal drugs should be treated differently from those who *sell* illegal drugs, or should they be treated the same?

1. DIFFERENTLY
2. SAME
8. DON'T KNOW
9. NOT ASCERTAINED

V211

D3(1). As I mentioned earlier, there are four basic responses that the court system can use when

dealing with juvenile offenders. Would you like me
to repeat those response categories?

    1. YES
    2. NO

D3(2).   *One. Regular probation,* where the juvenile is placed
on a **regular case load** and visited once or twice
a month.

Two. Highly structured probation, where the juvenile
is placed on a **special case load** with a small
number of other youths and is supervised closely in
the community with more **frequent visits** by a
specially-trained probation officer.

Three. Residential placement, where the juvenile is
moved away from his or her home and must live in
a **residential facility,** such as a **group home.**

Four. Secure placement in an institution, where the
juvenile must live in a structured, **very secure
facility.**

V212   D3a.   Suppose a juvenile is convicted of *using,* but not
selling, illegal drugs, and it is his or her *first*
offense. In your opinion, what would be the
appropriate way to deal with that juvenile? Would
you say regular probation, highly structured
probation, residential placement, or secure
placement in an institution?

    1. REGULAR PROBATION
    2. HIGHLY STRUCTURED PROBATION
    3. RESIDENTIAL PLACEMENT
    4. SECURE PLACEMENT IN AN INSTITUTION
    5. WARN AND RELEASE [IF VOLUNTEERED]
    6. PLACEMENT IN AN ADULT PRISON [IF
       VOLUNTEERED]
    8. DON'T KNOW
    9. NOT ASCERTAINED

V213   D3b.   What if a juvenile is convicted a *second* time of
using, but not selling, illegal drugs? (What would be
the appropriate way to deal with that juvenile?
Would you say regular probation, highly structured
probation, residential placement, or secure
placement in an institution?)

    1. REGULAR PROBATION
    2. HIGHLY STRUCTURED PROBATION

3. RESIDENTIAL PLACEMENT
4. SECURE PLACEMENT IN AN INSTITUTION
5. WARN AND RELEASE [IF VOLUNTEERED]
6. PLACEMENT IN AN ADULT PRISON [IF VOLUNTEERED]
8. DON'T KNOW
9. NOT ASCERTAINED
0. NOT APPLICABLE—V212 = 4

V214   D3c. Suppose a juvenile is convicted of **selling** *small* amounts of illegal drugs, and it is his or her *first* offense. (What do you think would be the appropriate way to deal with that juvenile? would you say regular probation, highly structured probation, residential placement, or secure placement in an institution?)

1. REGULAR PROBATION
2. HIGHLY STRUCTURED PROBATION
3. RESIDENTIAL PLACEMENT
4. SECURE PLACEMENT IN AN INSTITUTION
5. WARN AND RELEASE [IF VOLUNTEERED]
6. PLACEMENT IN AN ADULT PRISON [IF VOLUNTEERED]
8. DON'T KNOW
9. NOT ASCERTAINED

V215   D3d. What if he or she is convicted a *second* time of **selling** *small* amounts of illegal drugs? (What would be the appropriate way to deal with that juvenile? Would you say regular probation, highly structured probation, residential placement, or secure placement in an institution?)

1. REGULAR PROBATION
2. HIGHLY STRUCTURED PROBATION
3. RESIDENTIAL PLACEMENT
4. SECURE PLACEMENT IN AN INSTITUTION
5. WARN AND RELEASE [IF VOLUNTEERED]
6. PLACEMENT IN AN ADULT PRISON [IF VOLUNTEERED]
8. DON'T KNOW
9. NOT ASCERTAINED
0. NOT APPLICABLE—V214 = 4

V216   D3e. What about a juvenile who is convicted of **selling** *large* amounts of illegal drugs, and it is his or her *first* offense. (What would be the appropriate way to deal with that juvenile? Would you say regular probation, highly structured probation, residential placement, or secure placement in an institution?)

1. REGULAR PROBATION
2. HIGHLY STRUCTURED PROBATION
3. RESIDENTIAL PLACEMENT
4. SECURE PLACEMENT IN AN INSTITUTION
5. WARN AND RELEASE [IF VOLUNTEERED]
6. PLACEMENT IN AN ADULT PRISON [IF VOLUNTEERED]
8. DON'T KNOW
9. NOT APPLICABLE

V217   D3f.   What should be done if he or she is convicted a *second* time of **selling** large amounts of illegal drugs? (Would you say regular probation, highly structured probation, residential placement, or secure placement in an institution?)

1. REGULAR PROBATION
2. HIGHLY STRUCTURED PROBATION
3. RESIDENTIAL PLACEMENT
4. SECURE PLACEMENT IN AN INSTITUTION
5. WARN AND RELEASE [IF VOLUNTEERED]
6. PLACEMENT IN AN ADULT PRISON [IF VOLUNTEERED]
8. DON'T KNOW
9. NOT ASCERTAINED
0. NOT APPLICABLE—V216 = 4

V218
V219   D4a,b.   Please tell me whether you *strongly agree, somewhat agree, neither agree nor disagree, somewhat disagree,* or *strongly disagree* with the following statements:

Juveniles who are convicted of selling *large* amounts of illegal drugs should be *punished.*

A juvenile who is charged with selling *large* amounts of illegal drugs should be *tried as an adult.*

1. STRONGLY AGREE
2. SOMEWHAT AGREE
3. NEITHER AGREE NOR DISAGREE
4. SOMEWHAT DISAGREE
5. STRONGLY DISAGREE

8. DON'T KNOW
9. NOT ASCERTAINED

V220 D4c,d. (Please tell me whether you *strongly agree,*
V221   *somewhat agree, neither agree nor disagree,*
        somewhat disagree, or *strongly disagree* with the
        following statements:)

Juveniles who are *convicted* of selling *large*
amounts of illegal drugs should be *sent to adult
prisons.*

Juveniles who are *convicted* of selling *large*
amounts of illegal drugs should be *treated and
rehabilitated.*

1. STRONGLY AGREE
2. SOMEWHAT AGREE
3. NEITHER AGREE NOR DISAGREE
4. SOMEWHAT DISAGREE
5. STRONGLY DISAGREE
8. DON'T KNOW
9. NOT ASCERTAINED

V229 E0. The next questions are about juveniles aged 10
through 17 who commit *serious violent crimes* such
as murder, rape, armed robbery, and assault with a
weapon.

Again, as I mentioned earlier, there are four basic
responses that the court system can use when
dealing with juvenile offenders. Would like me to
repeat those response categories?

1. YES
5. NO

E1. *One. Regular probation,* where the juvenile is placed
on a **regular case load** and visited once or twice
a month.

Two. Highly structured probation, where the juvenile
is placed on a **special case load** with a small
number of other youths and is supervised closely in
the community with more **frequent visits** by a
specially-trained probation officer.

Three. Residential placement, where the juvenile is
moved away from his or her home and must live in
a **residential facility,** such as a **group home.**

Four. Secure placement in an institution, where the juvenile must live in a structured, **very secure facility.**

V230   E1a.   Please tell me what you think would be the appropriate way to deal with juveniles who are found guilty of a serious violent crime for the *first time.* Would you say it should be regular probation, highly structured probation, residential placement, or secure placement in an institution?

1. REGULAR PROBATION
2. HIGHLY STRUCTURED PROBATION
3. RESIDENTIAL PLACEMENT
4. SECURE PLACEMENT IN AN INSTITUTION
5. WARN AND RELEASE [IF VOLUNTEERED]
6. PLACEMENT IN AN ADULT PRISON [IF VOLUNTEERED]
8. DON'T KNOW
9. NOT ASCERTAINED

V231   E1b.   And, what about juveniles who are found guilty of a serious violent crime for the *second time.* (Would you say the appropriate way to deal with this should be regular probation, highly structured probation, residential placement, or secure placement in an institution?)

1. REGULAR PROBATION
2. HIGHLY STRUCTURED PROBATION
3. RESIDENTIAL PLACEMENT
4. SECURE PLACEMENT IN AN INSTITUTION
5. WARN AND RELEASE [IF VOLUNTEERED]
6. PLACEMENT IN AN ADULT PRISON [IF VOLUNTEERED]
8. DON'T KNOW
9. NOT ASCERTAINED
0. NOT APPLICABLE—V230 = 4

V232   E2a,b.   Please tell me whether you *strongly agree,*
V233   *somewhat agree, neither agree nor disagree, somewhat disagree,* or *strongly disagree* with the following statements:

Juveniles who commit serious violent crimes such as murder, rape, armed robbery, and assault with a weapon should be *punished?*

A juvenile who is charged with a serious violent crime should be tried as an adult.

1. STRONGLY AGREE
2. SOMEWHAT AGREE
3. NEITHER AGREE NOR DISAGREE
4. SOMEWHAT DISAGREE
5. STRONGLY DISAGREE
8. DON'T KNOW
9. NOT ASCERTAINED

V234   E2c,d.   (Please tell me whether you *strongly agree,*
V235   *somewhat agree, neither agree nor disagree,*
                  somewhat disagree, or *strongly disagree* with the
                  following statements:)

Juveniles should be sent to adult prisons for committing serious violent crimes.

Juveniles who commit *serious violent crimes* should be *treated and rehabilitated.*

1. STRONGLY AGREE
2. SOMEWHAT AGREE
3. NEITHER AGREE NOR DISAGREE
4. SOMEWHAT DISAGREE
5. STRONGLY DISAGREE
8. DON'T KNOW
9. NOT ASCERTAINED

V240   F1a.   The last few questions are about your own experience with crime.

In the *past year,* have you been a victim of a **burglary?**

1. YES
5. NO

V241   F1b.   Was it committed by someone 10 through 17 years old?

1. YES
5. NO
8. DON'T KNOW (DO NOT PROBE)
0. NOT APPLICABLE—V240 = 5

V242   F2a.   In the past year, have you been a victim of a **street robbery** *with a weapon?*

1. YES
5. NO

V243   F2b. Was it committed by someone 10 through 17 years old?

       1. YES
       5. NO
       8. DON'T KNOW (DO NOT PROBE)
       0. NOT APPLICABLE—V242 = 5

V244   F3a. (In the past year, have you been a victim of) a **street robbery** *without a weapon?*

       1. YES
       5. NO

V245   F3b. Was it committed by someone 10 through 17 years old?

       1. YES
       5. NO
       8. DON'T KNOW (DO NOT PROBE)
       0. NOT APPLICABLE—V244 = 5

V246   F4a. In the past year, have you been a victim of an **assault** where you were injured?

       1. YES
       5. NO
       9. NOT ASCERTAINED

V247   F4b. Was it committed by someone 10 through 17 years old?

       1. YES
       5. NO
       8. DON'T KNOW (DO NOT PROBE)
       0. NOT APPLICABLE—V246 = 5,9

V248   F5a. In the past year, has a *neighbor, friend, or relative* been a victim of a **serious violent crime,** such as murder, rape, armed robbery, or assault with a weapon?

       1. YES
       5. NO
       8. DON'T KNOW

V249   F5b. Was it committed by someone 10 through 17 years old?

       1. YES
       5. NO
       8. DON'T KNOW (DO NOT PROBE)
       0. NOT APPLICABLE—V248 = 5,8

V250   F6a.   In the past year, has a *neighbor, friend,* or *relative* been a victim of a **serious property crime,** such as burglary or auto theft?
                1. YES
                5. NO
                8. DON'T KNOW

V251   F6b.   Was it committed by someone 10 through 17 years old?
                1. YES
                5. NO
                8. DON'T KNOW (DO NOT PROBE)
                0. NOT APPLICABLE—V250 = 5,8

V252   F7.   How concerned are **you** about becoming the victim of *serious violent crime?* Would you say you are *not at all concerned, not very concerned, somewhat concerned,* or *very concerned?*
                1. NOT AT ALL CONCERNED
                2. NOT VERY CONCERNED
                3. SOMEWHAT CONCERNED
                4. VERY CONCERNED
                8. DON'T KNOW

V253   F8.   How concerned are you about becoming the victim of *serious property crime?* Would you say you are *not at all concerned, not very concerned, somewhat concerned,* or *very concerned?*
                1. NOT AT ALL CONCERNED
                2. NOT VERY CONCERNED
                3. SOMEWHAT CONCERNED
                4. VERY CONCERNED
                9. NOT ASCERTAINED

V254   F9.   Is there any area within a mile of where you live that you would be afraid to walk alone at night *because* you fear that a crime might be committed against you?
                1. YES
                5. NO
                8. DON'T KNOW
                9. NOT ASCERTAINED

V260   G1.   Are you currently married, living in a marriage-like relationship, separated, divorced, widowed, or have you never been married?

1. MARRIED
2. LIVING IN A MARRIAGE-LIKE RELATIONSHIP
3. SEPARATED
4. DIVORCED
5. WIDOWED
6. NEVER MARRIED
9. NOT ASCERTAINED

V261   G2.   What state do you live in?

                    1–51. ENTER CODE FROM STATE CARD
                    99. NOT ASCERTAINED

V262   G3.   Which of the following best describes where your home is located—(READ SLOWLY) a large city, a suburb of a large city, a medium sized city, a small city, a small town, or a rural area?

                    1. LARGE CITY
                    2. SUBURB OF A LARGE CITY
                    3. MEDIUM SIZED CITY
                    4. SMALL CITY
                    5. SMALL TOWN
                    6. RURAL AREA
                    8. DON'T KNOW
                    9. NOT ASCERTAINED

V263   G4.   Do you presently work for pay?

                    1. YES
                    5. NO
                    9. NOT ASCERTAINED

V264   G5.   On average, how many hours do you work per week?

                    1–95. ENTER NUMBER
                    99. NOT ASCERTAINED
                    0. NOT APPLICABLE—V263 = 5,9

V265   G6.   What is the highest grade of school or year of college you have *completed*?

                    00–12. YEARS OF SCHOOL
                    13–16. YEARS OF COLLEGE
                    17. GRADUATE WORK
                    98. DON'T KNOW
                    99. NOT ASCERTAINED

V266   G7.   We would we also like to know your race or ethnic origin. Are you White, Black, Hispanic, American Indian or Alaskan Native, Asian or Pacific Islander?

        1. WHITE
        2. BLACK
        3. HISPANIC
        4. AMERICAN INDIAN OR ALASKAN NATIVE
        5. ASIAN OR PACIFIC ISLANDER
        7. OTHER
        9. NOT ASCERTAINED

V267   **G8.** Do you have any children?

        1. YES
        5. NO
        9. NOT ASCERTAINED

V268   **G8a.** How many living children do you have?

        1–20. ENTER NUMBER
          99. NOT ASCERTAINED
        0. NOT APPLICABLE—V267 = 5,9

V269   **G8b.** How old is (the oldest/he or she)?

        1–95. ENTER AGE
          99. NOT ASCERTAINED
          0. NOT APPLICABLE—V267 = 5,9

V270   **G8c.** How old is the youngest?

        1–95. ENTER AGE
          99. NOT ASCERTAINED
          0. NOT APPLICABLE—V267 = 5,9 OR V268
            = 1

V271   **G8d.** Have any of your children ever been brought before the juvenile court for a juvenile offense?

        1. YES
        5. NO
        8. DON'T KNOW
        9. NOT ASCERTAINED
        0. NOT APPLICABLE—V269 = 0–7

V272   **G9a.** In general, when it comes to politics, do you usually think of yourself as a *liberal*, a *conservative*, a *moderate*, or what?

        1. LIBERAL
        2. CONSERVATIVE
        3. MODERATE/MIDDLE-OF-THE-ROAD
        4. DON'T KNOW/NO PREFERENCE/NEITHER
        9. NOT ASCERTAINED

V273   G9b. Do you think of yourself as a *strong liberal* or a *not very strong liberal?*
        1. STRONG LIBERAL
        2. NOT VERY STRONG LIBERAL
        8. DON'T KNOW
        9. NOT ASCERTAINED
        0. NOT APPLICABLE—V272 = 2–4,9

V274   G9c. Do you think of yourself as a *strong conservative* or a *not very strong conservative?*
        1. STRONG CONSERVATIVE
        2. NOT VERY STRONG CONSERVATIVE
        8. DON'T KNOW
        9. NOT ASCERTAINED
        0. NOT APPLICABLE—V272 = 1,3–4,9

V275   G9d. Do you think of yourself as more like a liberal or more like a conservative?
        1. MORE LIKE A LIBERAL
        2. MORE LIKE A CONSERVATIVE
        3. NEITHER
        4. REFUSES TO CHOOSE
        8. DON'T KNOW
        9. NOT ASCERTAINED
        0. NOT APPLICABLE—V272 = 1,2

V276   G9. Built Liberal/Conservative 7-Point Scale
        1. STRONG LIBERAL
        2. NOT VERY STRONG LIBERAL
        3. MODERATE, MORE LIKE LIBERAL
        4. MODERATE
        5. MODERATE, MORE LIKE CONSERVATIVE
        6. NOT VERY STRONG CONSERVATIVE
        7. STRONG CONSERVATIVE
        9. NOT ASCERTAINED

V277   G10. To get a picture of people's financial situation, we need to know the general range of incomes of all the people we interview. Thinking about your (and your spouse's/partner's) total income from *all sources* (including your job), did you (and your spouse/partner) receive $25,000 or more in 1990?

        5. NO
        8. DON'T KNOW
        9. NOT ASCERTAINED

| V278 | G10a,b. | Was it $35,000 or more? |
| V279 | | Was it $50,000 or more? |

    1. YES
    5. NO
    8. DON'T KNOW
    9. NOT ASCERTAINED

| V280 | G10c,d. | Was it $5,000 or more? |
| V281 | | Was it $15,000 or more? |

    1. YES
    5. NO
    8. DON'T KNOW
    9. NOT ASCERTAINED

V282 Built Total Income

    1. LESS THAN $5,000
    2. $5,000–$14,000
    3. $15,000–$24,999
    4. $25,000–$34,999
    5. $35,000–$49,999
    6. $50,000–AND OVER
    9. NOT ASCERTAINED

V300 Census Region

    1. NORTH EAST
    2. NORTH CENTRAL
    3. SOUTH
    4. WEST

V301 Sex by Age Categories

    118. MALES 18–29
    130. MALES 30–44
    145. MALES 45–59
    160. MALES 60 AND OVER
    218. FEMALES 18–29
    230. FEMALES 30–44
    245. FEMALES 45–59
    260. FEMALES 60 AND OVER

V302 Centered Weight Variable

    0.25–6.28

State Codes

01	Alabama	18	Maine	35	Oklahoma
02	Arizona	19	Maryland	36	Oregon
03	Arkansas	20	Massachusetts	37	Pennsylvania
04	California	21	Michigan	38	Rhode Island
05	Colorado	22	Minesota	39	South Carolina
06	Connecticut	23	Mississippi	40	South Dakota
07	Delaware	24	Missouri	41	Tennessee
08	District of Columbia	25	Montana	42	Texas
09	Florida	26	Nebraska	43	Utah
10	Georgia	27	Nevada	44	Vermont
11	Idaho	28	New Hampshire	45	Virginia
12	Illinois	29	New Jersey	46	Washington
13	Indiana	30	New Mexico	47	West Virginia
14	Iowa	31	New York	48	Wisconsin
15	Kansas	32	North Carolina	49	Wyoming
16	Kentucky	33	North Dakota	50	Alaska
17	Louisiana	34	Ohio	51	Hawaii

References

Alcser, K. H., Connor, J. H., & Heeringa, S. G. (1991). *National study of attitudes toward juvenile crime: Final report.* Ann Arbor: Survey Research Center, Institute for Social Research, University of Michigan.

Breslow, M., Connor, J. H., & Heeringa, S. G. (1990). *Study of attitudes toward juvenile crime in Michigan: Final report.* Ann Arbor: Survey Research Center, Institute for Social Research, University of Michigan.

Champion, D. J., & Mays, G. L. (1991). *Transferring juveniles to criminal courts: Trends and implications for criminal justice.* New York: Praeger.

Feld, B. (1987). Juvenile court meets the principle of offense: Legislative changes in juvenile waiver statutes. *Journal of Criminal Law and Criminology, 78,* 471–533.

Feld, B. (1988). Juvenile court meets the principle of offense: Punishment, treatment, and the difference it makes. *Boston University Law Review, 68,* 821–915.

Michigan Compiled Laws Annotated Sec. 712A.2 et. seq. as amended (1988). Prosecutors may seek waiver to the adult system for first and second degree murder; first degree criminal sexual conduct; armed robbery and armed assault in intended robbery; and manufacture, possession, or distribution of 650 grams or more of certain controlled substances. These laws also allow juvenile court jurisdiction over youths to the age of 21.

Schwartz, I. M. (1989). *(In) Justice for juveniles: Rethinking the best interest of the child.* Lexington, MA: Lexington Books.

Schwartz, I. M., Abbey, J. M., & Barton, W. H. (1990). *The perception and reality of juvenile crime in Michigan.* Ann Arbor: Center for the Study of Youth Policy, University of Michigan.

Cases

In re Gault, 387 U.S. 1 (1967).

12

Toward a National Juvenile Justice Agenda

Ira M. Schwartz

The chapters in this book include many important observations and suggestions about how the juvenile justice system in the United States could be improved. The challenge is to convert these ideas into public policy. This is not an easy task. However, it is a challenge that must be met. The stakes are high. Indeed, there is reason to believe that the future of the juvenile justice system, and of the juvenile court in particular, may hinge on the policy decisions that will be made during this decade.

Dozens of recommendations for improving the juvenile justice system and the quality of justice for children have been presented. While all of the recommendations have merit, a few deserve priority consideration.

The most significant and far-reaching issue that needs to be addressed is the future of the juvenile court. Barry Feld, a leading scholar and critic, presents a compelling case about the juvenile court's shortcomings. Frank A. Orlando and Gary L. Crippen, two thoughtful individuals with considerable judicial experience in family and children's issues, provide a chilling account of the inability of the juvenile court to ensure justice for children as well as quality treatment. Orlando and Crippen make recommendations for reforming the juvenile court. Feld, who is more skeptical because of the failures of past efforts to change this institution, raises the question about whether a separate court for children can continue to be justified.

The 1991 National Public Opinion Survey on Juvenile Crime indicates that the public favors providing juveniles with the same due process and procedural guarantees accorded adults. The public also favors adjudicating juveniles who commit serious crimes (particularly felonies) in the adult courts. The public does not want juveniles to receive the same sentences as adults nor do they want juveniles sentenced to adult prisons. This suggests the public would probably support a major overhaul of our system to provide a new system of justice for young people.

249

The time has come to begin giving serious consideration to alternatives to juvenile court. Elected public officials and other policymakers who may be inclined to adopt another model will need guidance and expert opinion on this crucial issue. In the meantime, policymakers should act to ensure that all young people accused of a crime have access to competent legal representation, and that they not be allowed to waive their right to counsel without prior consultation with an attorney. Criteria for diverting cases from formal juvenile court processing and dispositional guidelines emphasizing limited use of residential options should also be developed and implemented. Criteria for diversion should draw upon the excellent, but largely unused, research in this area by such respected academics as Delbert Elliott and his colleagues at the University of Colorado, William S. Davidson II at Michigan State University, Thomas Blomberg at Florida State University, and Mark Ezell at the University of Washington.

Policymakers, juvenile justice professionals, and child advocates should capitalize on the opportunity presented by fiscal problems at state and local levels to restructure state and local youth detention and correction systems. They should act to develop alternatives to secure detention, training schools, and private residential care, an approach that recent public opinion data suggest voters would support. In implementing these initiatives, consideration should be given to reallocating operating funds for training schools and contracted funds for residential treatment to the financing of community-based services. Again, policymakers and others should draw upon the research and experiences in various jurisdictions around the country for guidance.

There is a growing interest in service integration. In fact, policymakers in a number of states either already have created or are in the process of creating children's services agencies as a strategy for addressing this issue. Unfortunately, there is very little research on this topic. Such basic questions as which services should be consolidated, should services for children be separated from services to families, how should integrated services be delivered, would consolidating services lead to better outcomes, and what are the economics of service integration need to be carefully examined. Funds should be made available by the federal government and private foundations to address these and other important questions.

Much more work needs to be done in the area of delinquency prevention. In particular, we need to know more about how to prevent serious violent crime and the development of juvenile/adult criminal careers. The federal government, through the Office of Juvenile Justice and Delinquency Prevention, in collaboration with other relevant federal agencies and private foundations, should play a leadership role in funding, coordinating, and encouraging initiatives in this area.

Juvenile crime continues to be one of the most challenging domestic issues we face. Authors contributing to this volume have provided much food for thought. More importantly, they have put forward a promising agenda for policymakers and others who are genuinely interested in doing something constructive about it.

Index

About the Contributors

Yitzhak Bakal is the founder and director of the Northeastern Family Institute, Inc., a nonprofit organization based in Danvers, Massachusetts that provides care in the field of youth correction and mental health to eight states. Dr. Bakal received a B.S.W. degree from Hebrew University, his M.S.W. from Columbia University, and an Ed.D. from the University of Massachusetts. He has co-authored and edited three books and several articles on the subject of juvenile correction.

Meda Chesney-Lind is director of Women's Studies at the University of Hawaii at Manoa and president of the Western Society of Criminology. Dr. Chesney-Lind has authored monographs and papers on the subject of women and crime, and a book on female delinquency. She received a B.A. degree from Whitman College and a Ph.D. degree from the University of Hawaii at Manoa.

Gary L. Crippen, who has been an associate judge of the Minnesota Court of Appeals since 1984, has had a thirty-two year legal career, first as a general practitioner and an elected prosecutor, and then as a trial judge and an appellate judge. Throughout these years he has given special attention to personal-welfare law, including the fields of family law, juvenile law, and commitment law. Judge Crippen has a J.D. degree from the University of Minnesota Law School and an LL.M. degree from the University of Virginia Law School.

Mark Ezell is an associate professor at the School of Social Work, University of Washington. He received his masters degree in sociology as well as his M.S.W. and Ph.D. in social welfare from Florida State University. He has been taught classes in social work administration, juvenile justice policy, and advocacy. Dr. Ezell has had research findings published in *Social Service Review* and *Journal of Research in Crime and Delinquency* and has served on several agency boards such as the Washington Council on Crime and Delinquency.

267

Katherine Hunt Federle is an associate professor of clinical law at the Tulane Law School in New Orleans. She currently is an executive member of the ABA Family Law Section's Committee on Juvenile Law and the Needs of Children. She was director and founder of Hawaii's Juvenile Defense Clinic and coordinator for the Consortium on Child, Families, and the Law at the Center for Youth Research. She received her B.A. degree from Pomona College and J.D. from University of Puget Sound School of Law. Her interests include children's legal rights, child witnesses, child abuse and the public schools, and institutionalization of juveniles.

Barry C. Feld is professor of law at University of Minnesota. He received his B.A. degree from the University of Pennsylvania, J.D. degree from the University of Minnesota Law School, and his Ph.D. degree in sociology from Harvard University. Professor Feld has served on the National District Attorneys Association, Juvenile Justice Advisory Committee and as a visiting scholar at the National Center for Juvenile Justice sponsored by the U.S. Department of Justice.

C. Ronald Huff is director of the Criminal Justice Research Center and professor of public policy and management at the Ohio State University. He received a B.A. in psychology from Capital University, an M.S.W. in social work from the University of Michigan, and a Ph.D. in sociology with a specialization in criminology from the Ohio State University. Dr. Huff taught at the University of California, Irvine and Purdue University. His interests are in American gangs, gang intervention, and wrongful conviction.

Barry Krisberg is president of the National Council on Crime and Delinquency (NCCD) located in San Francisco, California. He holds a Ph.D. from the University of Pennsylvania. Previously he was on the faculty at the University of California, Berkeley. He is a member of the California Attorney General's Advisory Committee on Criminal Justice Policy. His research interests include the future of the juvenile court.

Harvey Lowell develops Northeastern Family Institute's community-based programs for people with complex emotional, family, and legal problems. Formerly executive director of the Children's Law Center of Massachusetts, he is the author of several articles and monographs on structural problems in human service systems.

Franklin A. Orlando is director of the Center for the Study of Youth Policy at Nova University in Fort Lauderdale, Florida. Judge Orlando has been employed as general counsel and executive director for the Legislative Committee on Delinquency, and served as assistant attorney general as well as a circuit judge for the State of Florida. Other appointments were as special advisor to the Governor and Legislature on youthful offender issues, and vice-chairman of the Florida Bar Association Corrections Committee.

Dwight Price is director of Governmental Affairs for the National District Attorneys Association (NDAA) and directs the Juvenile Justice Prosecution Program for NDAA, presenting policy development programs in juvenile justice, career criminal prosecution, and drug prosecution. Mr. Price graduated from the Georgetown University Law Center and worked as an assistant state's attorney in Maryland. His experience includes serving as executive director of Pre-trial Options Projects, Inc., a counseling program for youthful offenders.

James Shine is director of the American Prosecutors Research Institute and deputy executive director of the National District Attorneys Association. He was founder and director of the National Center for Prosecution of Child Abuse and served as acting director for the National Drug Prosecution Center. Mr. Shine received his bachelors degree and did graduate studies in criminology at the University of California, Berkeley, receiving his J.D. degree from Hasting College of Law and his masters degree in public administration from Harvard University.

Mark Soler is the executive director of the Youth Law Center in San Francisco, California, and an instructor in Mass Communication Law in the Journalism Department of San Francisco State University. After receiving his B.A. from Yale University and J.D. from Yale Law School, he taught at both Boston University and University of Nebraska School of Law. He has worked on improving the conditions for children in juvenile justice and child welfare systems nationwide.

Russell Van Vleet is a senior associate of the Center for the Study of Youth Policy. Mr. Van Vleet received his B.A. and M.S.W. degrees from the University of Utah and has served as a consultant for Community Research Associates in Illinois, NCCD in California, and the Hubert Humphrey Institute's Key Decision Maker Project. He was formerly the director of the Utah State Division of Youth Corrections and was a prominent figure during the "Quiet Revolution" that transformed Utah's juvenile justice system.

About the Editor

Ira M. Schwartz is professor and director of the Center for the Study of Youth Policy in the School of Social Work at the University of Michigan. Professor Schwartz was a senior fellow at the University of Minnesota's Hubert H. Humphrey Institute of Public Affairs, and served as the administrator of the Office of Juvenile Justice and Delinquency Prevention, U.S. Department of Justice. He directed criminal and juvenile justice agencies in Illinois and Washington and has worked extensively in both the public and private sector. Professor Schwartz has written extensively on juvenile justice and child welfare issues.